SHADOW AND LIGHT

SHADOW AND LIGHT

THE LIFE, FRIENDS AND
OPINIONS OF
MAURICE STERNE

EDITED BY
CHARLOTTE LEON MAYERSON

INTRODUCTION BY GEORGE BIDDLE

HARCOURT, BRACE & WORLD, INC.

NEW YORK

Thanks are due to the following for permission to quote from letters or published material: William McKnight Bowman, for quotations from reviews by Stark Young in *The New Republic,* December 25, 1929 and March 1, 1933, reprinted from *The New Republic;* Mrs. Edward Bruce, for letters from Edward Bruce; Crown Publishers, Inc., for material from *Journey into the Self,* edited by Edmund Fuller, copyright 1950 by the Estate of Leo Stein; Thomas W. Dewart, for a quotation from a review by Henry McBride in the New York *Sun,* May 9, 1947, copyright © 1947 by the New York *Sun;* Esquire, Inc., for material from "Sterne, Maestro in Art" by Harry Salpeter, © 1941 by Esquire, Inc.; John G. Evans and Yale University Library, for letters of Mabel Dodge Luhan; Charles H. Hapgood, for a letter from Hutchins Hapgood, and for material from *A Victorian in the Modern World* by Hutchins Hapgood; Harcourt, Brace & World, Inc., for material from *Movers and Shakers* and *Edge of the Taos Desert* by Mabel Dodge Luhan; The Jewish Publication Society of America, for material from *History of the Jews in Russia and Poland* by Simon M. Dubnow, and *Vilna* by Israel Cohen, with permission of the copyright owner, The Jewish Publication Society of America, Philadelphia; Kenton Kilmer, for material from an interview with Maurice Sterne by Joyce Kilmer; Mme. Lucy Krohg, for letters from Jules Pascin; Leon Kroll, for his letter; Prafulla C. Mukerji, for a letter from Basanta Koomar Roy; Lewis Mumford, for material from "Surprise-Party Wit In Water Colors"; New York *Herald Tribune,* for material from a review by Royal Cortissoz, "Maurice Sterne As Mural Director," © 1939, New York Herald Tribune Inc.; The New York *Times,* for material from an interview with Maurice Sterne by Joyce Kilmer, March 21, 1915, and reviews by Edward A. Jewell, February 28, 1932 and December 31, 1939, copyright 1915, 1932, 1939 by The New York Times Company; William H. Stein, for letters from Leo Stein; Beulah Washburn, for letters from Alexander H. Bullock.

TO THE MEMORY OF
VERA AND MAURICE STERNE

PREFACE

In 1956 Maurice Sterne wrote: "I have never been content unless I had some opus magnum to occupy me. Now that my illness keeps me from holding a brush, I can no longer hope to find myself in the pursuit of nature in art. My opus magnum must be my notes for an autobiography, and I race with time to set them down."

When he died in 1957 Sterne left suitcases filled with papers about his art, his friends and his incredibly full life. Yet by the time the notes were written, his mind was sometimes blurred with pain and drugs. His hand was unsteady and the physical drudgery of writing down page after page of recollections was too much for his failing strength.

In spite of these handicaps, there emerges from his memoirs the line drawing of a man with a creative intelligence, a warm and witty personality. The notes also throw new light on the lives and work of the large circle of well-known people with whom Sterne spent his life.

Perhaps, though, the most provocative aspect of this close examination of the career of a painter and sculptor lies in another area: very neatly and very poignantly it raises questions about art criticism, about passing fame, about the nature of fashion in aesthetics, etc. Sterne was convinced that his own fall from the highest place in American art to relative obscurity was based on sociological change rather than on the artistic merit of his work. This explanation might be put down as a self-protective rationalization, but the account of Sterne's life and career makes it difficult to brush away his claim lightly.

I have used the notebooks as a base and have built a connected narrative that is, I think, consistent with the style of expression Sterne used in the passages he was able to complete. He obviously worked over these finished pages several times for style and for accuracy. Other sections are sketchy fragments . . . the tantalizing beginning of an anecdote about a literary celebrity; nearly illegible paragraphs that are virtually undecipherable; copies of unaddressed and undated letters. . . .

Where large gaps remained in the history of his life or where vital details were lacking, I have drawn on letters, on art criticism, on published works, on old newspapers, and on the recollections of Sterne's wife and friends. Although their help has been indicated in the text, no footnote can cover the debt owed for the graciousness of such people as Veronica Gockel, Donald Gallup, Rachel and Horace Kallen, Mrs. Leon Kroll, Sidney Simon, Dolly Silverman, Cecil Wolman, and many others.

There would have been no book without Vera Sterne's generosity with the material, and her encouragement of my growing respect and love for her husband. For a long time Vera waited patiently to see the book. She died late in October, 1963.

Charlotte Leon Mayerson

FOREWORD

To an unusual degree, this book needs a short historical foreword. During the last few years of Maurice Sterne's life, when he was no longer able to paint, he lay propped up in bed for many hours each day, each night, writing in a handsome, spidery, almost illegible hand the story of his life. I visited him often during that period and always he would want to read aloud some of the new work and have me read, sitting there, other sections.

It became apparent that he was not writing a book with the usual continuities. He would render intensely a particular scene, the pursuit of a particular idea, or some meeting or conversation that was still vivid and important to him. Well before his death, he and I agreed that the book, which he knew would probably be completed only after his death, would require a very skillful editor to fill in the transitions, to select, cut and mold.

The problem was not solved until Charlotte Mayerson volunteered late in 1962 to tackle it. She soon stated her belief that to have a definite and effective shape, the book must be highly selective; moreover, she must resort to other sources of information about Maurice Sterne to fill in those periods and aspects of his life which he had not managed to cover. We agreed, and in little more than a year, Mrs. Mayerson produced the present book.

It is perhaps not proper, certainly not customary in a foreword of this kind to praise the editor, but in this case, I feel compelled to do so, for I know the extraordinary difficulties that beset the task. I feel that Mrs. Mayerson has overcome them with dedication, ingenuity and sensitiveness. Indeed, in an interesting and perhaps unique way, the book has become a collaboration, for she has done a great deal of cutting and of rewriting, yet with a rare fidelity to Maurice Sterne's own voice. It is my belief that the pages that follow thoroughly justify what I am saying here—and indeed, I am not alone in this feeling. One of the Sternes' closest friends said to me after reading the manuscript, "It is as though Maurice were speaking to me himself."

Hiram Haydn

LIST OF ILLUSTRATIONS

INTRODUCTION

by George Biddle

I n Paris during the winter of 1925 I had organized, with the help of Pascin (who had become an American citizen) a small group of American painters. Léonce Rosenberg wrote the introduction to the catalog. We exhibited at the Galérie Hubert-Robert in Paris and later at the Neue Galerie in Vienna. Pascin was a friend of Maurice Sterne's, who was living at the time in Italy. I greatly admired Sterne's work, which I had seen at the Bourgeois Gallery in New York. We invited him to join our group. Later that spring he came up to Paris.

Maurice was eight years my senior. By chance and not through intent the pattern of my life as an artist seems in retrospect to have followed in his footsteps by a decade. I won't say this drew us closer together. But its realization now gives me a deeper understanding of this gifted and complex artist.

In 1904 he arrived in Paris on a scholarship, his art-student days behind him, already a fine *déssinateur*—the only English equivalent is "master of the line." I only began my art studies at the Académie Julien seven years later. We were both equally influenced by the giants of the Impressionists, many of them then still living or working. Maurice met Rodin, once saw Degas at a Cézanne exhibition, and talked with Vollard. I had

xiii

also met Rodin, worshipped Mary Cassatt, was introduced to Vollard, talked with Durand-Ruel *père*, and watched old Monet at work in his Giverny garden. Youth's heroes often leave an indelible stamp on its impressionable clay.

In 1912, escaping from a tangled love affair, Maurice left for India, Burma and Bali. Here he spent a year and a half and painted his most explosive pictures. I left for Tahiti eight years later, bruised even more by the breakup of a war marriage than by the eighteen deadening months spent at the front in France. I remained there off and on for two years. It was here that I found myself. I had never heard of Sterne or Bali.

"From the very beginning I found . . . beauty that moved my soul. . . . The [island] I remember made of every phase of daily life a ritual in which all the people participated. . . . In my mind it has remained a paradise."

I, too, could have written these lines. For different reasons both of us were seeking serenity. We found it in the beauty of a primitive civilization—what was left of it—the harmony between man and nature. Art was a way of life and not a cult. Of course we could not remain forever. Later, when we met, we never talked together about this unique experience. And, of course, neither of us could ever apprehend that same serenity again.

Sterne was one of the half-dozen truly great American painters of his generation, those years that saw American art coming of age. I believe his finest paintings are comparable with the best that were painted in Europe at the time. Like all great artists, he was a complex man; full of shades, overtones and contradictions. He was innocent and devious; timid and impetuous. At bottom sweet and affectionate, he was occasionally vindictive and a little cruel. In his memoirs he is as ingenuously unabashed as Jean Jacques Rousseau.

I have always believed that artists are just like other men—but a little more so. Two qualities are indispensable to greatness whether in art or moral character: compassion and humility. In his fundamental approach to art and to life—below the shades and overtones—Maurice had, I think, these virtues. He also had integrity. The Latin word *integer* means "whole." In art and life Maurice was all-rounded, a whole man.

As a child Sterne lived in Libau, a small German-speaking Baltic port, one quarter of whose residents were Jewish. His family were orthodox middle-class intellectuals, amateurs of German music and German romantic literature. He recalls two incidents as a young child, perhaps four or five years old, which surely affected his entire life. This was during the reign of the cruel and bigoted Tsar Alexander III. In the streets "the derisive Cossack blare mingled with the sharp, thin scream of their victims' terror. . . . And my soul has recorded a deeper mark of the fear transmitted to me through my mother's shuddering body, which she used as a wall to protect me."

Later that week police officers and heavily armed guards broke into the house at night looking for his older brother Michael. Under one of the mattresses they found a book, banned for its democratic ideas. "My mother swayed and almost fell, because she had had no idea that my brothers' political activities went beyond the talking stage. . . . [She] fainted and the soldiers carried her downstairs."

Shortly thereafter occurred an even more terrifying experience. Among a line of convicts and political prisoners being exiled to Siberia he suddenly recognized a young cousin. "I . . . ran after him shouting, 'Kolia, Kolia, where are they taking you?' . . . One of the guards stepped out of line and hit me on the chest with his rifle. I fell to the street and lay in the gutter weeping."

Sterne was essentially a man of the world, recognized by his peers as such. I rather fancy he was a free-thinker, although I never discussed religious matters with him. He was incapable of bigotry. Only once I heard him allude to the so-called "Jewish problem." He mentioned—quite unconcernedly—that he had resigned from a certain semi-social organization because he had heard an anti-Jewish aspersion made by one of the members. But on two or three occasions he showed an attitude toward life—insecurity? a persecution complex?—which otherwise was difficult to understand in an apparently normal, vigorous and immensely successful person.

This was the inability to make a decision, a paralysis of will coupled with deep spiritual dejection and pessimism. Might one attribute this weakness to a scar left from the early terror, the terror of a child so young that he had no idea what it was all about?

I remember how surprised I was when Maurice, so deliberate and poised in speech and gesture, told me that for years he could not travel in the New York subways—such was his overwhelming dread of catastrophe.

Mabel Dodge, who had the portrait painter's eye for the significant facial trait, noted the one blemish to his beauty as a young man, his mouth. "Oh, dear! his mouth, when he forgot to arrange it, was not so good—more or less a thin, straight line, without curve or meaning." But, "What I liked about him was his handsome look of suffering." I, too, often observed the guarded demeanor in the slightly compressed lips and the grave, watchful eyes that must not give him away too hastily. There was the suggestion of a mask. I have noted the same expression sometimes in young people whose childhood has been unhappy.

I recall an occasion on which Maurice showed a kind of spiritual apathy when confronted by a challenge. In 1935 he began work on his murals for the Department of Justice Building in Washington. The theme of the twenty panels was the growth of justice in the law: "my . . . murals interested me more than any other job I had ever done, probably because of influences in my early childhood."

The murals, on which he had been working for five years, had been approved by the National Commission of Fine Arts and by the Section of Fine Arts of the Federal Works Agency of the Treasury, under the chairmanship of Sterne's loyal friend and admirer, Edward Bruce.

One panel, "Ordeal," showed "a victim of the Inquisition, his torturer, and a Church dignitary." The Catholic hierarchy in Washington objected to this panel. Sterne refused to alter it. Despite the strong protests of Bruce and the friendly interventions of Justices Harlan Stone and Felix Frankfurter of the Supreme Court and of Robert Jackson, then Attorney General, the hierarchy stood firm. Michael John Carmody, the Administrator of the Federal Works Agency, had charge of public buildings, an independent establishment which reported directly to the President. He refused to permit the installation of the panels. They remained stored in the basement of the Justice Department Building in Washington.

One day, visiting me in Croton, Maurice mentioned to me this disgraceful episode. I said, "What are you going to do about it? You can't take this lying down."

He answered me quietly, without passion, "George, I'm tired. There's no use. When things like this happen, I don't care any more."

I was surprised by his answer and his defeated resignation as much as I was shocked by the treatment he had received. My brother was at the time Solicitor-General in Washington. He also cared for freedom of expression in matters of art. He tells in his autobiography, *In Brief Authority*, how he "consulted Tom Corcoran, a Catholic himself, who knew his way round. As usual he at once suggested the next step. . . . Monsignor Michael Joseph Ready, the Assistant General Secretary of the National Catholic Welfare Conference in Washington, was the man. . . . We three lunched together." Monsignor Ready agreed hesitantly that Francis might quote him to Carmody as having said that although the murals were "pretty awful . . . he saw no objection to their being installed. . . . 'It won't do any good but you can say that if you want.' I waited two days and said just that to Carmody. The murals were immediately installed." But, it may be added, without official ceremony!

* * *

xvii

Most painters are sedentary by nature. Only a few of us have a touch of gypsy blood. We can sense romance beyond the horizon and feel the need from time to time to weigh anchor in search of the unknown. Of my fellow artists I cannot recall a half-dozen who ever needed to travel for inspiration farther from their New York or Paris studios than to Ogunquit, Maine, or to the Côte d'Azur. Today the "Mystic Isles of the South Seas" are gone forever. Travel has become nothing more than commutation. One can get to the Society Islands or the Leeward Group in a matter of hours. Such voyages used to take Maurice and myself upwards of a month.

Our little fellowship of world travelers—Sterne, Pascin, Adolf Dehn, Rockwell Kent, myself (who else?)—could think of ourselves as world citizens. Maurice experienced more serenity and spiritual ease among the unlettered peasants of the Abruzzi or the natives of Bali than in our automotive and electronic civilization. His friend, the artist Paul Dougherty, used affectionately to speak of him as the "Wandering Jew."

On the intellectual level, too, Maurice was a man of the world, of broad outlook and free of parochial prejudice. He could engage in a "hot dispute" with Sir Rabindranath Tagore "over the merits of Heine and *my* favorite poet, Goethe. Tagore felt that Goethe was too self-conscious and self-important to be really great." Sterne's return from Bali to Rome makes another charming vignette. He ran into Rodin. Sterne was just over thirty years of age, quite unknown, and Rodin was well on in his sixties. Together they "spent hours talking about art and its problems." Maurice, who had a low opinion of Matisse as a draughtsman, felt nevertheless that he was a fine colorist and "really did know what he was doing. . . . Rodin snapped, . . . 'We do not forgive a murderer for killing his wife, *especially* if he knows very well what he is doing' . . . and with a brusque, '*C'est assez maintenant,*' " he closed the conversation.

Such brief thumbnail sketches do more to illuminate the

personalities and aesthetics of great artists than many scholarly pages.

All his life Sterne flitted restlessly from one country to another. It seemed almost a neurosis. New York, Paris, Berlin, Potsdam, back again to Libau in Russia, Greece, the Orient, once more Rome, Anticoli, America, Italy again, Vienna, Anticoli and home to the States. Even then he never seems to have stayed long in one place, and he had many homes: Tarrytown, Croton, New York, Brooklyn, Taos, Connecticut, San Francisco, Provincetown. His two great loves, however, were Anticoli Corrado in the Abruzzi, and of course Bali.

I know Anticoli well. In 1930 Maurice suggested my joining him there. At the last moment he abruptly changed his plans but offered me his house, the Molino on the central piazza. Here my wife and I spent almost a year, our honeymoon. One gets to know a man well living with his books, paintings and furniture.

Anticoli Corrado is a typical little Italian hill town in what was once the Papal States. It is among the poorest, most ignorant, blighted and medieval in central Italy. I never understood what it was that drew Maurice back here like a magnet, off and on for twenty-nine years. Yet he constantly refers to the physical beauty of the place and people. He could work well here and was happy.

Only half a dozen of the houses in the village had running water or electricity. The sewage ran into the streets, many of which were unpaved paths for the goats, pigs, donkeys, cattle and chickens. Few of the peasants had ever seen a doctor or dentist. Nor had they money to buy shoes. They ate meat once a week and on church holy days. There was a run of cretins among the population. None of the peasants' houses was heated, although well before Christmas there was a coating of ice wherever water collected. Most of the peasants were unlettered. The children could not be kept in school and preferred trapping rats, which they took pleasure in dousing with turpentine and setting on fire. *"Le bestie non sono cristiane . . ."* * When it rained old Caterina, whom we had inherited with the house, arranged vessels and copper receptacles about the *salone* to catch the water dripping from leaks in the roof. She boiled a kettle of water for us every morning. This, with a tin foot tub, made do for a bath. In 1930 there were few American tourists in Italy and Il Duce's threats of bombing British vessels in *mare nostrum* kept the English away. Besides, the Depression had reached Europe.

On August 23, 1959, two years after Sterne's death, I attended a ceremony in the village for the dedication of one of the streets which was to be renamed in honor of Maurice Sterne. The world had changed in thirty years. So had Anticoli. As earlier in the nineteenth century, it had once more become an international art colony. There were Swedish, American, French and Italian painters among the crowd. The peasants all wore shoes and a line of handsome cars filled one end of the piazza. New studios and villas had mushroomed up among the older buildings. The mayor, a little drunk, was no longer of the Fascist party. An astute politician, he avowed his liberal and republican sentiments and was the acknowledged leader of the communist faction. Old Caterina was long since dead. But several of the peasants remembered us. When they spoke of Maurice and Vera tears came to their eyes. An old woman presented my wife with a bunch of flowers: *"Perchè era amica di Maurizio."* There was some chemical quality in Maurice that drew him close to the peasants of Anticoli. He always spoke of them with wry affection. They loved him, and he was their friend.

In the Orient Sterne's painting immediately matured. I believe myself that during those two years he produced his most

* One finds similar conditions today in South Italy and Sicily. To those interested, I recommend Norman Douglas' *In Old Calabria*, a masterpiece. It was one of the books in Sterne's Anticoli library.

original and powerful work. But it would be quite unjust to say—as many of his critics in the recent years affirm—that after that his work deteriorated. Hutchins Hapgood in his autobiography was "impressed by his mental force combined with a rich and deep temperament." * In the greatest periods, such as the Renaissance, art was a successful fusion of these two qualities. Sterne's earlier response to nature was immediate. As he matured, it became more calculated. In each period there is the best and also the less successful. I agree, however, with Lewis Mumford's criticism of him that often his hasty sketches were masterpieces and that sometimes his finished and more labored compositions were merely studies.

One would like to know more of Sterne's personal life in Bali. It is most unfortunate that he kept no journal. The many long letters that he wrote to his patron in Potsdam, Alard DuBois-Reymond, were either lost or destroyed during the Nazi regime. What he wrote half a century later emphasizes, however, the harmony, serenity and beauty of the Bali civilization and its permanent influence on his work, his aesthetics and his philosophy. "Life was an undulating spectrum of colors which played against the most lush and fecund background, which moved to the constant, exotic pulsing of the Balinese music. . . . Coming to the East was for me not a new discovery of an unknown place, but a return to a long forgotten scene."

He felt, too, in Bali the excitement and inspiration of seeing the human figure, not as in the artist's studio, but as it should be seen in all its unclothed and natural beauty in harmonious concord with the ritual of life. Only an artist who has lived among primitive people is aware of the ugliness and shocking deformity of the average, unclothed, civilized man. Sterne was a "painter's painter," but also a superb draughtsman. In the year and a half in Bali he made "ten thousand, . . . trunkfuls" of drawings and sketches of the natives.

* Hutchins Hapgood, *A Victorian in the Modern World*, New York, 1939.

Apart from their inspiration of his art Sterne has little to say of interest about the Balinese and their civilization. Nothing, for instance, about the language, which is hierarchic and subtle. One wonders if he ever learned to speak it with any fluency, although he was a fine linguist. Part of the time he must have lived quite alone. I have lived myself for two years a day's trip away from white civilization. I know the influence this can have on an artist's inner life. Who looked after Sterne's material needs? What was his social and intellectual life?

Karli Sohn, the young painter, was Maurice's only companion during the two years spent in the Orient. Yet he remains a shadow. Sterne was deeply attached to many of his friends, but few of them were artists. There is no mention in his memoirs of George Grosz, who for several years conducted a school for art students in New York with him. Nor of the young peasant-painter, Mario Toppi, whom Maurice befriended in Anticoli and later introduced to the Weyhe Gallery in New York. Nor, for that matter, of any of his brilliant New York contemporaries, whom he frequently saw at artists' gatherings such as the Society of American Painters, Sculptors, and Gravers. I can't recall a half-dozen names of professional colleagues in his memoirs and of only one of them does he speak with real affection. There was one exception, whom he really loved: Jules Pascin. Edward Bruce was a different matter. Though a fellow artist, he was in a sense a student and later a most generous patron. As an artist, Maurice was a lone wolf.

Maurice, for so reticent a man, is at all times candid—disarmingly so—about his sexual relations. "I was skillful and ruthless in my pursuit of physical pleasure, and not particularly concerned with the feelings of others. . . . It took many years for me to learn to see women as friends and not as prey, and I am still horrified and deeply ashamed of these moral debts that I cannot repay." He was now in his late twenties, yet he had only been in love once before—with a married woman whom he could not have supported even if she had consented to desert her husband and children. The Balinese girls had the same physical beauty and social grace as the men. I can only surmise that his relations with them had little effect either on his art or emotional development. They gave him what other women heretofore had—the satisfaction of his desires, packaged in a beautiful and exotic setting.

Solitary life in the tropics among primitive people can corrode and even destroy the least sensitive person. The time came, an incident occurred. He describes it in a beautiful and symbolic passage. Later in the night "I took down from a shelf a bottle of brandy I'd had for a year and drank a good deal of it, hoping it would calm me." Then he added a postscript to a letter. "This evening I have at last met the Serpent of Paradise. I, too, will probably be expelled from the Garden . . . because I have discovered that our Western world is not merely a memory that cannot be effaced."

Maurice was in love three times in his life. The rest were "ships that pass in the night." He was already thirty-five when he first met Mira. I doubt if his relations with women ever changed his character. They offer very interesting clues, however, in understanding this elusive personality. The second time he saw the sister of his friend Karli Sohn, he wrote, "I had fallen irretrievably in love with this woman. . . . From that first moment in her home I felt that a power stronger than I could cope with was robbing me of my will and of my freedom. . . . Women had been expendable before I met Mira."

He leaves immediately for the Orient for a stay of two years. He meets her again in Rome at the outbreak of World War I and finds himself more infatuated with her than ever. He goes to the German Consul in an effort to enlist in the German army "to be near her." But he is turned down. In desperation he begs her to leave her husband and join him in America with her two children. As he is practically penniless, his behavior can only be described as quixotic and irresponsible.

There is a pattern of behavior here which is recurrent in many crises of his life: the fear of being possessed, of losing his identity, and the consequent escape from the most passionate involvements. The weak or shabby behavior of many great artists is often a defense or shield to protect their creative life which, subconsciously, they realize is of more importance than conventional moral behavior.

Maurice's liaison—one can hardly call it marriage—to Mabel Dodge was something different. Judging from what they said about each other, and both are voluble, it was one of the most incongruous, incompatible and tempestuous adventures in the annals of love. From beginning to end it transcends reality. It transcends fiction. It is pure burlesque, Italian comic opera. On another level, it is a jumble of sentimentality, psychic experience, bad taste and sheer vulgarity. It is a five-year-long ring fight. No Queensberry rules. And many more than fifteen rounds. Both back in their respective corners, breathing messages of renewed affection and desire, as they regain their wind. And then in the ring again, hitting consistently below the belt. Mabel on the whole more aggressive—in her dogged efforts to renew the clinch, the more cool and knowledgeable in worldly ways. But Maurice, backed into a corner, can always sidestep—to another dwelling house in Provincetown, to Pottsville, Pennsylvania, Wyoming, Santa Fe, back to New York. Let us look at the two lovers, as they saw each other when they first met in the summer of 1916.

Mabel: "Well," I thought, "who might *that* be?" . . . His straight, fine black hair . . . fell back in long locks in the manner of Liszt, and his broad forehead had a pale, innocent look, especially at the temples where people show for good or bad. His long-lashed brown eyes were nothing more or less than *orbs*, there was such a splendor in their liquid regard. The nose, of a Biblical dignity, had a good bone ridge. . . . What I liked about him was his handsome look of suffering. A dark torture ennobled him. . . . The man might have been in a jungle, so watchful he was, so studied every glance and motion. . . . I always loved the slightest appearance of masterfulness in a man, because it hinted at an opportunity for me to exercise my strength.

And Maurice of Mabel: The woman I was then to visit puzzled and intrigued me, attracted and repelled me. She was entirely different from the kind of women I had always been attracted to before—robust, rather than tall and slender, without the fine bone structure in which I had always taken such pleasure. . . . Her most amazing feature was her eyes. They were cool, dark gray pools, shaded with long black lashes. They reflected her complex emotions spontaneously and honestly, could flash up with fury . . . or glow with rapture. But I loathed their flashes of cruelty. There was something inhuman in that particular look of hers! In contrast, her voice was like a viola, soft, caressing, mellow, with confidential overtones.

Mabel was a ruthless and sophisticated lion-hunter. She had already netted in her New York salon Walter Lippmann, Jack Reed, Robert Edmond Jones and Eugene O'Neill.

Maurice is drawn to her. "For the first time in my life I could relax, rest my will, and do what someone else decided was best." But he felt at other times that "she really disliked intensely" what he was, and was bent on destroying him. They both felt it was wiser to separate. He leaves for Pottsville, where he at once writes her that "it is no use Mabel. I *can't* stay away. . . . But *I don't want* to be possessed. . . ." They make another try at it in Croton. More quarrels and recriminations. He determines to leave her for good. Pottsville is not far enough away; so he buys a ticket for Wyoming. While he is packing his bags, she comes into his room, sits down and quietly watches him for some time. And then suddenly she says, "Let us finish this impossible impasse and get married." The "shotgun marriage in the hands of some perverse fate" takes place the next morning and he leaves—without her —for Wyoming.

Restless and lonely without her, he rejoins Mabel— possibly with misgivings—in New York. The belated honeymoon may have been all that could be expected, but he leaves again, alone, for New Mexico, which he seems always to have disliked.

A few months later, Mabel follows him. "The plain truth is I am just dying of loneliness without you and I have to come." But he is unhappy there and cannot paint. Mabel aggravates the situation by creating a triangular situation with Tony, "a no-good show Indian" who had once been on a tour with a Wild West at Coney Island.

Mabel lacked finesse. She had a tepee constructed on the lawn. Here nightly she indulged in what she considered psychic affinities with her Indian lover. Maurice borrowed a huge revolver, but "I never used the gun, only kept it under my pillow in a childish, rather pitiful attempt to play cowboy to Tony's Indian." One night there is a violent scene. "We struggled a few minutes, and I pushed her down, off the bed, and onto the floor. Mabel stormed out of the room and her parting words were, 'Tomorrow, you get out.'"

He did, though not immediately. When they parted she "kissed me, and repeated, 'You must not worry. Go East, and have a good time. Then come back and everything will again be as it was before.'" She was mistaken, although for a while she continued to support him.

Maurice fell in love with Vera Segal on the rebound. This seems to have become a pattern in his romantic life. What he says about their early relation was written as an old man and he probably showed it to her. But it seems quite sincere.

"It was at the Duncan School that I met Vera, the woman with whom I have lived so happily ever after. She was just a girl then, but has retained the strange quality which attracted me to her from the first. It was her innocence and simplicity . . . that made me turn from the intellectual and sensuous, . . . the egotistical and domineering, that I had found in Mabel. Vera was . . . like air and space. In her I found . . . nature in the process of formation. . . . [She] had hardly any psychic form at all. She was, instead, made of reflections of a Cellini sky."

What Vera wrote about him after his death is, I believe, equally sincere.

"Maurice and I met at the Duncan School, when I was fifteen. I was a very serious and precocious young girl, worked hard at my dancing, read Schopenhauer and Nietzche, and had no use for boys my own age. Perhaps the Freudians would say that I was looking for a father. . . . I fell in love almost at once with the magnetic older man who sketched us while we danced."

Maurice's behavior as a lover ran true to form. "I was still restless and reluctant to settle into a routine life even with Vera. I left the Duncan School and went back to Paris. . . ." The curtain drops on the first act. Three years later, Vera takes up the thread of the interrupted courtship. She has left the Duncan School and is studying in Vienna.

"Maurice heard about all the charming gentlemen pressing for my hand and very quickly left Rome and joined me." Maurice is equally candid. "For myself, right before we got married, I had been in the midst of a very intense and passionate love affair in Rome. I believed that my main reason for rushing to Vienna was that my Roman attachment was growing very serious, and I was determined to honor my promise to Vera, that if ever I married, it would be to her. I really did not understand at all, at the time, why I felt compelled toward Vera. My Roman friend, although she did not particularly interest me intellectually, was the most erotically stimulating woman." Was there ever such a lover?

The marriage was, I believe, a completely happy one. Each

one must have found in the other what was most needed. Since childhood Maurice had been in search of serenity, security and someone's unshaken faith. He found it in Vera's guilelessness and steady devotion. Vera was by no means unintelligent or naïve in worldly ways. But there was something a little fey about her. Even in her fifties she retained the innocence and buoyancy of a healthy child. They had no children. For her, Maurice could fill this want, and more than other men he needed maternal protection and reassurance.

Sterne's early years had been a struggle. He had known hardship and poverty. Shortly after coming to America when he was twelve years old he had determined to study art. "I took a job at Jake's saloon at the upper end of Third Avenue. My salary was to be a dollar and a half a night and I was given a place to sleep, since my hours were from six to eight A.M. and from eight P.M. to midnight." This paid his tuition through the old National Academy of Design.

All through his life, however, he impressed people with his talent and found patrons who were willing to support him when in need. Alard DuBois Reymond gave him the money to spend two years in the Orient, and during the Depression, Edward Bruce guaranteed him $4000 a year. Mabel Dodge, too, supplemented his earnings both before their marriage and after their separation.

Sterne was still unknown when he returned from Bali in 1914. He was thirty-six years old. By 1920 his prestige had grown and a few years later he had tremendous financial success. In 1926 at the Scott and Fowles Gallery his exhibition was sold out. By 1927 his earnings were such that he could turn down an offer by a wealthy Chicago tycoon to do two family portraits at $30,000 each. "I always hated commissioned portraits. I felt that I was prostituting myself when I did them." Even during a depression year he earned $60,000.

His prestige as one of the leading American painters and sculptors was on a par with his earnings. Museums bought his work. Critics considered his Rogers-Kennedy Memorial in

Worcester the finest in America. In 1925 he was invited to paint a self-portrait for the Uffizi Gallery in Florence, the first American so honored. Yet Sterne could never bring himself to execute this commission! Another example of the recurrent response to a crisis or challenge? He said to me once: "I somehow could never face myself on canvas; get started doing it." Yet he was a superb draughtsman and more than once mentioned this honor from the Italian government with obvious complacency. And in 1933 the Museum of Modern Art gave him a one-man exhibition—the first to an American.

In the United States more than in other countries there is little sense of tradition in the arts. Reputations are quickly forgotten. The past fifty years, too, have seen a constant shift of taste and a jettison of the aesthetic criteria that have guided Western art since the fifteenth century. During the 1920's Sterne's paintings seemed a complete expression of the so-called "modern movement." "When I was a young painter myself, my work was considered 'ultra-modern'; as I reached maturity, the ultra-moderns called me 'old-hat.'"

In the best sense of the word Maurice Sterne was a traditionalist. So was Cézanne, his greatest influence as a young man. Both painters believed that a study of the classics and the understanding and reverent interpretation of nature are the foundations of great art. Sensitive and highly intellectual, Sterne was completely aware of the importance of the revolution in the arts which was taking place. He had, however, too much mental independence and honesty to swallow the movement whole. And I believe he was blind to, or at least he depreciated, two of the most important contributions of the École de Paris—the creation of a new idiom of design, the most important since the Renaissance superseded the Gothic five hundred years before; and, secondly, the acceptance of abstraction as a valid art form. "I admit the possibility that I am intellectually incapable of appreciating abstract art."

Little by little, on the other hand, he began to realize the two weaknesses in the movement that have culminated in the present universal chaos, and the breakdown of criteria of reference in art throughout the world. The first—the general assumption that technical innovation is *per se* in any way related to aesthetic excellence. "I have seen Picasso's innovations for the past fifty years, and each time I . . . have liked them less." The second—the extreme emphasis on self-revelation, which today, in much of our literature as in much of our art, seems almost a neurosis. "Great pictorial images arise from the discovery of previously unknown aspects of nature. They [the avant-gardists] were deluded into thinking that by turning their vision inward and exploring personality, they would create new masterpieces."

As he grew older Maurice felt more and more out of touch with contemporary trends. By the forties he was no longer fashionable. A decade later, already an old man, he believed that he was forgotten and left behind.

Fifteen years before his last illness Maurice was operated on for cancer. From then on he grew weaker. He had increasing spells of the dejection and pessimism which had haunted him from childhood. Old age seemed to him "a slow and painful ordeal . . . made infinitely worse by the terrible loss of friends and my own physical inability to comfort those who are left." He once said to Dr. David M. Levy, the psychiatrist, who had grown to know him during these years: "All my life I have on occasions behaved like a son-of-a-bitch. But my illness has changed me and made me a more decent man."

Several years before in one of his singular flashes of self-scrutiny Maurice observed that "my recollections of [Tagore] are meager, not because my memory is bad, but because I never really benefited very much from intercourse with celebrities. My own drive to make an impression on them, myself, shut me off from any really sensitive perception. I had a tremendous need to be judged 'someone to be reckoned with.' Even their words of wisdom were to me a challenge to say something in response which would be impressive. After these interviews I would remember little that the famous person had said, but every one of my own clever replies. I blush now to admit this."

This effort to impress and please others was part of Maurice's undeniable charm. One evening in Provincetown a year or two before his death he was wheeled from his sickbed to a *soirée* in a neighboring cottage. A number of his friends were gathered, among them several earlier students, now middle-aged women. How envious I became of his hypnotic charm. His voice was feeble but when he talked or recounted some anecdote the guests remained silent.

During these last unhappy bedridden years Maurice was too ill and weak to paint. When he had the strength he worked consistently on his memoirs. They would be his credo and *apologia sua* to posterity. I visited him once or twice during the summer in his Provincetown cottage, when he would sometimes read me a chapter. Hiram Haydn, who had agreed to publish the memoirs, saw him much more frequently. He became a very close friend and, in his role of editor, perhaps a confessor.

"When I left each time, he would say, 'Now come back soon.' Then there came a day in late July of 1957 when he seemed to be saying, though rather obliquely, that he thought he had done all he could do on the book. In fact, I remember his saying, not as though pleading, not even questioning—but saying—'It's really finished, isn't it?' He didn't look well and I noticed, too, that as we said goodbye, he didn't say anything about coming back soon. When I had gone to the door, he called me back and asked me to bend down and kissed me and said, 'I love you as much as any man I know because you know all the bad of me and still love me.' He died a little over a week later."

One late spring day a few months previously I had driven over from Croton to his home on Byram Lake Road in Mt. Kisco. In a corner of his bedroom where he lay there was a half-finished flower-piece of gladioli standing on an easel.

Maurice had asked my son Michael, who had come with me, to bring along some of his drawings. He looked them over and said some generous words. He seemed in one of his gay and whimsical moods.

He spoke with his deliberate and carefully articulated pronunciation and with his slight Russian accent. He said, "When I was a young man I was quite beautiful and rather proud of my body. But for several years now it has been behaving very badly. For a long time I was angry with it and resentful. Recently, however, since I have been ill we are forced to lie in bed together. So we have gotten to understand one another better, and are once more reconciled."

Vera told me that she was uncertain whether even then Maurice was aware of the nature and gravity of his illness. This cannot be true, for Maurice was not stupid or addicted to self-deception. A human being who can mature and mellow through suffering, and show fortitude, humility, sweetness and humor as he faces life's ultimate challenge, has become truly great.

SHADOW AND LIGHT

M·S

I

*In 1902, the work of Maurice Sterne was shown at an
exhibition of the Country Sketch Club in New York. From
that time, until his death in 1957, interviews and articles about
the artist appeared in the international press. During those
fifty-five years of public notice, it would be difficult to find
even one piece for which Sterne supplied the background
material which did not lay stress on his Jewish childhood in
Latvia. His notebooks, his letters, the conversations his friends
remember, are interlaced with recollections of his early life
and with speculation about its effect on his work and on his
personal motivation. Like so many creative men, Maurice
Sterne, painter and sculptor, seems to have carried his childhood with him as a very conscious and tangible part of his
adult life:*

Until I was a grown man, living in New York and about
to marry, I was not sure of what day I came into this world.
My mother was always vague about the date, and even the
month and year of my birth. When eventually I pressed her
to remember, she confessed that she had kept the date hidden
from me all those years because in 1878 I was born on the
Jewish holiday *Tischa B'ov*, a summer day set aside to mourn

3

the fall of the Temple in Jerusalem.[1]

The day seemed ill omened altogether. My mother had received a telegram, notifying her that her beloved sister Sarah Ita was dying and was calling for her. The two women had been very close since their childhood, when they were cruelly mistreated by their mother's second husband and were thrown upon each other for comfort and affection. Now Mother insisted on making the difficult journey immediately, in spite of the many hours of travel and the fact that she was in the last month of her pregnancy.

She traveled eighteen hours from Libau, the Latvian city in which we lived, to Königsberg, over the German border. She arrived only in time to see her sister die, and in a dazed and grief-stricken condition got back on the stagecoach and headed home. The shock and the rough road soon took their toll, and while the coach rattled on, my mother felt her first labor pains. She tried very hard to conceal her distress from the other passengers so that she might get home in time, but they realized what was happening and put her off the coach at Memel, a Latvian hamlet. I was born two hours later in the cottage of a local peasant. My mother was in no condition to care for me, and when Father arrived that evening he found her sitting on the floor and chanting prayers for the dead according to the Jewish mourning tradition, and in complete disregard of the child she had just borne. Luckily her baby's needs soon intruded upon her grief and she came back to reality, but this highly emotional reaction was typical of the kind of person she was.

All through my childhood my mother exacted obedience by

[1] Although few births of Jewish children were legally registered in the Russian world at that time, family traditions or records usually noted at least that a child was born "when David went to America," or "the year the wheat crop failed," etc. Even though *Tischa B'ov* is a day of partial fasting and mourning, it is unusual for a mother to suppress the fact that a child was born on this holiday. Jews are more likely to speak of the good omens of various births, and a child is believed to bring "his own good luck" to families rather in need of it. It was more likely her other bad associations with the day Maurice was born that gave her a superstitious feeling about it.

4

the impassioned plea, "I will suffer much more than you if you misbehave." She had a great flair for storytelling and for getting all the drama she could out of a situation. Her sense of humor was famed in the Jewish community of Libau, and sometimes, as when she named our cow after a neighbor, the jokes had a very sharp edge. I am afraid that my own lifelong inability to resist a wicked *bon mot* is a direct inheritance from her.

Mother was almost entirely in charge of the children, since my father was either away at work or at the synagogue discussing scholarly Talmudic problems. Although he was well educated and intelligent he was interested less in scholarship than in mystical concepts. He encouraged his children in this sort of speculation, and was much more patient with the many questions I asked during my childhood than was my mother. I remember one such incident after my first exposure to the Bible in the cheder, or religious school, to which I was sent when I was six. The rabbi had read in Yiddish, "In the beginning God created Heaven and Earth" and I wondered who, if that were so, had created God. I was absolutely bewildered and pondered over the question for days. I finally took the mystery to my mother, who very characteristically replied, "What questions he asks! How can I tell who created God, if I can't even tell what makes my own child ask such foolish questions?"

At that, Father put down his book and looked over the lamp beside him, into the shadows of the room beyond. "It is not a silly question," he said, "because God himself makes the boy ask it. It is a question I have often asked, though not of others." And looking over at me he added, "No one else can have that answer for you."

Mother wanted to know if he had ever found the right answer after all his years of asking and he replied, "Not yet, but I have not given up hope." He returned to his books then, as he had sent me back to mine.

It was certainly Hirsch Zwi Sterne, my father, who instilled

5

in me the need and the patience that have allowed me to spend all the years of my long life in the pursuit of my art. Whenever I think of him, I am reminded of Jacob wrestling with the Angel of the Lord. Jacob, at least, had a practical objective—to obtain a heavenly blessing. Father wrestled only for the sport of it, and it was this characteristic that most infuriated his wife. She had struggled with poverty all of her life and her battles were of a very practical kind: to find a decent life for Joel, Michael, Carl, Rosa, Lena, and myself. Obviously, this took all her energy.

My father's love of abstract ideas had been of little use in supporting such a large family. As a young man he had been a rabbinical student in Vilna, and according to the tradition of that city, had been supported at the Talmudic school by members of the community. He was engaged to marry the daughter of a wealthy manufacturer of Lodz when he met the beautiful and penniless Naomi Schlossberg. They were married, much to the indignation of Father's patrons, who taunted him with the old phrase against such folly, *"Hule, kaptsen,"* "Rejoice, you pauper." They continued to support him however, and during the years when my brothers and sisters were born, Father became a rabbi. However, Vilna was full of struggling young rabbis and I think that he must have understood that, in that city, his own intellectual gifts were insufficient to allow him ever to earn enough money to support a family. As an added complication, his thinking was much influenced by the German Jewish progressive movement which Moses Mendelssohn had originated the century before. Conservative Vilna was hardly the place for a young man of liberal views to prosper.

The family decided to move to Libau, a Baltic port with a population of about forty thousand, of whom about one quarter were Jews, and most of the rest German-speaking. Libau was the provincial capital of Courland, whose peasant population spoke only Lettish. Thus, although the area had been under Russian control since 1795, there were few Russians there and almost no Russian influence as to language or custom.

There were, however, more than enough rabbis in Libau, and my parents were again faced with the difficult task of feeding all their hungry children. At that point, my father's own father died and left enough money to enable him to buy a small brush factory. Unfortunately, he sold that business and bought another which failed disastrously. For years after, the unfortunate man was unable to earn a living, and it was my mother's small farming activities which kept us all alive. Then, just before I was born, my father became a grain merchant and finally began to prosper, though we did not realize then how short that prosperity would be, or how dangerous.

It was clear to me even as a young child that my mother and father, in spite of their temperamental differences and their quarrels, were very dear to each other. Our home was poor and simple, yet my brothers and sisters knew and loved good music and I remember best the long winter evenings when Lena and Rosa played Mozart, Haydn, and Bach over and over again. Mother would pay me a kopeck for each composer I could identify from a small part of the piece one of my sisters would play, and although I loved to get the money, I don't think that it had any great influence on my appreciation of music. In my adult life I haven't worried too much about struggling for money, but my love of music has grown every year.

The graphic arts had absolutely no place in our lives. Religious Jews took very seriously the Biblical injunction against "graven images" and I was punished badly one day by the rabbi of my school for drawing his picture on the ground with a stick. He said that I had broken the Second Commandment, but I suspect his reaction was quite close to that of the Balinese who years later were somewhat afraid of letting me draw their likenesses on the ground where they might be abused by passers-by. In my own home, paper was a precious commodity, and probably it was for economic rather than religious reasons that there was none for me to scribble on. Yet, even as a very small child, I loved to watch the snowflakes on our window, and I spent hours in the courtyard next door, fascinated by the cooper who started out with some scraps of wood and finished with a handsome barrel. Even then, it was the creative *process* in which I was interested and I had endless patience with it.

Moreover, my father was very clever with his hands. He had no training of course, but he could make all sorts of charming paper animals, and would amuse me by creating birds on perches or flying through the air, or by folding boxes, boats, and what, to my charmed eyes, seemed like a hundred other creatures. I learned the trick of making those things from him, and to this day, when I fold and cut the little paper toys for the grandchildren of my friends, I feel Father's presence vividly.

Though our lives had little graphic decoration, they were filled with the ceremony of religion. My parents were not as strictly Orthodox in their religious practice as were many of their neighbors, but my mother, in particular, loved the ceremonial observances and the holidays. All my days ended, not with lullabies, but with the solemn sound, in the bed beside me, of my mother calling her God in the traditional words, *"Sh'ma Yisrael, Adonoi Elohenu, Adonoi Echad"*—"Hear O Israel, the Lord our God, the Lord is One."

On Yom Kippur, the Day of Atonement, I used to visit my parents at the synagogue where they spent the entire day in fasting and in prayer. I would watch the congregation solemnly beat their breasts with their clenched fists in the ritual counting off of their sins of the year that had passed; and even now, I can think of no sound more awe-inspiring than the hollow gale of despair that issues forth from the *shofar*, the curved ram's horn, at sunset on Yom Kippur.

My education in Judaism was not confined to the synagogue or to my rabbi's teaching at school. I had a practical lesson one day while my mother and I were walking in a street of small

8

shops. A great noise of shouting men and horses' hoofs exploded behind us and without once looking back my mother ran with me into the shelter of a nearby doorway. A small company of Cossacks charged around a corner and into the narrow street where they laughed and cursed and swung their *nagaikas*, those infamous long whips. The crowd scattered in panic beneath their feet, and though that day no one was caught under the horses, the whips lashed out with agonizing accuracy. I have never forgotten the dreadful sound of that street, when the derisive Cossack blare mingled with the sharp, thin scream of their victims' terror. And my soul has recorded a deeper mark of the fear transmitted to me through my mother's shuddering body, which she used as a wall to protect me.

That day was a scene old in Mother's memory. She was born in 1838 midway in the reign of the merciless Tsar Nicholas I. While the rest of Europe was awakening to new concepts of freedom and the dignity of man, he had turned his face and his nation to the despotic past. The death penalty was revived, all freedom was suppressed, and minorities, particularly the Jews, were ruthlessly persecuted. Alexander III, the Tsar of my own time, was faithful to these terrible ideals, and by the 1880's all Russians of liberal thought lived in the shadow of fear. The secret police were everywhere, and what they did not discover for themselves might be revealed by some frightened neighbor. The sound of soldiers on the street, the midnight knock on the door, were as feared then as in Hitler's time, or in the worst days after the Bolshevik revolution.

Of course, the Jews of my parents' generation who knew personally what suffering was involved were the most fearful. Once when my brother Carl brought a forbidden book into the house, my mother grew hysterical and made Carl promise to dispose of it.

A week later, her worst fears were realized. My father was away on a business trip, Carl had returned to the university in

Dorpat, and Michael was gone for the evening. Two police officers and two heavily armed guards came into our house late at night. They declared quite simply, "We want Michael Sterne," and they commanded my mother to get him. Now, at this distance, I realize how brave she was, for she firmly replied, "Michael Sterne is away from home. I do not know where he is and can tell you nothing of him."

The officer advised my mother that as a pious woman she should not lie about a son who attended meetings where students spoke of treason. My mother swayed and almost fell, because she had had no idea that my brothers' political activities went beyond the talking stage. The guards began to search the house and my mother followed them from room to room, with me trailing after her. Lena and Rosa fled upstairs to the large bed they shared and there they sat throughout the night, clasped in each other's arms.

As it turned out, Carl had not disposed of the banned novel, for the guards found it under a mattress in the room he and Michael shared. The officer glanced at the book and passed it to his small companion who somehow caused it to disappear in the huge coat he wore. This moment returns to me with special clarity, for although he probably put the book in some inner pocket, the effect was so much like a trick of sleight of hand that I almost giggled.

The Russians assumed that the book was Michael's, and the danger to him was greatly increased. My mother fainted and the soldiers carried her downstairs and placed her on my cot. They ordered the lights turned off and a watch set up lest Michael return. They waited for him all through the night and ceaselessly questioned my mother in low insistent voices. The quiet and dark were strangely peaceful and I think I fell asleep. I remember starting up at one point, when footsteps sounded on the street outside, but they went past our house and the waiting began again. Michael had still not returned at dawn. The soldiers and officers left, apparently confident that they would soon get him.

But with the help of loyal friends and my mother's silver candlesticks, Michael escaped over the border into Germany where he began to train for a career in opera. His participation in the political ferment of the time ended that night. My mother must have been relieved to have one of her sons away from it. In any case, she could never understand what stake they, as Jews, could have in the Russian political struggle.

There is a good explanation of this late nineteenth-century Russian-Jewish revolutionary activity in Dubnow's History of the Jews in Russia and Poland:

> The Russian school and literature pushed the Jewish college youth head over heels into the intellectual currents of progressive Russian society. Naturally enough a portion of the Jewish youth was also drawn into the revolutionary movement. . . . In joining the ranks of the revolutionaries, the young Jews were less actuated by resentment against the continued [persecution of the Jews] than by discontent with the general political reaction in Russia. . . . Jewish students began to "go to the people"—the Russian people to be sure, not the Jewish. . . . It was taken for granted [by the Jewish youth] at that time that the realization of the ideals of Russian democracy would carry with it the solution of the Jewish as well as all other sectional problems of Russian life.[1]

After this crisis, our family had a period of good fortune. The grain business continued to prosper, my oldest brother Joel was well established in business in Moscow, Carl was doing brilliantly at the university, and Michael had gone from Berlin to America where he hoped to realize the promise of his splendid voice. Rosa, Lena and I lived at home with our parents. It was a happy time.

[1] Semen Dubnow, *History of the Jews in Russia and Poland* (Jewish Publication Society of America, 1920), Vol. II, pp. 222–23.

Yet my mother, who kept insisting that good luck was to be distrusted, turned out to be right. After about two years in the grain business my father began to be bothered by a dry, hollow cough which grew worse all the time. On the days when the peasants brought their grain into the warehouse he would have paroxysms of coughing that lasted far into the night. He insisted that it was only the dust which bothered him, and that a glass of wine would wash it out of his throat. But the dust swirled about him day after day, so thick that no wine could wash it away, and at last the dust became death.

My father went to bed one week during the last grim days of winter and stayed there until my brother Joel came from Moscow in the early spring to be with us for the Passover. Joel had not seen our father for months, and when he stepped into the room to say some cheerful greeting, he stopped in stricken disbelief. I also saw my father then, though Joel's fresh eyes, and understood for the first time, though I was only seven years old, that he would die. We all knew that this Passover was to be my father's last; that this Seder was the last one for all of us as a family. My mother and sisters prepared the meal with a special tenderness and Joel tried to explain to me the symbolic meaning of our celebration: the marking of spring as a joy that succeeds the winter's sorrow, the hope of daily deliverance from death. I saw in my brother's face how the pain of that day was made sharper by remembrances of other Seders the family had shared.

At last everything was ready, the table was set, the ceremonial candles lit and blessed by my mother. All the traditional symbols were there: the shank of roasted paschal lamb, the roasted egg, the horseradish, the unleavened bread, the *Charoseth* made of apples, wine, and nuts to recall the bricks and mortar our forebears had been forced to labor with in Egypt. Bright in the center of the table was the glass of wine which is set out for the stranger, for the Prophet Elijah who is expected on that night.

My father had been forbidden by his doctor to get out of

bed and we began the service without him, all of us painfully conscious of his absence. Joel took Father's place at the table, uncovered the *Matzoh*, and read the ancient words:

"This is the bread of affliction which our forefathers ate in the land of Egypt. Let all who are hungry enter and eat of it, and all who are needy, let them come and celebrate the Passover."

Father came through the door then. I looked up at him, and through the halo of light around Elijah's silver goblet, I saw the figure of the Prophet himself. He stood tall and gaunt in a white robe that fell to his feet. His long black hair and beard framed his pale, sad, still face, and his great eyes burned with a terrible and beautiful life. If I did not really doubt then that it was my father, neither have I ever doubted since that night that the Prophet may come to the feast.

My father conducted the service, though his hand shook as he held his prayer book and fever stained his cheeks as red as the wine on the table. At last the meal was over, but he stayed a minute to tease me about how well, as the youngest son, I had asked the Four Questions on which the service is built. "Who ever taught you, Moshe, to say them so well?" he asked. "It must have been your rabbi."

I was very proud of my accomplishment and told him I had not only learned the Four Questions, but had taught myself the Kaddish. My mother and brother gasped when I said this. What I did not know was that the Kaddish is the mourner's prayer for the dead. Father broke the shocked silence and gently said, "Let us hear how well you remember this long and difficult prayer. Stand up and recite it for me, my son."

I began, "*Yiskadal v'yiskadash shmay rabah . . .*"

I did not understand what I was saying, but I knew that something terrible was happening and I ran from the room in bitter tears.

Passover lasts for eight days and Father seemed to want to

see it through. He died on the ninth day, with some words on his lips for my mother, which she could not understand.

I was unprepared for the violence of her grief when Father died. In my childish ignorance, I had been looking forward to the funeral as a special sort of holiday, but my mother's anguish was a reality I could not cope with. She flung herself on the coffin and shrieked for my father to take her with him. She made of her cries of his name—"Hirshele—Hirshele—" a desperate appeal, a moan of finality.

I did not know what to make of it all and began to wail myself. I somehow believed that the undertaker was the cause of all our problems and I bit and kicked at him. Only when I heard Joel say that I was in no condition to go to the cemetery did I calm down, so anxious was I to get my first long carriage ride.

Our family never returned to its old peace, nor did anyone ever seem the same to me. During her husband's long illness Mother had lost her gaiety. She performed her chores in silence, and though I teased and tempted her, our humorous chats were gone. This detachment became much worse after my father died. Then her day passed either in housework or in chanting prayers for interminable hours.

I remember how shocked I was when I overheard her telling her closest friend that she herself was responsible for Father's death. She said that from the time he entered the grain business she had had a premonition of impending disaster, though he had scoffed at her worrying. She blamed herself for having enjoyed the prosperity, and not having insisted that he give up the business.

Months later a business associate of my father had a long chat with her and explained that since she had never even set foot in the granary, she could not have had any inkling that the dust would cause tuberculosis. After that conversation her guilt feelings seemed to subside and she slowly came back to herself.

As to my own mourning, I said the Kaddish in earnest at the

Maurice Sterne at an early age, with his mother and sisters

The young Maurice Sterne

grave on the day of the funeral and according to Jewish law, continued for many months to say the prayer every morning and night at the synagogue. It was really a remarkable attendance record for a seven-year-old boy, and I was quite proud of its unblemished perfection, until one day I was on some excursion with my mother and missed the evening prayer. I was terribly upset, and right out on the street began to cry and hit out at her with my fists for making me miss it. I shouted, "It's all your fault! Yours, yours!"

Mother looked at me with a surprised and pitying expression and said, "Please don't make such a spectacle of yourself, Moshe. Everyone is shocked." When we got home she added, "Your outburst back there almost makes me feel like dying right now, while you're still so eager to say Kaddish. I know that if I wait until my old age to die, there will be nobody to say the prayers for me."

From that day on I did not particularly care whether I missed the Kaddish or not. I suppose I had considered my attendance as a sort of sports record rather than a religious duty.

We received religious training at the cheder I attended but I thought of the Bible more as a good story than anything profound. I have never during my life been of a particularly religious turn of mind, but shortly after my father's death my own "Jewishness" made a deep impression upon me. My mother had taken me to Vilna to visit with my father's brother David and his family. They were Orthodox Jews and my uncle was scandalized that Mother did not wear a wig, as was customary for married women, and that I was dressed in indecently short pants.

However, in spite of Uncle David's disapproval, I felt a sense of harmony and relaxation in Vilna that I had never felt before. For a while I longed to live there permanently. Although we spoke Yiddish in our house in Libau, the moment we stepped out into the street we had to be sure to speak another language. To the small boy I was, it seemed as if

I myself had become a translation. In Vilna, Yiddish was spoken openly on the streets and the Jews made no attempt to disguise their customs or hide their identity.

Israel Cohen's classic work on Vilna [1] *gives us some further insight into the city's impact on the young Jewish boy:*

> The area within which they [the Vilna Jews] lived was so circumscribed that they were obliged to exploit it to the utmost. They thus created inner streets in the court-yards behind the houses. . . . Every door and every window was utilized by tradesmen and artisans for their stores or workbenches. . . . [2]

> Physically, the Jews of Vilna were in a Slavic country that had been a stronghold of paganism until the Four-teenth Century; spiritually, they were in close daily communion with ancient Palestine. . . . The devotion to this religious lore was not confined to the rabbi or to the professional student, but was shared by the merchant and the artisan. . . . [Even the material needs of the Yeshiva students were looked after by the community.]

> [Vilna] gave birth to the most famous of Talmudic luminaries in Eastern Europe. . . . Moreover, Vilna pro-duced countless eminent rabbis for other communities and other countries. . . . [3]

> A city in which every third inhabitant was a Jew had an unmistakably Jewish character; and this was enhanced by the fact that . . . 98.9 per cent of the Jews in . . . Vilna used Yiddish as their ordinary medium of intercourse. Vilna could claim to be not only the "Jerusalem of Lithu-ania," but the cultural capital of Russian Jewry. [4]

[1] Israel Cohen, *Vilna* (Jewish Publication Society, 1943).
[2] Ibid., p. 91.
[3] Ibid, pp. 182–87.
[4] Ibid., p. 334.

Before my father's death, Joel and Carl had gone to Moscow to make their way. Then, a few months after Mother and I returned from Vilna, Rosa graduated from the gymnasium and it was decided that we should all go to Moscow where she could get a teaching job and the family could be together again.

Moscow vibrated with excitement in those days before the drab and stultifying influence of Communism. There were Chinese merchants in long dark robes, with pigtails and thin white mustaches above scraggly goatees; Uzbeks from Central Asia, who shaved their heads and wore colored skullcaps and long striped robes; strong-faced Tartars from the Black Sea. I would stare at the large bundles they carried through the streets and shiver at the illicit things they probably concealed.

My favorite walk was along the banks of the Moscow River on a wide street called Hunter's Row. In winter huge frozen sturgeon were piled in front of the shops, like logs in the deep snow. I would dodge through the crowds of peasants in their picturesque sleighs and sniff at the strong smell of their shaggy-coated horses.

But it was Zaradye, the small and poverty-stricken Jewish ghetto, that fascinated me most. Only a stone's-throw from the mighty Kremlin, it was a dirty and noisy place whose inhabitants lived crowded together below the level of the streets, and had about them the vibrant energy of a people who belonged. My mother and brother Joel were shocked that I went into such a bad and shameful neighborhood, but I could not stay away, for in Zaradye I, too, felt that I belonged. It was the only place in Moscow I could walk without the fear of some derisive voice calling "Szyd," "Szyd."

Perhaps my own experience with persecution was the reason I stood spellbound whenever lines of guarded men on their way to Siberia passed through the streets of Moscow. Those among them who were criminals walked with bowed heads and slid furtive glances at the silent crowds. The political prisoners, many of them banished to a life of slavery for expressing their views, walked proudly; yet no one among the spectators dared acknowledge them, or even meet their eye.

Children do not have such "discretion." One day as I was talking with my mother, we passed a group of these men trudging through the snow. Suddenly I saw that my young cousin Nicholai was among them and I was terribly frightened. I tore away from Mother and ran after him shouting, "Kolia, Kolia, where are they taking you?"

Kolia did not turn his head, but one of the guards stepped out of line and hit me on the chest with his rifle. I fell to the street and lay in the gutter weeping.

Nicholai was my favorite cousin. The family was very proud of him because of his brilliant work at medical school, but I admired his dark blue student's uniform, with its row of proud silver buttons. To see this beloved hero in the misshapen cap and ill-fitting khaki coat of the convict was more than I could bear.

I pestered my family for days to tell me what had happened but they considered Siberia and Nicholai's anti-Tsarist political activities too terrifying to speak of to a young child. Like other adult secrets, this one was unsuccessful and we children knew that Kolia had been exiled from life.

For all its problems, it was in Moscow that I had my first encounter with the art that was to become my life. When I was about ten years old my sister Rosa took me to the Tretiakoff Art Gallery to see some of its famous paintings. On our way out of the museum we passed through a small gallery where I saw something that interested me far more than had any of the exhibits. A man stood before a painting of a seated Christ and—wonderful to behold—he was copying it! Rosa could not tear me away. Eventually the young artist asked me if I wanted to become a painter when I grew up. I was stupefied by the question and answered, "I don't know." He asked me whether I liked to draw, but I could not be bothered with conversation, so engrossed was I in comparing the original with the canvas on the easel. It was like a miracle to me to watch the colors on the palette being transformed into a painting.

"How do you like my copy?" the artist suddenly asked.

"I think it's better than the original, but . . ."

He urged me to continue and I told him that I didn't know what was wrong but that something about the left eye disturbed me. The painter patted me on my cheek, and when I asked if I could hold the palette, indulgently told me that I might put a few dabs of paint in the background of his work. I thanked him and said, "If you don't mind I'd rather fix that eye. Now I see just what's wrong with it. The one on the wall has a much dreamier expression than yours."

At that, my embarrassed sister whisked me away but I went home from that gallery determined to be an artist.

My family gave me no encouragement in this burning desire. I had been registered in a trade school and was expected to learn a useful skill, but every moment I could I spent in drawing and I gave very little attention to the teachers who tried to make me a locksmith.

The Jewish trade school I attended was established by the famous Baron de Hirsch.[1] It had an academic as well as a vocational program and I acquired there a love of fine literature, strangely, from the dourest, strictest teacher of the school. One day, as he read a poem "The Scholar" in sensitive and moving cadence, Dimitri Petrovich was transformed from an ogre, and I loved him thereafter with all the passion an intense child can bring to such relationships. With his guidance I read Lermontoff, Gogol, and Pushkin, and literature soon took the place of religion in my life. As a matter of fact, very often I would be mumbling poetry when I was supposed to be

---

[1] Baron Maurice de Hirsch, 1831–96; Jewish philanthropist who sponsored a plan to colonize Jews in Argentina, and subsidized Jewish education in Galicia, Russia, and the United States, with special emphasis on manual and technical skills which Jews had not heretofore studied.

reciting my Hebrew prayers.

In 1888, Joel became a "First Guild" merchant and went into the wholesale dry-goods business. We all prospered. It was decided, with some reservations about my ability, to take me out of the trade school and send me to the more advanced polytechnical school. I was not as happy with the change as I had expected. For the first time in my life, my classmates were not Jewish and until I was befriended by a big boy, I was teased and tormented for being a Jew.

I did poorly in geometry and mathematics, the very subjects the school stressed. However, in "free drawing" I was always the best, and eventually my art teacher and the school's director summoned me to ask why, with such talent, I was studying engineering. I explained that my family considered that I would starve as an artist.

However, their encouragement gave me added incentive to draw, and the moment I finished my daily homework, my real life began. I drew everything around me: my mother with her Bible, or at the stove, or blessing the Sabbath candles with mysterious gestures; Lena at the piano; my childhood memories of Libau. A favorite subject was the lanky, black chimney sweep with his stovepipe hat, and, slung over his shoulders, coils of rope with large iron bells attached to their ends. He was very long-legged and carried a tall, thin ladder. He had the most picturesque silhouette I'd ever seen.

As the end of the school term approached, even my drawing could not console me. I knew that although I had received the highest marks in all my other subjects, I would never master the mathematics.

I went to my art teacher in despair and asked him if he could help me since he continued to be enthusiastic about my painting. By the end of the week he had arranged an interview for me with the director of the Kommisarsky Art Academy. The Director examined my work and cautioned me to study hard. The following week I was awarded a scholarship!

My family was amazed and not at all approving. Joel,

especially, thought that my work was extremely ugly and that I should not be permitted to accept the scholarship. However, my mother intervened and everything was arranged. Then, only two days later, the newspaper announced that all Jews who were not university graduates or First Guild merchants had to leave the city. Joel was a First Guild merchant, Carl had a university degree, and Rosa was married to a lawyer. However, my mother, my sister Lena, and I were ordered out of *Matushka Moskva*, "Mother Moscow." We did not know where to go, since more and more of Russia was being closed off to Jews.

The History of the Jews in Russia and Poland *gives some of the details of this Imperial Russian order:*

It was on . . . the first day of the Jewish Passover, when the synagogues of Moscow were filled with worshippers, that an alarming whisper ran from mouth to mouth telling of the publication of an imperial ukase ordering the expulsion of the Jews from the city . . .[1]

People who had lived in Moscow for twenty, thirty, or even forty years were forced to sell their property within a short time and leave the city. Those who were too poor to comply with the orders of the police . . . were thrown into jail or sentenced to the transportation prisons.

The heads of various local provincial administrations published circulars calling the attention of the police to the "audacious conduct" of the Jews who, on meeting Russian officials, failed to take off their hats by way of greeting. The governor of Moghilev instructed the police of his province to impress the local Jewish population with the necessity of "polite manners."

In 1890, the provincial authorities, acting evidently on a signal from above, began to change numerous little townlets into villages, which, as rural settlements, would be

---

[1] Dubnow, *History of the Jews in Russia and Poland*, Vol. II, p. 401.

closed to the Jews. As a result, all the Jews who had settled in these localities after the issuance of "Temporary Rules" of May 3, 1882, were now expelled [as were older settlers who could not prove their claims].[1]

We wrote to Max[2] in New York, who cabled us that steamship tickets were on the way and early in August, 1889, Mother, Lena and I sailed for America on the SS *Suevia*.

[1] Ibid., p. 405.
[2] Formerly referred to as Michael.

We had arrived at last in the promised land, and although much has been written about immigration to America, only those who have known the agony of repression can appreciate the blessing it was to be here.

It was also absolutely bewildering to me. We lived at first with my brother Max and his family, on a street near the Metropolitan Opera House in what was then a predominantly Negro neighborhood. I was keenly aware of the vibrant life around me but, as in my previous transplantation to Moscow, I had no inner contact with my new surroundings. I seemed to live in a sort of no-man's-land.

As a matter of fact, probably because of my uprooting, my whole adolescence was dull and abstracted. When I look back now, I seem to have been asleep. All I can recall is an exaggerated self-consciousness that got in the way of my perception of outside things. I suppose it was an unconscious mourning over my childhood and also a marking time, a waiting period until I could go back to painting. I never talked about this but I believed that I would be an artist as fervently as any true believer—it was the religious faith I could never muster.

I studied English and went to school for a few days, but my family was in bad financial condition. With the money Joel had given her, Mother bought some used furniture, and Lena, she, and I moved to the Lower East Side, where among other European Jewish immigrants, we felt less disoriented.

Lena gave up her studies and got a job as a seamstress and after a very short time, I also left school.

Sterne wrote of his early days in the United States in a piece for The New Yorker *published on January 29, 1955:*

I put on the drab factory apron of a Jewish immigrant. My first job was stripping tobacco in the rear of a cigar store on Eighth Avenue. The next year, I worked in a bronze factory on Varick Street, helping to produce those elegant Spanish cavaliers that adorned the black-marble clocks that were so popular on Victorian mantels. When I tried to improve upon the design of the cavaliers, I was fired. This led me, in the summer of 1892, when I was twelve,[1] to go to work in a flag factory on the lower West Side.

The year 1892 was particularly memorable for me. Gentleman Jim Corbett defeated John L. Sullivan for the heavyweight championship of the world. The United States celebrated the Fourth Centenary of its discovery by Christopher Columbus. Grover Cleveland was elected President, and the country's greatest poet, Walt Whitman, died. I took an interest in all these events. I won fifty cents on the fight. I marched up Riverside Drive in a Columbus parade. I promoted, as we shall see, the election of Grover Cleveland, and I discovered Walt Whitman, whose *Leaves of Grass,* . . . made me aware, at least in theory, of the essential difference between the Old World and the New.

During the Presidential campaign, there was a great demand for small American flags that could be carried in parades. In five months at the factory, I, as a sticker boy, glued one and a quarter million paper flags to small wooden sticks. All those flags, I felt, would be used to help elect Cleveland. (That they might just as well be used to help reelect Benjamin Harrison

[1] Sterne was fourteen or fifteen at this time.

did not occur to me. I was, for some reason, a staunch Cleveland man.)

The factory was on the third floor of a four-story loft building. The only light came from gas jets burning overhead, the heat in summer was stifling, and there was the sickening odor of fish glue at the boiling point. To add to the discomfort, the whole building vibrated from a machine shop on the lower two floors. I could hardly wait for the 6 P.M. siren. The sticker boys—there were about a dozen of us—worked under the stern and often bloodshot eye of a foreman named Meyer, a former sergeant in the German Army. He was a short, wiry man with a straggling walrus mustache, and pale-blue eyes gleaming under bushy brows. He knew by name only the two boys he was fond of, Hans Bauer and Johnny Tweedy. All the rest of us he called "*Verfluchter Hund,*" "*Schweinehund,*" and "*Lausbub*" (cursed dog, pig-dog and louse-brat). I was almost always a "*Lausbub.*"

The flags, each about the size of a postcard, were printed twelve dozen to a sheet, and Herr Meyer's job was to cut them apart, using a heavy, brass-edged ruler, and then to arrange them in gross lots for the sticker boys. It was tedious work. Herr Meyer was a gambler and a heavy drinker. All day long, Johnny Tweedy ran back and forth between the factory and the corner saloon, fetching pints of lager beer in a tin pail. He also fetched slips with numbers on them. These slips resulted in Herr Meyer's either shouting with joy or cursing like hell. When he won—it was the policy game—he would get drunk because he felt good, and when he lost, he would get drunk because he was angry. Almost invariably, when he was angry, he would shuffle across the floor and hit one of us sticker boys on the head with his brass ruler.

My chief balm at this time was Walt Whitman. The poet had died a few months before, and the wonderful tributes paid him in the newspaper obituaries had made me want to find out about his poetry. A friend of mine, a theological student much older than I, had lent me *Leaves of Grass.* Although Whitman's poems did not exactly celebrate the America I was familiar with, I felt in them an elemental power, a beauty, and a sense of comradeship that I had never known before. At work, to raise my spirits, I would recite, sotto voce, the few poems of his that I had managed to memorize.

Then, one night at home, I copied some of my favorite Whitman poems on small sheets of paper; the next day I took them with me to work, slipped them beneath my stack of flags, and referred to them whenever I had a chance. This way I learned a great many by heart.

One night, when I came home from work, my mother noticed a bump on my head and asked how it got there. I had never told her about Herr Meyer's brutality, but now I did. He had struck me that afternoon because he was drunk and had lost at policy.

"Does he beat the other boys, too?" my mother asked.

"All but the two he is fond of."

"How often does he beat you?"

"This was the first time," I lied. As a matter of fact, it was only the second.

"And it will be the last. Tomorrow, I will go with you and repay him with interest." She paused. "What did you do when he hit you?"

"I don't remember. I think I cried."

"I cried," she repeated in a whining voice. "Look at him. A big, strong boy, almost a man, and he thinks he cried. You should have taught him a lesson he'd never forget." When I gave her my word that I would quit the job on Saturday, she agreed not to accompany me to the loft.

I didn't even stay until the end of the week. The following day, I was glancing covertly at one of my sheets of paper, mumbling some lines from "Song of the Open Road," when Herr Meyer suddenly appeared at my side, armed with his ruler. He had lost again at policy and was in a furious mood.

"*Lausbub!* I'll learn you to read poetry," he shouted, and

26

with the ruler delivered a vicious blow on my head. Almost maddened with rage and pain, I grabbed up a five-pound weight we used in our work and hit him between the eyes. He dropped to the floor.

One look at his sprawling figure was enough for me. I rushed to the door, where I pulled my hat and coat from a hook, and then went leaping down the two flights of stairs. I didn't stop until I was a couple of blocks away from the building. Then I hid in a doorway; I knew that one of the sticker boys, a friend of mine, would soon be passing on his way home. When he walked by, I spoke to him, asking about Herr Meyer, and he said, "Too bad you didn't kill the old bastard. But you certainly did a good job. He bled like a pig." The gash, it seemed, had been bandaged hurriedly with several of the flags. "He was a pretty sight, with his head all wrapped in stars and stripes," the boy said, laughing.

When I reached home and told my mother what had happened, she said, "It's about time you woke up."

"Supposing I had killed him?"

"But you didn't," she replied. "Anyhow, it would have been in self-defense."

For the next four years, I worked at a variety of factory jobs, and took a mounting interest in the life of the city. One day, in 1896, I read that a new store, Wanamaker's, had opened at Tenth Street and Broadway. This was a considerable distance from Madison Street, where I lived, but, anxious to see the new store, I made the trip, on foot and through the snow, on Christmas Eve. After I entered the building, I began rambling around the huge main floor, and presently came to the book counter. I glanced at the rows of volumes—they were mostly current novels and books for children. Suddenly, I thought of Walt Whitman. Through the years, my admiration for him had grown steadily, even though I had never owned a copy of *Leaves of Grass*, feeling that I could not afford one. Now I looked around for a copy of the book. There wasn't a single one to be seen.

27

When a salesgirl came up to me and asked if she could do anything for me, I said, "I wonder if you have Walt Whitman's *Leaves of Grass*."

"We had quite a few, but they were sold," she replied. "I think we have one copy left of an earlier, more expensive edition." She looked at my rather shabby overcoat, and added, "It costs three dollars and seventy-five cents."

"Would you mind if I look at it?"

"Not at all." She found the book on one of the shelves and handed it to me. Then she moved down the counter, leaving me with the book and the distressing thought that I could not afford the luxury of buying it.

I opened the volume, and as I turned the pages I remembered how, four years before, the poet had been a comfort to me when I worked under the tyrannical Herr Meyer. Then something else stirred in my memory. I thought of Russia in the eighties and of how much another writer—Dostoevsky—had meant to my brother Carl and my sister Rosa. Dostoevsky was their favorite author. They were always discussing his novels, and they often quarreled over *Crime and Punishment*. My brother condemned the main character, Raskolnikov. "Murder could never be justified, even if it would benefit all mankind," he would claim. My sister was a few years younger than he and believed that the end justifies the means. She saw no harm in killing and robbing old women if it would benefit a gifted young student who was handicapped by poverty. I agreed with her. My mother sided with Carl. "Raskolnikov was a fool," she once said. "Only they who have no conscience can afford to kill and steal."

Thinking of this now, as I thumbed through the pages of Whitman, I was startled by some lines which I had never read before:

> *Whoever you are holding me now in hand . . .*
> *Put me down and depart on your way.*
> *Or else by stealth . . .*

Why not by stealth? I felt, all at once, that I could not depart without the book—why not steal it?

Yes, Mama, I know I have a conscience, I thought. But stealing is not killing. And to steal from a store is not like stealing from a person. A store has no heart. It cannot suffer.

A popular German proverb—*Wer wagt nicht, der hat nicht* (Who dares not, he has not)—flashed through my mind. My desire for *Leaves of Grass* was stronger than my conscience. I saw my chance, presently, when a number of people gathered at the book counter, and the salesgirl was kept very busy. I picked up the book and tried to slip it into the right-hand pocket of my overcoat, but was horrified to find the pocket too small. The book fell to the floor. Trying to seem nonchalant, I casually picked it up again, put it on the counter, and looked over several other books. Relieved at not having taken the volume, and yet disgusted with my bungling, I decided to go home. I was about to leave when an elderly lady, with stooped shoulders, came up to the counter, looked around, and then picked up *Leaves of Grass* and gave it to the salesgirl, along with a ten-dollar bill.

"Please wrap it up nicely. It's a Christmas present for my son-in-law," the old lady said. When she got her change and the book, she left.

On my way across the store, I saw the lady again, buying neckties, and I stopped to watch her. Presently, she moved to another counter and bought a pair of pajamas, and then went on to the handbag counter, where she put down her parcels and began to examine the bags. She bought one, finally, and walked away.

It's impossible! I thought. It can't be true!

She had taken her other packages but left the book behind; it was partly covered by a large bag made of Paisley. I went over and without hesitation picked up the book. I reasoned that the old woman's negligence and my presence at the crucial moment could not possibly be mere coincidence. It must be a pattern woven by a fate chiefly concerned with my welfare. I watched her as she made her way slowly through the crowd, toward the main entrance. Suddenly, she seemed to me to be very old and helpless and pathetic. I hastened after her. I had gone only a few steps when I felt a light tap on my shoulder.

"I wouldn't do that, if I were you," a voice said. "What is this parcel?"

I looked around and saw a large and severe-looking man who, for a moment, brought back thoughts of Herr Meyer.

"A book," I said.

"Where did you get it?" the man asked.

"I found it."

"Yes? We'll soon see about that."

Gripping me by the arm, he took me back to the book counter, where I confronted the salesgirl.

She unwapped the parcel and stared at me, and then at *Leaves of Grass*. "My God!" she exclaimed. "How did you get hold of it? I sold it to an old lady only a little while ago."

"I've had my eye on him for some time," the man holding me said. "When I caught him, he was about to sneak out with the book."

I was amazed to hear that I had been watched.

"Come along," the man said, picking up the book.

I can never forget the long march through the crowded store. Fortunately for me, the shoppers were not aware of my disgrace. But the employees knew that I was in the grip of a store detective. They stared at me.

At last we reached the manager's office, at the back of the store. He was sitting behind a desk. When the detective reported that I had stolen a book, the manager asked him the name of it.

"A book on botany," said the detective, placing it on the desk. "It's called *Leaves of Grass*."

I saw a faint smile cross the manager's face.

"Are you familiar with *Leaves of Grass?*" he asked me.

"Yes, sir," I replied.

"Do you own a copy?"

"No, sir."

He then asked me my name, age and birthplace. I told him. "You must have learned English as a child, in Russia," he said. "You speak it quite well."

"No, sir, I picked it up since I came here."

"What do you mean, picked it up?"

"From Shakespeare, Dickens, and Walt Whitman, mostly," I said. "I also know German, Russian, and Yiddish and can translate the five books of Moses from the Hebrew."

"If you are so familiar with the Bible," he said, "I am surprised that you have forgotten the Seventh Commandment, 'Thou Shalt Not Steal.'"

"I beg your pardon, sir. You mean the Eighth."

"I beg your pardon," he said, with a smile. "I made a mistake." He leaned back and looked at me intently for a moment. "You say you are familiar with Walt Whitman's poems. Can you recite one?"

He evidently thought to trap me. Confidently, I began:

*"A woman waits for me, she contains all, nothing is
    lacking,
Yet all were lacking if sex were lacking. . . ."*

The manager smiled again. "All right. Now try another," he said.

I replied:

*"Give me the splendid silent sun with all his beams full
    dazzling. . . ."*

"I see you are quite a scholar, and your memory is excellent," the manager said. "But I advise you to pay more attention to the Eighth Commandment."

He turned to the detective and told him he could go. When the detective left the room, he turned back to me. "Now, I

31

find all this very confusing. Sit down in that chair and tell me about it."

Sitting down, I told him exactly what I had done while in the store. Then the manager said, "There is something I would like to clear up. You claim that you were about to return the book to the woman when the detective stopped you. Why didn't you tell him that?"

"I was confused and scared, I guess."

"Now tell me truthfully, did you really intend to return the book to its owner?"

It took me some time to answer. "I was sure until now. Since you asked me, I am not so sure."

The manager looked thoughtful. "Well," he said, after a minute, "I believe you did intend to return it, and I think that that mitigates your crime. In view of your youth and the circumstances, I am going to let you go home. There is one condition, however—you must promise never again to take anything you are not entitled to."

I promised.

Then the manager picked up the book and said, "Unfortunately, I can't give you the splendid silent sun you so ardently desire, but perhaps you will accept this gift from one admirer of the poet to another." He handed me the book.

I was too dazed to do more than mumble a "thank you," take the gift, and rush from his office. It was closing time, and the store was almost deserted. A few shoppers were being directed to a side exit. Suddenly, the detective came up beside me. He did not grip my arm, but, apparently knowing what had happened, he said, with a smile, "No hard feelings?"

"None," I replied.

Leaving Wanamaker's, I walked home in the snow, under halos that swirled around the street lights, carrying my copy of *Leaves of Grass*. I still have it.

———

My last factory job was in the shop of a map engraver where I ran errands and learned the rudiments of the trade.

However, my frustration at not being able to paint grew unbearable and I began to search the want-ad columns for "artist apprentice" jobs which I imagined would be common in such a large city.

Weeks went by and I did not see even one such advertisement. I determined to call on the artists' studios in Carnegie Hall and on West Tenth Street. At 51 West Tenth Street I knocked on every door in the building. Most of the occupants stared at me as if I were joking, but at one door a young man told me to wait and I heard him say to someone in the studio, "You know, Mr. LaFarge,[1] we could use another assistant, though this boy does look rather young."

An elderly man called me in, looked at me, and asked how old I was and how long I had studied art.

I told him that I was fourteen and added, "I never have studied art at all. I want to study. That is why I have come here."

"I'm sorry," he answered. "I can use an assistant but not an apprentice. You have the right idea, only you were born five centuries too late. The days of apprenticeship are over. Go out and study for five or six years and then come back and I may be able to use you."

The next day I tried Carnegie Hall and met with the same bad luck, and the added difficulty of an encounter with a predatory homosexual who was looking for a different sort of apprentice. I had about given up when I heard voices from behind a studio door, speaking Russian. I knocked and in Russian asked the tall man who answered whether he could use an apprentice. His name was Kramer and he invited me in, gave me some tea, and asked me about my background. Like LaFarge, though more gently, he explained that there were no longer apprenticeships in art and that I ought to enroll in an art school.

I later learned that he was a successful portrait painter but

[1] Probably John LaFarge, well-known and respected American artist and muralist; 1835–1910.

33

although I was just a boy he was very generous to me and talked to me that day about various technical problems, gave me some tubes of oil paints, and told me to bring some of my drawings for him to see.

Both LaFarge and Kramer were responsible for my enrollment in the night classes of the local art school, but it was the ultimatum of my foreman at the map-engraving shop which gave me the final push that left me sprawling on the threshold of freedom and a full-time, lifelong involvement with art.

My boss came up to me one day when, glazed with boredom and despair, I had been doing an unusually clumsy job. "Look here, kid, I had great hopes you'd make a first-rate engraver, but since you were bitten by your art bug, you've been no good at all to us. You'll have to choose between your job and that other damn nonsense."

I flung off my hated apron and headed for the door, shouting back at him, "I choose the damn nonsense."

By the time I got home my bravado had worn off. I had found that it was almost impossible to work during the day and paint at night; even if I were not too tired, the gas-light of those days was insufficient. I had no idea of what to do next.

The next night my sister Lena told her fiancé about my problems and he got me a job at Jake's Saloon at the upper end of Third Avenue. My salary was to be a dollar and a half a night, and I also was given a place to sleep since my hours were from six to eight A.M. and from eight P.M. to midnight.

My routine was established. When the boss came in at eight in the morning, I rode the Third Avenue El down to Twenty-third Street to the old National Academy of Design. I lived two separate lives, and though I had some exciting adventures in the saloon, I did not look or feel like the typical bartender of the Gay Nineties, nor did the two years behind that bar contribute to my development, as the romantics would have it.

As a boy I had been able to ignore the lurid life at the

34

factories, but from the moment I began my art studies, I came to loathe the sordidness of my personal life. My eyes had seen a vista of wonder and I hated the ugliness of my daily surroundings, though I liked many of the bums and prostitutes who frequented "Jake's," and had more sympathy with them than with my teachers at the N.A.D.

They taught us nothing that a student could not have learned by himself. Indeed the shrouds of their academic techniques made the task even harder for us. The criticism we received was purely corrective, delivered according to rule, and centered on obvious, unimportant things. I can still hear the eternal questions of one of my instructors, a Mr. Ward: "Did you use your plumb line? Are the feet well planted?" Another teacher, Mr. Turner, found fault with my shadows which were always too dark, or else too light. He never said a word about their shape as a revelation of form. I should have learned that during the first year of art school; left to my own resources, it took me five years.

We heard that Thomas Eakins had been asked to join the N.A.D. faculty and my hopes rose, because I considered him the best painter in America. However, he was assigned to teach anatomy and seemed as bored with the subject as we were. Eakins was a wise and sympathetic man who could have given the students a great deal, but he was not permitted to teach painting or drawing—I suppose, because the mediocrities at the Academy did not consider him good enough.

We were left pretty much to ourselves, as long as we followed the rigid routine of study at the school. Beginners were expected to spend their first months sketching from plaster casts of classic sculpture. I was completely dazed when I entered the long hall that was filled with ghosts of Venus de Milo, Apollo, and the Discus Thrower. I did not know how to begin and when I asked to speak to the professor was told by his assistant to pick out a statue I liked and to start drawing. I walked up and down the hall and finally began to sketch the only figure that appealed to me. I was doing well and was fired

with my work, until the professor arrived. He was enraged
that a novice should dare to tackle Michelangelo's "Slave" as
his first attempt and sent me off to draw feet and hands.

The next day I stole back into the gallery and the professor
inspected a drawing I was making of the Venus de Milo. He
did not recognize me, but told me that my work had progressed to the point where I could leave the antique class and
enroll in the life class.

Thus, I jogged along, learning from my own mistakes and
more from the galleries of the Metropolitan Museum of Art.
My family, my instructors, and even some of my fellow
students urged me to give up, but nothing that anyone said
could discourage me.

The only one who showed the least interest in my work was
Alfred Maurer, who studied at the N.A.D. at the same time I
did. Alfie shared my disgust with the quality of teaching at the
Academy. A few years later we had studios in the same
building and he was later very kind to me, when he had
become the most celebrated American painter in Paris. When
I myself returned to New York in 1914, after a ten-year
absence, I looked Alfie up again. He told me that his aged and
irascible father had tricked him into leaving the Paris he loved
and coming to New York. Alfie freely admitted that he was
waiting for the ninety-nine-year-old scoundrel to die so that
he might be free and financially independent. A couple of
years later, shortly after his father's death, Alfie, that unpre-
dictable and irrepressible man, committed suicide—the same
tragedy that was to take so many of my friends.

In 1901, of course, I had no inkling of such horror and I, as
well as Alfie, spent the days in work. At the end of each school
year I would select what I thought was the best of what I had
done and submit it in the N.A.D. competitions. I think now
that I hoped to win at least an honorable mention in order to
convince my mother that I was not wasting my time. I myself
was never satisfied with my work. From the very beginning I
looked at it as if it were a long journey, with each day and each

painting important only as a record of progress.

I did not win anything for several years, but by my fourth year I had come suddenly into bloom. I was sure that even fools would see that my work was superior to anything else there. A few days before graduation, the Director told me to be sure to attend the commencement exercises and to bring my mother with me. He added, "You'd better get yourself some decent clothes too."

The clothes were a problem. I borrowed my brother's cutaway coat, a white waistcoat from someone else, and a vibrant tie from a neighbor. I had no decent pants and no shoes that were formal enough for the rest of my outfit. My mother borrowed ten dollars for me and down on Baxter Street I completed the ensemble with light blue trousers and russet shoes.

On graduation night I was very proud of the fact that everyone seemed to notice my elegance. Toward the end of the exercises, the awards were announced and I heard the President say, "Drawing from the Nude, First Prize awarded to Maurice Sterne." In a daze I walked up to the platform, held out my hand for the silver medal, and stumbled back down the aisle toward my seat. Halfway there I heard, "For Composition, First Citation, Maurice Sterne." By the end of the evening I'd received first prize for Drawing from the Nude, Painting from the Nude, Composition, and Etching; and honorable mention for Portraiture.

My mother wept and the rest of my family was triumphant, especially because, in addition to glory, I'd brought home that night the "bacon" they approved of, a very kosher three hundred and ten dollars' worth. I even had the medal weighed and was told that it contained eight dollars' worth of silver.

I left the Academy in 1899 feeling rich and confident. It had been affirmed that I could draw correctly, use paint intelligently, etch, and, in general, was prepared for any challenge the art world could offer. The trouble was, the art world offered the young artist no challenges at all, ignored his existence, in fact. There were not even any dealers, in those days, to whom the unknown painter could show his work.

The only alternatives were to stick to painting and starving, submit your work to the Annual Academy or the Society of American Artists, or to do what most gifted people did—get a job on a newspaper or magazine and try to save enough money to get to Paris. Paris was the goal of every student of my generation, though few of them made it.

I tried this latter course, trudged from one art director to another with no results at all. My prize money was almost gone and there seemed to be no hope. The only bright spot was that I had a place to paint. Some of us who had been at the Academy together founded a group called the Country Sketch Club, with a huge loft on Broadway and Thirteenth Street in New York and an old shack across the Hudson River in Ridgefield, New Jersey, where we spent our weekends.

Thanks to people like Glackens[1] and "Pop" Hart,[2] those weekends were amusing and lovely. Hart didn't talk much, but he sang wonderful songs, which he seemed to make up as he went along, for it is almost certain that his mother didn't teach them to him. My favorite was a ditty about a turtle who went "mucking in the fountains" while her friend, a mountain goat, went "roaming in the mountains."

Had I not gone abroad at about that time, we would have remained good friends. Aside from my enjoyment of his vibrant presence, we each had something to give the other in our work. Hart had a way of calling a spade, in art as well as life, a "god damn shovel" and I, perhaps, of romanticizing it.

His work, at its best, reminded me of the seventeenth-century Dutch so-called "little masters," with their rather naughty humor. At his worst, he showed the distinct influence

[1] William James Glackens, 1870–1938, American landscape and genre painter and illustrator. Achieved fame as brilliant painter of the contemporary scene.
[2] George Overbury Hart, 1868–1933, American water-color painter, etcher and lithographer, who later achieved wide recognition, particularly for his water colors.

of the *Police Gazette*. When the critics first began to notice Hart, they thought that his talent was essentially illustrative. They did not know what I saw from the beginning, that Hart's sense of form was no less instinctive than his dramatic flair.

The Country Sketch Club was permitted to have a show at the N.A.D. in 1902 and we caused quite a stir. I even sold a canvas, to a fellow student, for ten dollars.

Sterne had maintained contact with the National Academy of Design and early in 1903 James D. Smillie, an instructor of etching, asked him to act as a teaching assistant. Later in the year the school received an endowment for a traveling scholarship to be awarded to a promising young painter. In 1904 Sterne received this first Mooney Award, for composition, and left immediately for Paris.

3

At the beginning of the century Paris was swarming with art students who had come from all over the world to complete their studies. I was surprised that, of them all, it was the Americans who were the most conservative. Their ambition seemed to be, first, to pass the examinations at the École des Beaux Arts, and then to exhibit in the old Salon des Artistes Françaises. The only radical American artists in Paris were Alfred Maurer, Jacob Epstein, Max Weber, Samuel Halpert —who died very young—and myself. Of course, Maurer was the only one who was born in the United States; the others of us were Russian Jews who had migrated to America in our early teens.

Degas, Cézanne, and Renoir, the great masters of the nineteenth-century French Renaissance, were still alive in France, yet few realized or acknowledged their greatness, least of all, the American students. As a rule they studied at the two famous art schools, the École des Beaux Arts and the Académie Julien.

My own scholarship had been awarded with the condition that I continue my studies abroad, but I found little to choose from between these two schools, although the Beaux Arts was the more conservative and the Julien more under the influence of the local mediocre celebrities. I visited their classes and was disappointed to find that the work of the best Paris students was no better than the output of students anywhere in the world. I went to the galleries to see the painting exhibited by the teachers of these schools and again was disappointed at the lack of fresh vision, vital perception, or sensitive reaction to contemporary life. The painters of Paris, right and center, had the greatest respect for the old masters, but from their own work it was evident that they had learned nothing important from the masterpieces at the Louvre.

I knew that it would be a mistake to study with these teachers, but I did not know what else to do about my own training. However, as soon as I paid my first visit to the Luxembourg Gallery things began to happen. I had gone there to worship Whistler's "Portrait of His Mother," which I then believed to be the greatest of modern art. Whistler had had a strong influence on my work in New York, unfortunately to the extent that an unscrupulous dealer sold a small panel of mine as a twenty-five-hundred-dollar "original." Now, I stood before his painting for a long time, trying to convince myself that I was in the actual presence of a supreme masterpiece. The longer I looked at it, the less I saw in it; indeed, rather than revealing anything new, the original itself seemed like a life-size reproduction.

Across from the Whistler room was a gallery that my fellow students at the American Club called "the lunatic asylum." It housed the Caillebot collection of the then notorious Impressionists, the insurgents, the nonconformists. Out of curiosity I went in, and what I saw threatened my own confidence badly. I was confronted with a strange, unfamiliar world which could not be understood in terms of the language of painting that I had patiently studied for twelve years, and which I believed to be universal. There was a safety within that familiar, restricted zone and unlike the child who is afraid of the dark, I was fearful of the light in that gallery. It revealed large, open spaces of which I knew nothing.

I decided to postpone my enrollment in an art school and,

whenever I was not actually working, to spend all the time I could in the Louvre with Degas, and in the gallery I had just seen. Through long and painful study I learned to give up my fear that the new painting would undermine my foundations, and that Cézanne and Renoir were not lawless rebels but builders, who worked from time-honored and time-tested bases themselves.

Years later, Sterne wrote of this early encounter with the Impressionists:

To be misunderstood and ridiculed was the common lot of the masters of the nineteenth-century French Renaissance, but only Cézanne aroused hatred. He became the symbol of everything that was anathema to his contemporaries, the target of bitter recrimination. The public, the critics, even his fellow artists joined in unanimous attack. . . .

I first heard of Cézanne in 1904 when I arrived in Paris. I must not fail, I was told, to see the Salon d'Automne, where Puvis de Chavannes, the most successful and famous painter of his era, was honored with a one-man show. Another gallery was devoted to a comparatively obscure painter called Paul Cézanne. This was unfortunate. The outcry against Cézanne dimmed the rather feeble luster of Puvis. . . .

I visited both many times. I did not learn anything from Puvis and I did not laugh at Cézanne. I was too horrified and upset for laughter. But I noticed something strange. The more I saw of Cézanne, the more Puvis shrank in stature. Yet Cézanne still remained a mystery I could not fathom.

. . . [My] most strenuous struggle was against preconceived, deeply rooted traditional art standards, that so often interfere with an open mind and heart in our approach to the art of others, especially when it happens to be radically different from our own.

Cézanne was the Gordian knot I felt I must untie because his art attracted and repelled me. . . . It took me many years before I more or less succeeded. . . . Each painting was a new problem and required an individual solution. . . .

My second round with the master took place at Vollard's little shop on the Rue Lafitte. My friend Leo Stein, who was interested in my art education, introduced me to Vollard who was very obliging and showed us half a dozen canvases, two of which I liked: a very early portrait and a landscape with nudes. . . . Those figures, hurled against the background with utter disregard for surrounding space, were alive in spite of the listless, airless world around them because of the intensity of his [Cézanne's] tactile perception. But I was still blind to his later, far greater period, from which Vollard had a large number of paintings.

My third encounter took place at the 1905 Salon d'Automne, where again a room was devoted to Cézanne. I visited that show many times but made no progress. Late one afternoon I found two elderly men intently studying the paintings. One, who looked like an ascetic Burmese monk with thick spectacles, was pointing out passages to his companion, murmuring "magnificent, excellent." His eyes seemed very poor, and he was very close to the paintings. I wondered who he could be—probably some poor painter, to judge by his rather shabby old cape.

Suddenly a pompous, portly personage appeared on the threshold. His gray Van Dyke beard, his well-fitting clothes, the wide black ribbon from which hung a gold pince-nez, his red button of the Legion of Honor—these proclaimed him a successful artist. He paused at the door, fussed with his beard, put on his pince-nez and rushed from one painting to another. He was in a state of extreme indignation. Suddenly losing all self-control, in a shrill voice he shouted, "I protest against such *cochonnerie* being shown to the public. I protest against such vile daubs that idiots call art. I protest, I protest!" His face was so purple that I feared the poor man would have a stroke. The first two visitors turned sharply to face him and he recognized one of them. "You, Monsieur Degas!" he gasped. "What the devil are you doing here?" Without a word, Degas (the man with the thick spectacles) and his companion hurriedly left.

I was shocked and astonished when I learned that the man in the cape was Degas—that the painter I held in the highest esteem was an admirer of what appeared to me to be uncouth daubs. Suddenly this dramatic scene appeared comical and I burst into laughter. The aesthetic protestant looked at me ferociously and hastened out. He must have misunderstood. How could he know that I laughed at myself, for I was indeed in a quandary.

Those words of Degas—his "magnificent, excellent"—cut deep. When I mentioned this episode to a friend, a young painter who had won the Prix de Rome, he shrugged his shoulders. His only comment was *"Chacun à son gout."*

What right has a painter to have taste! Only a layman can indulge in this dubious luxury. The painter must have judgment and perception in his approach to the art of others. . . .

The next day I . . . was back in the Cézanne room. . . . And when I looked at the paintings on the wall I realized that I really had not seen them. . . . They now took on life. . . . Until then I had been a conscious critic and an unconscious devotee (quite a common ailment). . . . Cézanne was a realist who observed reality not only with his eyes, but with his body and soul too; a realist who penetrated within his motif. How could a public (this includes both the artist and the critic) brought up on the superficial notion that realism consists of the depiction of obvious appearances be expected to possess the inner eye to see at a glance an image it took the artist sometimes many weeks to project, and the outer eye a lifetime to evolve?

To Cézanne the appearance was not a point of arrival; it was a point of departure, a journey not away from the motif, likely to turn into a joy-ride by oneself (so freely indulged in at present), but a journey of exploration into the hidden secrets that reality may hold. . . .

[However] it is not only what the creative artist succeeds in expressing but what he perceives beyond his horizon, what he cannot materialize in visual images, what his creative antennae can *almost* touch, that is of equal importance. As he grew older, he (Cézanne) shrank more and more from human contact; his motifs replaced human relationships. They became his constant companions, always together, either whispering secrets or fighting ferociously. Sooner or later he would reach the boundaries of human perception. Convinced that his motif had betrayed him, that it had kept some inner truth from him, he abandoned it in disgust and, in a fit of desperate frustration, cried, "I cannot realize." He would often leave a . . . painting behind to rot in the field.

All this became clear to me only when I had suddenly seen his paintings as a whole, free from the deficiencies one is bound to find in new forms when one's approach has been too much influenced by the old. As long as our reaction to so-called revolutionary art is dominated by taste cultivated by tradition, we are bound to be shocked by the new, and its positive values appear negative. . . .

Only when I realized that his distortion was not due to his inability to draw "correctly" or to optical imperfection, but to reasons purely compositional—only then did I comprehend that his malformations were in reality transformations. Cézanne was not a nihilist; there is no interim between the past and the present. He was both an innovator and a resurrector of worthwhile values which had been lost sight of.[1]

I studied Cézanne, Renoir, Degas, Courbet, Sisley, Monet, Pissarro . . . and I became a witness to one of the great periods in art history. Those years in Paris were devoted to work, and although I had love affairs and spent time with friends, all my real energy was in my art.

I moved into a studio on the Rue Vercingetorix and found a model whose visiting card read, "Juliette La Bastarde." Juliette had no shame about her origins, but she refused to pose in the

[1] Maurice Sterne, "Cézanne Today," *The American Scholar*, Vol. XXII, No. 1 (Winter, 1952–53).

nude. I was surprised because she seemed to have a lovely figure. Months later, when our relationship had grown much closer, I found out that her reluctance was based on no false modesty, but on her fear that her bosom was too small, like *"oeuf sur le plat"* was the way she put it. She knew lovely Brittany folk music from her childhood and I have heard nothing since so sweet as her small voice singing those volatile and elusive old French songs.

Juliette was a lovely model and she posed for two of my best portraits of that period. I grew very fond of her, and to that other question she asked whenever we were together, *"C'est bon, n'est-ce pas?"* the answer was a charmed and contented, *"Oui."* Then one day Juliette announced that Charles Cottet, the well-known Parisian painter, wanted her to pose exclusively for him. She told him that she would do so as soon as I was able to finish the head I was working on, which I planned to enter in the Spring Salon de la Société Nationale des Beaux Arts.

One day while Juliette was posing, the portly red-bearded M. Cottet appeared at my studio. He glared at my portrait for a moment and then asked if I would be kind enough to stop work and to let Juliette pose for some important work he was doing for the Spring Salon. I told him that my own work was equally important to me, and that it would take at least a week to finish. Cottet stormed out and later sent word with Juliette that I should not submit my portrait since he had three likenesses of her in the exhibition.

When the portrait was finished I put it in a lovely antique Dutch frame and sent it off to the Salon. M. Lucien Lefebre-Foinet, who owned an artists' material store and who was a loyal friend of the young artists of Montparnasse, told me that my painting had been accepted and was hung in a place of honor in one of the best galleries. This was wonderful news, since "the hanging" in a large exhibit is of utmost importance —it can make or break the artist. I went to the Vernissage that day in an exalted state, and hurried to the proper gallery.

Sterne in Bali costume, *from an article by Joyce Kilmer in*
The New York Times Magazine, *March 21, 1915*

Sterne in the European days

My Juliette was not there. In her place hung a silly portrait of an aristocratic lady, décolleté. I rushed from gallery to gallery looking for my painting. In one room I ran into M. Lefebre and Alfie Maurer, neither of whom could understand what had happened. About an hour later, Alfie came back to tell me that he had found my painting. Without a word, he took me down to the basement lunchroom, where my lovely Juliette was hanging right over a counter.

It was a public execution! Later we learned that the aristocratic lady, labeled Comtesse X, had been painted by Cottet and that Juliette had posed for the painting. He also submitted a full-length portrait of a Madame de F, and a painting of a Baroness W; Juliette la Bastarde had posed for them all. Cottet used these paintings to try to get portrait commissions, and even I, who knew Juliette so well, did not suspect that she had been the model. Even worse than his banal performances on the walls of the Salon was his shabby behavior toward a much younger colleague.

I had other reminders of the difficulties for unknown artists in Paris. Shortly after I had moved into my studio, a little monkey appeared on the roof of a courtyard shed, and he would sit there mournfully in the sun day after day. The concierge told me that he had belonged to the former occupant of my studio, a M. Paul, a painter who had brought the monkey from some Pacific island. He had lived in Paris for a few years and then decided to go back to the Pacific. She could not remember her tenant's surname, but did remember that his island was called Tahiti.

I made some inquiries around the city and found that for the two years between his first and second trips to the Pacific, Paul Gauguin had indeed lived in my studio. I wondered whether we also shared a love affair with the pink-cheeked laundress who remembered him so well.

There was no question of sharing the friendship of pretty young girls with Leo Stein, whom I began to know in those early Paris days. Although Leo was very attractive, both to

47

women and to men, his female friends were never of the pretty, feminine type. They were intellectuals with fine minds and dull bodies, and were awed by Leo's keen intellect. Leo was, himself, more interested in ideas than in earthy experience. His abstract creative urge was stronger than any physical creative instinct. Until he met Nina, when he was about thirty years old, he had had no amorous adventures at all.

During those years, however, he was definitely the head of his own household. He and Gertrude still lived together, and it was Leo who was then the undisputed ruler of the Stein clan. Gertrude had no taste or judgment in the visual arts; at best she was a reflection of her brother Leo. Never in those early years of the century did she take the initiative herself in the purchase of a painting. It was always Leo. However, before the painting could be transferred to their walls, Leo had to get Gertrude's consent, because they had pooled their incomes. It was only when a considerable amount of money was at stake that she even bothered to see a painting before it was acquired.

I remember very well one occasion like this, when Leo was taking a long time to decide whether they could afford to spend fifteen hundred dollars for a life-size portrait by Cézanne. He asked me and Gertrude to come to Vollard's with him to take a look at it, and when we got there, Gertrude had little to say in the matter.

Anyone interested in the facts would have to discard as pure invention all that Gertrude wrote about her important role in building the collection. I have not read her autobiography of Toklas, but I have been told that she hardly mentions Leo. The book was written, of course, after their break; these other things took place long before, when Gertrude and Leo appeared as the happiest couple on the Left Bank.

Gertrude did have excellent perception in literature. I remember a vigorous walk I took with her in Italy shortly after our Paris acquaintance. The three kilometers we had to cover in the midday sun were accomplished at a rapid pace.

Gertrude's tempo was not like Leo's *adagio;* it was *vivace allegro.* Her mind moved rapidly and the quicker her thoughts, the greater her physical speed. Although she was stout, her spirit did not suffer from fatty degeneration; it was alive, keen, and active.

I asked her that day whether she had ever thought of becoming a critic, since she spoke so intelligently about writing. She replied, "It's funny that you should say that. As a matter of fact, I did, long ago, but I found that analysis is not in my line. I'll leave that to Leo—he loves to chew the cud. I want to do something more vital than write about the writings of others. Writing about it doesn't interest me. I want to do it, and when I do, I'll give the chaps who can't do it, but 'know all about it' plenty to chew the rag about. I'm writing a book now . . . been at it for some time . . . long before I wrote down a word."

I congratulated her and asked whether it was a novel she was working on.

"I hate labels. It's just a book, a book about different characters, three different people I knew long ago. It's almost finished, I'll send you a copy."

Quite a while later, when I was in Greece, I received from Gertrude a copy of her *Three Lives.* I wrote her that although I enjoyed her keen penetration of character, the constant repetition of what I supposed she considered important was extremely irritating. I told her that her technique made form more important than content, and that it was this same self-consciousness in painting that had driven me from Paris. Our friendship did not survive that letter, which I realize now was cruel and unfeeling.

I think that Gertrude was the one who was primarily to blame in the quarrel with Leo since she needed to free herself from the Oedipal hold Leo had on her. She was definitely not the clinging female type who might have enjoyed living under his authority. Of course, some of her criticism of Leo was quite justified. He was, in a sense, a split personality: cold, annihilating, analytic toward others and blind as a bat about himself. Eventually he realized that he was unhappy and began his interminable self-analysis. For about thirty-five years, every time we met or wrote he would proudly announce, "I have practically finished my analysis."

Years later his friends and relatives all asked how anyone of Leo's intellectual powers and breeding could marry a person like Nina. I had never met her before they married, but she was well known in Montparnasse and I had seen her on one memorable occasion. From down in my courtyard, I had heard a fine voice accompanied by a violin. I looked out the window and saw a powerfully built, handsome girl with brown skin and a shock of unruly brown curls. When she finished her song she held out her beret for coins and I dropped her the few sous I could spare. Someone threw a rotten apple at her feet and she let forth with a stream of curses and swearing more colorful than I had ever heard before. When her taunter merely laughed, she went mad with anger and had to be led away by her accompanist and the concierge. When I asked the concierge about her, I was told, "She is *méchante*. Don't you recognize her? I thought all Americans knew her. Nina is crazy about music and Americans."

I later learned that although Nina seemed completely immoral from a conventional point of view, she had a strict sense of a morality of her own. Love was sacred to her and she dedicated her youth and beauty to its cultivation. Although she was studying voice, she occasionally posed for American artists and it was in this way that she met Leo. She was fascinated by his self-absorption and detachment, and not a little shocked to learn of his absolute inexperience in the matter of love. Nina was determined to get him, and she did, and I think that in spite of many difficulties, they never regretted it.

To understand what Leo was, and what he was not, one had only to see Nina. She was the living being of the abstraction he longed for, and he avoided marrying her for many years in order to keep his conception private and untouched. Theirs was a truly complementary relationship: Nina a woman ruled by her passions, Leo a man whose emotions had been overruled by his brain.

By the time I knew them, Leo and Gertrude were familiar figures in the avant-garde world. One day they invited me to go with them to Pablo Picasso's studio where they were taking Etta Cone, a visiting Baltimore friend. We climbed up three steep flights of stairs to get to his studio, and when we reached the door we found a note on Manila paper, pinned there with a thumbtack. It read:

Je suis
A   K
A   K
A K K

In place of the signature was a drawing of a gentleman in a crouching position, with his pants down. It was a "spittin' image" of the master.

Leo looked angry and Miss Cone was embarrassed, but Gertrude, with the sudden eruptive laugh that had become famous in Montparnasse said, "Isn't he cute!" My own reaction was, "Behold, King Pablo the First, on his throne."

I suggested to Gertrude that she add this example of intimate art to her Picasso collection, but she didn't seem to appreciate the humor of my remark. However, if there should turn out to be a present-day controversy among the critics about the period or authenticity of this work, I will gladly testify that it was executed in the spring of 1905, and perhaps I can provide a scholarly background anecdote for the latest historical study of the great man.

I feel that Picasso's eulogization is most ironic, especially because, in a certain sense, he bears the greatest responsibility for the artistic malady of our time—the glorification of inventiveness. In technology this quality is a blessing; in art it is a curse. The modern public has come to look eagerly for some new innovator to spring up each season; or, what is more distressing, for the well-established inventor constantly to market new thrills. This is why Matisse, who continued to *produce*, was eclipsed by Picasso, the arch-inventor, who could be counted upon by a grateful public to come up with new "gadgets" year after year. Matisse's color is infallible; Picasso may well be color blind; in any case his use of color is limited, and dissident rather than effective or harmonious. Rouault had profound depth and sense of form; Picasso's distortions are neither poetic nor constructive. Bonnard had sensitive spatial perception; Picasso's space adds no decorative qualities nor force to the content. Ironically, these eminent contemporaries must take second place to the master *"sans pareil."*

The Steins were, of course, Picasso's important "promoters," although Leo's taste later moved in other directions. Their sincere admiration for Matisse and Picasso was bound to be misunderstood. People in Paris raised skeptical eyebrows when it became known that Leo, Michael, and Gertrude were buying work by these artists exclusively. There was open speculation as to whether the Steins bought the paintings because they admired them, or admired them because they had bought them.

I had one experience of this sort with the "Stein Corporation," as the local gossip named them. In the spring of 1907 Leo and I attended an exhibition at which Matisse's "Joie de Vivre" was first seen. I was shocked by what I considered its poor drawing and crude color and I am afraid that I agreed with the judgment of the laughing crowd in front of the painting. I asked Leo what he thought and he replied, "I don't know yet. I must first study for a while before I can make up my mind." I told him that it was his first impression that I wanted, since I knew that he had at first disliked intensely another Matisse which he later bought.

A week later I asked Leo if he had made up his mind and he curtly replied, "Not yet." Still another week passed and then

BENARES (1912)

The Phillips Collection, Washington, D.C.

Leo informed me that he had come to the conclusion that "Joie de Vivre" was a superb painting, and had purchased it.

This made me very angry and I said, "It took you a hell of a long time to make such an astounding discovery!"

"It took *you* much longer to see Cézanne," he replied.

However, I don't think the two situations were the same. When I first saw Cézanne I was fresh from America where I had been fed only the benign fare of Whistler. I had a lot of ground to cover, and yet, even by that time, my judgment was not so sluggish. Van Gogh swept me off my feet the first time I saw his work; Seurat, Gauguin, and Toulouse-Lautrec aroused my instantaneous appreciation. It has never taken me two weeks to decide whether a girl *or* a work of art attracts me.

Picasso himself is reported to have said years later of the Steins, "How they exploited me." Truthfully, Leo did at times act like the patron saint of both Picasso and Matisse. He persuaded Matisse to begin an art school so that he might become, in the true sense of the word, a *"chef d'école."* The school did not last long because Matisse was never really interested in teaching and was disturbed when his students insisted upon caricaturing their master's work. Several young painters I knew attended the school, among them Max Weber and my most intimate German friend, the gifted painter, Hans Purrmann.

In an article for The Dial *magazine, Purrmann tells of how he came to the school:*

I met in a café an American painter, Sterne. Our views on painting were similar, with the result that he took me to the collection of a friend of his [Leo Stein]. Embarrassed and curious, I went with him to a studio where the walls were hung with pictures. . . . It was a blow to me; how could a man collect such pictures! and pay out good money for them! For the first time I awoke! I spent so much time on one picture that it attracted attention; as a result, I was introduced to the painter. He was Matisse.[1]

Another beloved friend, the Russian actress Alla Nazimova, came to join me in Paris in 1905. We had an idyllic two weeks together, enhanced by love and also by Alla's wonderful dramatic readings. The night she arrived we sat up until dawn while Alla "acted" *Uncle Vanya* for me. On another night she read a scene from *Eugene Onegin* and I saw then with deep intensity how gifted she was. Every nuance of the poetry was dramatically expressed, not only in the many different vocal inflections, but in the constant change and movement of her body. Her face and hands, too, were remarkably mobile and expressive.

Alla told me that, outside of Russia, she found her accent a great handicap. She could be wholly conscious of the character she played in her native language, but in English she became, instead, *self*-conscious. I was most impressed with her intense emotionality. When she played Chekhov and pronounced the line, "I am a sea gull"—"*Ya, tchaika,*" the tears were rolling down her cheeks. At dinner the next day I praised her and marveled at how deeply she must have felt to bring those tears from her eyes. Alla laughed at my naïveté and proceeded to illustrate her point.

The waiter had come up to our table to ask if we would have a cognac with our demitasse. With tears spilling out of her eyes Alla whispered, "No, thank you, no cognac." The waiter was startled and asked her what was wrong. Alla's face was lit with a sad smile. She said, "I am crying from happiness. This is my first honeymoon." The spiritually uplifted waiter left and I nearly exploded with laughter.

She left Paris two weeks later, promising to return in the spring when we were to be married. In America, Alla got

[1] Hans Purrmann, "From the Workshop of Henri Matisse," trans. from the German by Kenneth Burke, *The Dial* (July, 1922), p. 32.

involved with her career and I received a few passionate letters
from her, the last of which announced her decision to stay in
the United States. After a few years, I heard that she had
married a handsome Englishman. When I saw her again, many
years later, I asked her whether she loved her husband. She
admitted that she did not, and when I pressed her further she
said, "I can't get rid of my strong foreign accent and it is a
terrible handicap in my career. I thought having him around
would improve my English."

Nazimova had a humor about herself that was very attractive, nor did she take her gifts so seriously that she was not
able, for example, to laugh at her own love of publicity. Sarah
Bernhardt, on the other hand, expected constant worship, and
was herself full of homage for her own person. Her genius was
perhaps marred by this self-adulation and by an excessive
reliance on art. I had a letter of introduction to Bernhardt and
she received me graciously in Paris in 1904. She must have
been about sixty at the time, but she looked quite young and
beautiful in the soft golden light that filled the room. Either by
accident or design, the light on her head was always dim, so
that as she reclined on her couch, her pale face was framed in a
mass of glowing dark red hair. In her home, as on the stage,
Sarah dominated the performance.

Duse could not efface herself because no one else on stage
even remotely approached her genius. With Bernhardt, it was
a careful artfulness. I wondered whether Sarah's Jewish
heritage and her Catholic education had not accentuated her
self-consciousness. Perhaps when European Jews are able to
break out of the ghetto, they have an added incentive to call
attention to their own success, and their formerly restricted
sense of competition bursts forth with an accumulated vigor.

I was not free of this attitude myself when I was a young
man. I was immoderately proud when a very early review in
the *New York Evening Sun* said that "the drawings of M.
Sterne dwarfed all the other drawings around them." I was
insufferably exultant when, while I was still a newcomer in

Paris, my Coney Island etchings were exhibited at the Salon d'Antoine and mentioned most favorably by the distinguished critic Roger Marx.

My small successes led me to some wild excesses in publicity-seeking. I wore my hair in a bang like Julius Caesar and enjoyed being pointed out in cafés in the Latin Quarter. The worst of it happened when Alfie Maurer urged me to send a group of my small marine paintings to an exhibition at the American Club on the Rue Notre Dame du Champs. I sent several paintings along and told Alfie that since they were each extremely small, I wanted them hung in a group. When I got to the galleries I found that the panels were scattered throughout the hall. Some English artists who were with me assured me that mine were the best paintings there and that it was outrageous that they were not hung properly. Fortified by their praise and by several liters of Vin Grey we had shared, I marched back into the gallery, pulled my paintings off the walls, and left an indignant and impolite note in their place.

It caused a terrible rumpus. A few people who thought the club was too conservative applauded me, but the majority, including Alfie Maurer and other friends, condemned my rashness. I knew I had been wrong and that my gesture of bravado was stupid. What hurt more, however, was my own suspicion that it was exhibitionism rather than artistic motives that had prompted me. I suppose it took two years in all for my cheap indulgence in the pursuit of fame to fade and to be displaced by a craving for real achievement. This lesson has served me well in my old age, when each year marks again the passing nature of popular fame.

Even worse than this professional foolishness was my behavior toward women during those years. I was skillful and ruthless in my pursuit of physical pleasure, and not particularly concerned with the feelings of others. My love affairs never lasted very long, not because I grew tired of my partners, but because I dreaded becoming too involved. My conscience always acted retrospectively; it never kept me from the next cruelty. I am afraid that it took many years for me to learn to see women as friends and not as prey, and I am still horrified and deeply ashamed of these moral debts that I cannot repay.

I loved Paris and when I received the last installment of my scholarship, I felt as if I had been sentenced to banishment. Fortunately I sold a small painting to Mrs. Gertrude Whitney and a larger one, "The Entrance of the Ballet," to the annual exhibition of the Art Institute of Chicago. They did not bring much—only about one hundred and fifty dollars—but this was enough to give me two more months in Paris. Spring came, the money was almost gone, and with a very heavy heart I began to wind up my affairs and plan for returning to New York and resuming the dreaded struggle to earn a living.

However, as it turned out, the two months' delay changed my life and enabled me to stay abroad and paint for ten more years. A voice student I knew told me that she had met someone who admired my painting at the Salon and who was very anxious to meet me. She added that he was so shy and nervous that she did not know whether he would summon the courage to come to see me.

A few days later, a tall, untidy man appeared at my studio unannounced. He stood at my door and without waiting for me to speak said, "My name is Harris. Mabel Gibberson told me that I could come to see you. I saw your painting at the Salon and I would like to buy it, if you care to part with it. I don't know anything about prices, but could you let me have it for one thousand dollars?"

I stared at the strange creature and gasped, "Did you say francs or dollars?"

He smiled, then. "Dollars, of course."

Then he awkwardly pulled out of his pocket, peeled off, and signed ten one-hundred-dollar Travelers' Checks. He handed them to me with great embarrassment, and when I looked into his childishly innocent blue eyes, I felt like an unscrupulous cheat. Had he inquired about the price beforehand, I would surely not have asked more than two hundred dollars!

After the sale was completed, we sat in uneasy silence. He got up as abruptly as he'd come, and uncertainly stammered that he'd better leave. I tried to make him comfortable and urged him to stay and chat. He refused a cigarette, and when I offered him a glass of *vin ordinaire*, he told me he only took wine at mealtime. With that sad expression, he added, "I'm afraid you will find me a bore."

We talked about art and I was amazed to learn that mine was the first painting he had ever bought. His main interest was apparently poetry, and he had been attracted to my picture at the Salon because its scene of workmen tearing up a street seemed to him to be symbolic of Walt Whitman's work which he loved. He had spoken to Mabel Gibberson who told him of my admiration for Whitman and that common interest apparently gave him the courage to come to see me.

I invited him to come to dinner with me and this caused still more embarrassment. He confessed that he was unable to swallow food in public and always dined in his hotel room. We drove to an exclusive hotel on the Right Bank and a waiter soon appeared in Harris's room with a menu. Harris marked off enough food to feed a huge family, but the waiter did not appear surprised. He soon returned with a helper, wheeling two huge tables of food into the room. There were two separate portions of fish, roast chicken, Chateaubriand steaks, lamb chops; two tureens of soups; all sorts of vegetables and salads; and a huge platter of cheeses. As the waiter was leaving the room, he said, "Kindly ring when you are ready for dessert."

I could hardly believe my eyes. I asked my host how we would manage to eat all the food he had ordered. With a sheepish look he explained that he could not choose his meals from the bill of fare, but had to see the dishes in order to get his gastric juices operating. After several moments of deliberation he chose one chop, a little salad, and a portion of cheese. I ate handsomely, but even so, at least three-quarters of the elegantly prepared food remained untouched.

As for the dessert, another full table was wheeled into the room. I had a delicious raspberry tart, but apparently nothing there worked on his "juices," for Harris had only coffee. That meal dispelled any bad conscience I might have felt at the high price of my painting. Evidently Alan Harris could afford to pay generously.

The dinner had another strange and much more important result. I invited Harris to join me at the Louvre on the following afternoon and took him to see what I considered its finest statue, the bronze reproduction of the "Charioteer of Delphi." I told Harris about my enthusiasm for the sculpture and how I hoped someday to go to Greece to see the original. He said, "Why wait? Why not go now? I should also love to go, but I hear that the ships are dirty and full of bugs, and I hate even the best of sea voyages."

We continued to tour the Museum and when it was time to part he turned to me and with a shy eagerness said, "If you should decide to go to Greece, do you think I could come along?" I assured him that if I could go I would enjoy his company, but that I could not afford such a trip. Alan then timidly proposed that we go as "companions" and that he would assume the expenses for the trip. I was amazed and did not know what to make of the man.

I got in touch with Mabel Gibberson and she told me that Alan was very wealthy but that he had had a tragic life. A disastrous marriage had left him in a sanitarium. Just as he was recovering, he and his nurse had been caught in a hotel which was destroyed by fire. They were among the very few survivors and had a harrowing escape. Harris was traveling to try to forget these experiences and Mabel assured me that he really was in need of companionship.

The next day, a beautiful two-and-a-half-foot reproduction of the "Winged Victory" arrived at my studio, and a few days later he sent a complete set of large photographs of the frieze and pediment figures of the Parthenon. I was convinced that this generous man did not regret his invitation and we began to make plans for our trip.

We were advised that Greek summers were terribly hot and that we ought to wait until fall to go. It was decided that we would spend the summer in Italy and go on to Greece in October. We stopped at Menton, on the Riviera, on the way down, but I found the bourgeois atmosphere depressing and I was anxious to get back to my work. Alan noticed my restlessness. He suggested that I go on to Florence where he would join me before we left for Greece.

Alan did not join me there, nor ever again, though he very generously continued to finance the trip. When it was time to leave Florence he wired that he was delayed and would meet me in Athens. Later, other delaying letters arrived. Finally, after my Greek stay was over, I received a painful telegram from him. I had been sending him all the paintings I was doing as recompense for his support. His message said that upon reading a book I had recommended and on seeing my latest painting, he realized that he had not understood my character before, and now wished to sever our relationship. This was a financial as well as an emotional blow to me and it was not until years later that I realized that Alan had fallen under the complete domination of an unscrupulous older woman who had sent those telegrams. I saw him with her, and although he was bitterly unhappy, that childlike man was unable to summon the courage to break away.

All this happened later, of course. In 1907 I was busily making plans to leave Paris for the trip. The night before my departure, my friends gave me a wonderful farewell party. An interesting commentary on the kind of life we lived in Paris is to be found in the fact that as I looked around the table, I saw not one French face. I realized with a shock that although I had had many transient relationships with French men and women, there was no French Parisian I could really call a friend. I attributed this to my poor knowledge of the language which makes the French, in particular, most impatient. Bali and Italy were the only countries I ever visited where the heart speaks louder than the lips and where the people eagerly help you to make yourself understood. Especially in Italy I formed friendships in a very short time that have outlasted the very lives of my companions, and affections that still warm my own aging heart.

Leaving France was made easier also by the climate of the art world at that time. I was not in sympathy with the new direction that was being indicated by Matisse and Picasso. I felt that it was wrong to break with the tradition of the nineteenth-century French Renaissance, which had not spent itself at all, but needed a younger generation to bring it to full growth. The new artists were instead intent upon self-exploitation and experimentation with new forms. They denied the basic fact that the great pictorial images arise from the discovery of previously unknown aspects of nature. They were deluded into thinking that by turning their vision inward and exploring personality, they would create new master-pieces. I am afraid that in this departure from nature in art, an ingrown soul is as perverse as an ingrown toenail.

M·S

4

THE trip from southern Italy to Piraeus was dreadful, as Alan Harris had predicted. There were bugs at dinner, bugs in bed, and noisy passengers in the lounge. Long before the boat arrived in Greece I was regretting my decision to leave the civilized West. I arrived at my Athens hotel after midnight and slept for ten hours, and when I awoke and looked out the window I was even more disappointed. Were these ugly houses, this Balkan banality, the Athens I had dreamed of, the Hellenistic culture I longed for?

The maid brought breakfast and the rancid butter on my rolls merely confirmed my decision to leave this dreadful country. Then I saw what I had come for, and almost wept for the joy of it. The maid had pulled open another blind, and there in the brilliant sunshine, the Parthenon gleamed like pure gold against a lapis lazuli sky. But even the Parthenon seemed to be choking in its surroundings, its slender columns like bare arms raised in supplication. I knew then that I would have to seek the glory that *had* been Greece to be reconciled to its modern ugliness.

One feels no continuity in Greece between the ancient world and the present. In Athens, in particular, the ruins stand like relics of a strange culture now set down among alien people. It is very different in Italy where, in spite of superficial changes in costume or transportation, there is a tangible connection from modern days, through the Renaissance, back into the ancient empire. I hated Greece for many weeks, and was sorry indeed that I had stayed in Florence only a month or two, instead of stopping there permanently.

It was not only the physical aspect of Athens that bothered me. Fifty years ago it was the deadest, dullest capital in Europe—a Balkan town without even the murky Balkan glamour or its nightly dramatic chiaroscuro. Its only diversion was in petty gossip, focused on the diplomatic corps. The *cause célèbre* during the 1907 season had to do with the mating of a French-owned and a German-owned pedigree dog, which was interfered with by their diplomatic owners.

I would surely have left the place had things continued as they were. However, on a chilly November afternoon I had been sketching Mt. Hymettus from my window and my fingers grew stiff with cold. Since my room had no heater I decided that the only way to get warm was to take a brisk walk, and I set out in the direction of the mountain I had been drawing. I soon left the city behind me, as I followed a dirt road that led to Hymettus' slopes. The landscape was dreary, the gray-brown earth streaked with a few patches of green and some burnt brown brush. There was not a living thing to be seen for miles, though when I passed near some isolated farmhouses, sheep dogs set up a furious howling, more like wolves than domesticated animals.

I had been watching a distant house surrounded by a low cement wall, and as I got closer I saw at the gate a slight old man, with a gray shovel-shaped beard. He was dressed in a long brown robe, tied round the middle with a hemp rope, much like a Franciscan friar. Bowing low, he greeted me, and in very formal address, said, "Welcome to our monastery. Come in and refresh yourself with the life-giving nectar from our spring. It is a drink that made the ancient gods human, and can make humans godlike."

The water was cold and good and I thanked the old

gentleman although I felt no godly effects. However, as I turned to go back down the mountainside I did have an awesome, religious experience. For the first time since I had come to Greece, I saw the Parthenon in its ancient purity, arising from a valley filled with mysterious shadows, with not one ugly slate roof to mar its setting. The Propylaea and the Erechtheum were in deep violet shade, the columns of the Parthenon like a crown reflecting the rose of the sunset against an opal sky. It was a glimpse of a resurrected glory. I thought longingly of what a vision it would be at dawn, arising from the night; or in the dazzling midday when the marble turns to mellow gold; or moving silently in and out of the moonlight. I told the old man, "I envy you your view. I wish I could stay here."

I was very surprised when he replied, "Why don't you?" He explained that the monastery had been abandoned and that he and his wife were custodians hired by the Church. To prove that there was plenty of room for me, he showed me the inside of the building which had about six cells, each furnished with a cot, a chair, and a small table. There was also a tiny chapel adorned only with a Greek cross and an antique bronze bell suspended from a fragment of a Corinthian column. The former dining hall was now used as living quarters by the old man and his wife. He urged me to stay, and said that the only problem might be that I would not care for their simple meals. I assured him that they would be fine and soon was taking a daily repast with them of goat cheese, milk, and bread, with fish on Fridays, mutton stew on Sundays, and numberless overripe black olives all the time.

Thus began what I now see was the most formative period of my life. The days passed in rhythmic uniformity. I worked most of the time, but spent a few hours a day with the caretaker. He had an extensive classical library and patiently taught me to read in ancient Greek the works I had only known before in their English or German translations. On Saturdays I went to Athens to study the sculpture at the museum and to attend a Professor Dorpfeld's [1] lectures on the Acropolis. He was a trained architect and his approach was simple and instructive. I had met the Professor and his colleagues one exciting day on the Acropolis. Athens had had its first snowfall in years. As soon as I saw it, I rushed to the top of the city to see the ruins in the snow. I was feeling quite drunk with all the dazzling light and form and I decided to make a statue of Athena right in the Parthenon where the ancient colossal effigy had stood. I began piling up the snow, and when the German archaeological team saw what I was doing, they pitched in to help. Orange peel and wood shavings provided splendid archaic decorations for face, nipples, and navel. We all stood there in the sun and snow admiring my *chef d'oeuvre* for quite a while. A picture of the sculpture appeared in a Berlin weekly soon after, thus immortalizing a rather impermanent art medium.

After this frolic, we became good friends, and shortly after our meeting the Germans invited me to join them on a tour of the Peloponnese. My companions were anxious to see Sparta and we traveled over snow-covered mountain roads in a crowded and ancient carriage to get there. When we arrived I could hardly believe that this commonplace village of low stucco houses was the modern offspring of the powerful ancient city that had conquered Athens. The location, of course, remained magnificent, with a mountain range to the east and the dramatic Mt. Taygetus to the west. There was no hotel but we found a prosperous peasant's wife who was willing to take us in. Her husband, as was very common, was in America, but the family expected to be called to the promised land momentarily. We had a delicious meal, with a lot of resinated wine. When we got to our room, Wentscher, my roommate, proclaimed that classical Greek was the most beautiful language in the world, and, to prove his point, began a dramatic recitation of the Iliad. To me it seemed that any

[1] Probably German archaeologist Wilhelm Doerpfeld, who later became famous for his excavations at Olympia.

language is beautiful when it is the vehicle of a great poet. I was in a terrific emotional state myself. The graveyard scene from Hamlet seemed to be pouring from my soul, and when I leapt into the grave of Ophelia, shouting, "Now pile your dust upon the quick and dead, Till of this flat a mountain you have made"—there was a sharp click at the door. The landlady had locked us in and Wentscher got very excited about that. He hammered at the door and shouted until the police arrived, and we only got off because Dr. Jacobstahl, our other companion, explained that we were actors rehearsing a new role.

The next morning we climbed the hills above Sparta to go to the monasteries and see the frescoes of the Byzantine ruins of Mistra. When we reached the village, there was a crowd on the square, dancing and singing in the brilliant sunlight. The recurring theme of their song was, "Anathema Amerika" and when Dr. Jacobstahl asked an old man why they were cursing America, he repeated several times, "Just look around, look around you." We saw again the tragedy of Greece at that time: there were no young men anywhere in the village, since all of them had migrated. During the dance a buxom, black-eyed young Hera tossed her thick dark braids in my direction and I was eager to stay and console her for the lack of male companionship, but my archaeological friends were tireless in their pursuit of ruins.

As I saw more of the ruins and art, I realized how anemic my conception of ancient Greece had been, based as it was on second-rate Hellenistic copies and Winkleman's plaster casts of original sculpture. This was true even of the Delphi Charioteer whose replica I had so admired in the Louvre. In Paris I had not been able to judge the importance to the statue's beauty of the silvery, light green patina. But replica or original, that sculpture continues to fascinate me to this day. In spite of the grooved drapery that completely covers the figure, it has about it a starkness that is close to nudity. We are accustomed to outer embellishments or "tricks" that cover truth and falsity alike. This sculpture was conceived not as the

66

bronze portrait of a man of flesh and blood, but as a symbol of man, conceived *directly* in the bronze. It achieves, because of this, a perfect, stark reality.

The Greek artists did not concern themselves, as did the later Christians or the Egyptians, with problems of the soul or of eternity. They did not try to solve the riddles of existence in their art, but found their inspiration in the beauty of form and movement, in the glory of the flesh. Neither crucifixions nor elaborate mummy cases had a place in their way of life or their art.

Months went by in work and study. I had no interest at all in the modern Greek scene, I lived only in its past. When spring came, I grew restless. I found myself reaching out to caress the marble statues, but I lacked the Pygmalion touch and was rewarded not with pulsing flesh, but with angry looks from the museum guards. I took to walking the streets, hoping that some Athenian beauty would speak to me, for in spite of considerable experience in the general field, I had never learned the art of the "pick-up." Late one afternoon I followed a pretty girl for what seemed like miles until she finally went into a small side street and stopped. I hastened joyfully forward to meet her but as I approached she shouted, "Don't come any nearer! If you don't stop following me, I will call the police!"

I felt like an inept fool and to get the fair sex out of my mind, had a bottle of Rezina wine and then some of their anise-flavored brandy, ouzo. On my way home, my befuddled consciousness came up with the old advice that needy Americans abroad should get in touch with their diplomatic representatives. I'd been away from home for four years and the occasion had not yet arisen to exercise this right of citizenship and since I was passing the American Consulate at that moment, I decided to give it a try. I rang the bell long and hard until a sleepy attendant came to tell me that the office was closed for the weekend. My problem was too urgent for delay and a five-drachma note got me the Consul's home address. At his residence, my noisy quarrel with the housekeeper brought the Consul downstairs. Luckily he had heard about the American artist on Mt. Hymettus and invited me in. My courage almost failed as I sat opposite that imposing man, but the ouzo and the Rezina must have propelled me forward, for I blurted out my need for female companionship.

As soon as the words were out I realized that what I was doing was requesting that the Consul-general of the United States of America act as my personal procurer! He was furiously angry, and I don't know what would have happened had my dulled wits not grasped at a way out. I interrupted the Consul's scathing reply to tell him that he had misunderstood, that what I really was asking for was the name of a woman who might pose for me before I had to leave the country. Whether he believed me or not I do not know, but the Consul himself introduced me to Elena, a lovely young Turkish woman who later made a warm and intelligent companion both in my private life and in my work. (As a matter of fact, some of the nicest Greeks I met turned out to be Turks!)

That night was full of important surprises! While walking back to the monastery I seemed to be surrounded by howling farm dogs and I decided to take a short cut through the fields. The barking got closer every moment and in the darkness I found myself dodging back and forth away from those fearful snarls. I was lost and scared and sure that the beasts would get me. One came very close and, as I veered sharply away from him, my foot slipped and I found myself plummeting into one of the deep pits that pocked these meadows. The growling dogs circled the hole endlessly, and I spent a dreadful night down there. At dawn, the padre found me and got me safely out, with the dry comment that "Good folks stay indoors at night."

My meeting with Elena and the fresh proof that pit had given me of my isolation from humanity convinced me that it was time for me to leave my monastery. The padre and I said sad farewells. Before I left he asked my advice. He had saved almost all the money I had given him for board and had amassed about a thousand drachmas which he wanted to invest. I reminded him that in ancient times, Mt. Hymettus had been famous for its honey, and that since the same flowers that covered the hillside then would appear each modern spring, the bees might be expected to produce the same wonderful honey. He seemed pleased with the idea, and although I often thought of him in the following months, I did not know what had become of the plan. In Rome about two years later, I had a call from American Express, informing me that a crate had arrived for me from Greece. When the package was delivered I found two containers of Mt. Hymettus honey, as delicious as the ancients had described it.

M·S

5

I RETURNED to Italy in 1908 and went to a small village I knew, outside of Rome, called Anticoli Corrado. The place had a hold on me from the first time I saw it. I was reminded of Sydney Smith's first reaction to Scotland when he wrote, "The place is uncommonly beautiful, and I am in constant balance between admiration and trepidation: taste guides my eye where'er new beauties spread while prudence whispers 'look before you tread.'" The people of Anticoli were extremely beautiful. They had been used as models for centuries and their statuesque carriage and noble faces would inspire all but the most "non-objective" painter.

I had received the last check I would be getting from Alan Harris, and it was supposed to last me for three months. If I lived in Anticoli, the three months could be stretched to six, and there would be wonderful conditions for work besides.

I found a large studio and with the help of Gigi, a dashing neighbor, I was able to heat it fairly well. Gigi was the most exciting local character: handsome, vain, boastful, and always acting a part. He got into all sorts of scrapes, and tricked me badly several times, although I always seemed to find him out before too much damage was done. Gigi remained my friend through it all because I greatly enjoyed watching his play-acting and I think he respected me for not being taken in by

70

him. The Italian has only contempt for those he considers stupid, and it is the one thing you cannot accuse him of without drawing blood. My greatest Italian compliment came one afternoon when I was having a drink with Gigi and he looked speculatively at me and said, "You know, for an American you're pretty smart." The poor man didn't know that he was dealing not with a born American but with another Mediterranean.

Anticoli taught me many lessons over the years I lived there, perhaps none more lovely and poignant than the sanctity of bread to the poor. I am very fond of fresh bread, and in Anticoli it is about the best you can get. It has a dark golden color and an earthy bouquet. Whenever I smelled a fresh baking in the air, I would ask Caterina, the woman who kept house for me, to fetch a loaf. She usually objected that we already had some, but I could not resist.

There was a starving dog that hung around the piazza, and one day while I was feeding him his daily portion of stale bread, a thin middle-aged woman passed. She stared at me for a few minutes, and then in an angry voice told me, *"Signore, pane e per Cristiani e non per cani."* I realized that she was right, that in spite of the poverty in my own life I understood nothing about the anguish and physical exhaustion of growing one's daily bread. Since then, I have seen peasants curse the sun for burning their young wheat, wet the earth with their tears during a drought, stare helplessly at the sky when day after day the rain soaks the harvested stalks and the fear of hunger first appears in their frightened eyes.

The harvest fascinated me, and I plunged into sketches for a major work that I envisioned as a huge frieze of the Anticoli harvest. I did hundreds of sketches and carefully finished studies of human figures. I had planned to rent a large studio to execute my work, but now, with Alan Harris no longer free to help, all this had to be abandoned. I was back where I had been four years before, with no income and no really salable work, since I had neglected that sort of painting during these protected years. I was terribly depressed. I had no money, no paintings, no hopes; only a bunch of male nudes which I would not dispose of even if I were starving, since I needed them for my opus magnum, my only justification for these years. Even if I were to abandon all hope and decide to return to America, I had not the money for the passage home.

At that point a letter arrived from my mother. She was in Moscow, visiting my sister and brothers, and begged me to come see her before she returned to America. I had left Russia nineteen years before and from time to time had thought about visiting my family. I could hardly afford the trip at that time, but I calculated that since, when I got there, I could live a few months with my family, it might be feasible to go.

I traveled the cheapest way I could and had a hard, uncomfortable journey. The closer we got to the Russian border, the more nervous I became. I had heard that there was rigorous persecution since the 1905 revolution, and I worried even more because I knew that anyone born in Russia was considered eligible for military service, whether or not he had other citizenship. I decided to speak Russian to the inspectors since my Russian friends in Paris had told me that my speech had a strong American accent. I hoped this accent would also come through to the officials. Everything apparently went smoothly at the border during a brief interrogation and I leaned back in relief when the official left my compartment. However, a few moments later an army officer wearing black glasses entered the compartment with his orderly. He was apparently blind and had to be led to his seat. He introduced himself and when I told him that I was an American, he asked how I had learned Russian so well. I explained that I had learned Russian in order to be able to read their great literature in its original. He questioned me about my work, about where I had been living for the past several years, about the Russians I knew abroad. As he got up to leave the compartment he said, "Your accent gives you away." I panicked and would have given *myself* away had he not added, "For an American, you speak good Russian, but there is no doubt you have a strong foreign accent."

His orderly led him out of the compartment, to my great relief, though passing through the train later in the trip, I saw my "blind" officer again. He was playing cards with some other men, was in civilian clothes, and obviously could see very well. He was not embarrassed that I recognized him, but said to his companions, "Here is our American." I was startled for the moment, but I suppose that there was never any doubt that he was with the Secret Police.

Christmas was only a few days away and the train was crowded with holiday travelers. I had decided to take a first-class seat for this reason and was dozing peacefully when suddenly I heard the conductor shouting, "Kishinev, Kishinev." We were entering that city which had been the scene of one of the most cruel pogroms in Russian history.[1] I restlessly left my seat and went into the corridor as an elderly couple and their young daughter entered the train. The women were wrapped in sable coats and they were evidently members of the very wealthy Jewish community of that city. As they passed down the corridor the man looked into my compartment and, seeing an empty seat, beckoned to his wife saying, "Hannah, we're in luck. Here's a seat for you."

Someone in the compartment shouted that the seat was already taken, but I hurried in to tell the woman that since I had been sitting for hours I would be pleased if she would use the seat. The usual polite dialogue ensued—they insisting that I sit down, I that she remain where she was. The other people in the compartment were staring at me curiously—the interesting foreigner, the glamorous American, had turned out to be nothing but a Jew, and their scornful glances and cold silence showed too plainly how the mighty had fallen!

If non-Jews ever wonder about the clannishness and cohesion of the Jewish community, this is a perfect example of how it comes about. I felt strangely drawn to these newcomers and

[1] 1903.

we were soon deep in a moving, intimate conversation. We spoke in German to protect ourselves from the Russians in the compartment and I told them all about my life and my work. The beautiful young daughter was very bitter about their lot in Kishinoff and said, "My only wish is to finally get away from this country." We parted when the train reached Moscow, but I have often thought about these "relatives" of mine, and wondered how they fared in all the terrible events after our meeting.

I went directly to my family's home and we had a happy reunion, but I found it very difficult to adjust to the strangeness of being back. Moscow, after Paris and Rome, seemed like a small village. The Kremlin against the winter snow was beautiful in its play of faded colors and lovely towers, but St. Basil's Cathedral was much smaller than I had remembered it and seemed a shapeless, rather grotesque mass.

Russia had changed not only in appearance; the 1905 revolution had disrupted every phase of its life. There was brutal repression of all liberal thought, which was by no means limited to the political area. However, these conditions had little effect on the Moscow Art Theater, because the artistic revolt of Stanislavsky and Nemirovich-Danchenko had preceded the political revolution by about twenty years. Those men had realized that the star system limited the impact of the theater, and that it could achieve great things only if individuals submerged their own personalities to "the play."

This revolutionary concept soon elevated the Moscow theater to an unrivaled world position. When I met Stanislavsky in 1909, we talked about the problem of individualism and art. He had inquired about why I left Paris and went to Italy and I explained that I felt that in the art world of Paris there was too much emphasis upon uniqueness of expression, rather than on what was expressed, that the problem was not unlike what he, himself, had faced in the theater.

We talked about Alla Nazimova and Stanislavsky commented, "She was a very talented young woman, but found it too difficult to become a member of a group. She was too fond of publicity, but I think that in America, with its accentuation of the star system, she will be quite happy."

At the New Year's Eve performance of the Art Theater, an usher brought me a card from Stanislavsky inviting me to a party after the performance. It was very gay, with much caviar and champagne. What impressed me most was my introduction to a very handsome and distinguished-looking gentleman who turned out to be Prince Dolgoruki. It was a Prince Dolgoruki who had been responsible for the expulsion of the Jews from Moscow when I was a boy. I had had enough champagne at the party to give me courage to plan the joke of going up to my fellow guest and telling him a fable about a little Jewish boy, thrown out of his sacred city, who made good in America and was now celebrating in his own August Presence. Fortunately the champagne had not completely loosed my inhibitions, for surely the joke would have backfired badly in the Moscow of 1909.

It was a cruel winter in Moscow, and I went to St. Petersburg seeking comfort. The cold there was even more penetrating and unbearable. I suppose, having come from sunny Italy directly into this climate, I felt it more, since the streets were filled with people who did not seem to notice that their beards and eyebrows were white with frost. They seemed not to notice, either, a scene that etched itself on my mind and became, for me, the bitter symbol of oppression and persecution. On a busy St. Petersburg street, a soldier saluted a huge officer he passed, but evidently the salute was not satisfactory. The officer shouted, "Stop," and as they stood facing each other, he clenched his fist and struck the soldier full on the mouth. "*Vinovat* (I beg your pardon), Your Highness," said the soldier. Again the right fist landed on the young man's mouth; again the humble, "*Vinovat*, Your Highness." The officer smashed his mouth a third time, and with blood flowing from his lips, he again said, "*Vinovat*, Your Highness."

75

No one else on the crowded street had stopped or even seemed to see what was happening. The officer stormed off, shouting, "Wait, that's only a small sample of what's going to happen to you." The soldier's cap had fallen off and as he stooped to pick it up, some drops of blood and a tooth fell to the snow. He picked up the tooth, rubbed it against his sleeve, and put it in his pocket.

I wondered how long the people would stand for such outrages. I could have wept with relief that I had left all that horror behind me and had become a citizen of a country where such disregard for human decency did not exist. Later, I learned better. When I read of lynchings in the South, saw the Fascists in Italy, heard the horrors of the German Nazis, I realized that such degradation is not the exclusive property of any place or people. But that poor boy's face, its clear blue eyes and bleeding lips, the crimson blood staining the Russian snow, remains with me as a painful symbol.

The only one in my own family who seemed to be taking an active interest in the political unrest was my niece Ida, a lovely young medical student. Ida begged me to take her with me to Italy, as much, I am afraid, out of schoolgirl infatuation as political considerations. However, she stayed and became a successful doctor, and then I heard that she and her young physician husband died tragically together during the World War I typhoid epidemic.

As for the rest of my family, they appeared politically reactionary, apathetic and dull. I had been looking forward to seeing them again, but too much had happened to all of us since our last meeting, for us to have much in common. They were much more bourgeois than I had become. Rosa, in particular, was a typical Victorian matron: proper, stiff, and much concerned with sentimental possessions and memorabilia. However, this interest of hers gave me one of the most poignant insights of my Moscow visit. Rosa had saved all sorts of things from her childhood and youth: pictures, water colors she'd done at the gymnasium, and even her old diaries. I persuaded her to let me look at the diary entries about our parents, and I copied out a few because of the fresh understanding they gave me. Although Yiddish had been the language of our home, Carl and Rosa were rather snobbish about it and tried to get us all to use German. It was rather amusing to read the old diaries, since Rosa, in recording my parents' conversations, had translated them from Yiddish into the more approved German. By 1909 I had learned to think in English, and I found myself copying the entries out of the old book in English translation—all very much removed from my parents' simple speech.

Two of the diary notes I found most illuminating and moving were these:

September 28, 1883: Papa is the eternal student. He sneers at material accomplishment. When Mama said, "Zakheim contributed a thousand rubles toward the building of a synagogue," Papa said, "I know the old hypocrite." Mama said, "By their deeds thou shalt know them." Papa laughed then, "Good deeds only too often hide evil thoughts. You don't expect people to show off their wickedness, do you?"

October 5, 1883: Mama talks very fast especially when she gets excited and her tempo tries to keep up with her emotion, then her voice gets higher and higher until she screams the climax—but when Papa tries to emphasize a point, his voice becomes a whisper, as if he were imparting a secret. . . .

I was rather surprised that my mother and Rosa were on such good terms that year in Moscow. Years before, my mother had been told by a notorious scandalmonger that my sister Rosa had converted to Christianity, in order that her husband be permitted to pursue his profession as a lawyer. Mother's reaction had been "I'd rather see Rosa dead than buried in a Christian cemetery." I teased her about this remark when we were together again in Moscow, and told her it hadn't seemed to make much sense, and, in any case, it now looked as if she had been reconciled to Rosa's baptism. My mother was very dignified about the whole thing and replied, "Rosa is my child. My love for her has nothing to do with her religion. I would of course rather see her *alive* than buried in a Christian cemetery."

Rosa's diary seemed to be my only connection with my old home. I had expected that my past would be resurrected during this visit. Instead, I found myself in an alien world, disliking the snowy landscape, the people, even my own family. Rosa, who had been beautiful and sensitive, had grown heavy, spiritually as well as physically. I had always disliked her husband Michael, and he had become loathsome. He had a long red mustache like an empty carrot, a Germanic, stubborn neck, and a political conservatism which disgusted me. Joel, my gay, quick-witted, older brother, had become morose and silent. He looked like a Mongol, with slanting eyes, high cheekbones, and low forehead, bent over his vodka night after night.

My greatest disillusionment was with my brother Carl. I remembered him as a highly intelligent, enthusiastic student with a passionate interest in chemical research. He had loved the best in German and Russian literature, and would spend hours in passionate argument over the relative importance of Tolstoy and Dostoevsky. Now, I hardly recognized him; his hair was clipped close, his ears stuck out, and his pointed skull looked like a queer vessel with protruding handles.

My brother owned a factory which made certain products which depended on chemical skill, but when I asked him if he had kept up his interest in science, he answered, "I am no longer interested in anything. I am a *milovar*" (a soap maker).

I reminded him of the six Browning revolvers he had written me to send him from Paris four years before. While I was painstakingly concealing them in cans of olive oil I had been sure of which side would use them. Now he snarled, "It

The Rogers-Kennedy Memorial to the Early Settlers of Massachusetts,
Worcester, Massachusetts (*Worcester Art Museum*)

Detail, "The Prayer," Rogers-Kennedy Memorial (*Worcester Art Museum*)

would be better for all of us if you would forget about that. Evidently you have not heard about Stolypin's neckties." [1]

I was disgusted with him at that time, although I was later very proud of Carl when I heard of his brave action on the Kerensky side of the revolution, and his long refusal to cooperate with the Bolsheviks. Only after he and his family were starving did he consent to return to the laboratories of which he was part owner.

In 1909, none of this fervor was evident. The winter was cold and grim. I was listless, apathetic, and, in a real sense, disinherited. I sat in the overheated house, overpowered by the smell of kerosene and sauerkraut within, the cold oppression and suspicion outside. I was aching to return to Italy, to its warmth and its free-flowing rhythms of life. Before coming to Russia, I had met the DuBois Reymond family of Potsdam and they had invited me to visit them and to do a portrait of Mrs. DuBois Reymond. I could not stand Russia another moment; I cut my visit short and went off to Germany.

The DuBois Reymond family was extremely wealthy and cultured, and they were well known for their support of the arts. The husband, Alard, was an imposing-looking man, who had about him an air of suppressed violence. His family and his acquaintances treated him with the greatest respect, but it was a respect that came very close to fear. Lili, his wife, was almost his antithesis. Her grandmother had been the gifted sister of Felix Mendelssohn, and she inherited from that part of her family a gentle spirit and a worship of beauty, though apparently none of their extraordinary talents. She had a fine, sensitive mind, and was sweetly humane.

Instead of merely commissioning the one painting we had discussed, the DuBois Reymonds asked me to do a portrait of each of them: of Lili and Alard, of their two sons, their young daughter, and Mrs. DuBois Reymond's brother, the distin-

[1] P. A. Stolypin (1863–1911), Russian premier and minister of the interior (1906–11); he was responsible for the exile and execution of thousands of people. He was eventually assassinated by a revolutionist.

guished philosopher, Paul Hensel. They were all intelligent and generous and their lives were in sharp contrast to the atmosphere I had just left in my own family's home. I had been shocked by their materialism, their crude manners, their beefy overfed look, and their narrow political views. This family was obviously different, and had I come into their home five years before, I would have been charmed. Now I felt hemmed in by their middle-class, professorial attitudes toward life and art. They condemned everything that was alive in music, painting, or literature, but I had heard the music of Debussy, the poetry of Verlaine and Baudelaire; I had seen the painting of Cézanne and Degas, and I could not condemn them, nor forget them.

I did not belong. I had been brought up in a different milieu, not at all properly, according to their standards. While I had long since learned about good manners and drawing-room niceties, I could not understand or tolerate a culture founded upon the premise that the highest good was to be found only in the past. Once, in a rather heated discussion about Debussy, Mrs. DuBois Reymond exclaimed, "But I thought you loved Bach and Mozart!" I replied, "I do, and although what was good enough for my father is also good for me, it is not good *enough*."

I had yearned for a home, yet after a few weeks in Potsdam I felt like a caged animal. I was too young and fired with my ideals then to realize that one's friends do not necessarily have to share one's artistic tastes, and in my usual restlessness I left Potsdam and went to Berlin.

There I met several old friends, among them Bernhard Kellermann. He mentioned my work to Paul Cassierer, who was the most important art dealer in Germany and made an appointment for me to see him. I took some drawings to his gallery where he greeted me with extraordinary personal rudeness and disdain for my work. I gathered up my drawings and started to leave but Cassierer called me back, told me the drawings were "not bad," and that he would arrange to show

them. A few weeks later I received a printed invitation to an
exhibit at his gallery of "Five Master Draughtsmen: Graf von
Kalckreuth,[1] Ferdinand Hodler,[2] Maurice Sterne, Honoré
Daumier, and Edgar Degas." Not bad company, I felt! Max
Liebermann [3] praised my work to Cassierer, which was rather
ironic for me. Some time before, Mrs. DuBois Reymond had
shown Liebermann some of my work and he had scornfully
called me a young man completely "without talent." Although
his judgment did not affect my own opinion about my work, it
made me sad to think that my generous friend had been made
to feel foolish in her choice of protégé. I told Cassierer the
story and that sharp-tongued fellow hurried back to tease
Liebermann with it.

I was pleased with this artistic success and with the carefree
life I had resumed in Berlin. One day as I sat in a café with two
friends, a handsome young man at a nearby table was pointed
out to me as a painter, the grandson of Sohn-Rethel, a
prominent German artist. His name was Karli Sohn; we were
introduced, and he invited me to his home. We sat in his studio
talking about our work, and from a nearby room I could hear
someone perceptively, and rather stubbornly, practicing a
Beethoven sonata. Karli explained that it was his sister Mira,
who had at one time studied for the concert stage, but had
retired when she married two years before. A few minutes
later Karli took me in to tea and I saw before me a beautiful
woman, whose grace and charm struck me with great force. I
had noticed her on a Berlin street a few days before and had
been immediately enchanted and haunted by her.

Seeing her again, in my new friend's home, gave our
acquaintance a magical beginning. I had fallen irretrievably in
love with this woman who seemed unable to move or speak or
act in any way that was not perfect. She had a self-assurance
that came from deep within her, and although she must have

[1] Leopold Karl Walter, Graf von Kalckreuth (1855–1928), German
painter, one of the founders of the Secessionists.
[2] (1853–1918), Swiss painter and lithographer.
[3] Leader of the German Secessionist painters.

been aware of her extraordinary beauty, she was never self-conscious about it or vain. She never made light chatter, spoke only when she had something important to say and then in a voice of low intimacy that seemed to come from the depth of her womanhood. From that first moment in her home I felt that a power stronger than I could cope with was robbing me of my will and of my freedom. I would vow to stay away from her, would run off to my work or to another woman, only to be drawn back. When I was with her, I was terribly restless, unable even to enjoy her music, because when she played, she would become detached, unaware of my presence.

Women had been expendable before I met Mira. They answered temporary needs, but never provided the deeper satisfactions I found only in my work. Mira was my completion; I was a fragment away from her, in tangible physical pain.

We were completely sensitive to each other; it was as if she shared my thoughts. Our passion for each other grew each day, but Mira would not be unfaithful to her husband nor to the life they had begun together. She loved him and could not bear the thought of doing anything to jeopardize the happiness of her young child. There was another difficulty; one night when we were both ill with unfulfilled desires, Mira told me that she believed that I had so idealized our relationship that if she were suddenly to agree to come away with me, I would be disappointed and would tire of her as I had of the other women of whom she had heard. It was an impossible situation, without hope of solution. I was unable to work because of my anxiety about Mira. I grew tired of Europe and I longed to be traveling again.

Sterne left Berlin in May, 1910. He went to Rome and then to Anticoli where he spent the summer. In the fall, he returned to Rome, took a studio, and apparently went earnestly back to work. Leo Stein discusses this brief Italian visit in a letter he wrote to Gertrude Stein at about this time:

Dear Gertrude,

Yesterday I looked over Sterne's drawings quite extensively. That wasn't the least bit like guessing weather at Perugia, but I really surprised myself by the acuteness of my connoisseurship. I could date the drawings with quite unfailing accuracy, . . . Sterne is in regard to drawing a little like [Edward] Bruce as to color. . . .

He is making the great discovery of why Cézanne and Matisse and others draw the way they do. His own drawing is tending in that direction too.

I started cooking today. Sterne and I take supper together at the studio. I supply the vegetables and fruit; he supplies the oatmeal, butter, cheese, alcohol, salt, sugar, etc. I did some stewed tomatoes today in Sterne's boilerette and they certainly were the most delicious stewed tomatoes I ever ate. Sterne did the oatmeal today but he didn't boil it enough and it was a little raw so I'm going to take charge of things tomorrow.[1]

In October, 1910, Sterne accidentally ran into Mira and Karli Sohn in Rome where they were also visiting. The painful relationship was resumed, and by Christmas, he was back in Germany to spend the holidays at the home of the DuBois Reymonds.

During that period I talked constantly of finding a Garden of Eden where life would be simple, where beauty might exist as a part of daily living, rather than as an escape from it. I burned to paint the human body in unclothed naturalness, but the models who came to my studio were awkward and self-conscious once they undressed. The DuBois Reymond family was unbelievably patient and kind to me. They felt that I would never come back to myself if I stayed so close to Mira, and they very generously offered to pay my expenses on a lengthy trip abroad.

[1] Edmund Fuller (ed.), *Journey into the Self, being the letters, papers, and journals of Leo Stein* (Crown Publishers, 1950), p. 32.

I was already thirty-four, an age when other men are firmly settled in a particular place, yet I was thrilled with the idea of traveling again. I doubt that this love of travel can be traced to all the moving around my family did during my childhood. My sister Lena is only eighteen months older than I, and she was subjected to exactly the same changes of environment, yet Lena loathed it as I loved it. I suppose that some people are nomads by nature, and I, for one, have always craved to sail the seven seas. I disliked being rooted to one place because I felt that my roots were in all of nature and that I must, therefore, explore every part of it.

It was not that I rushed, like a tourist, from place to place, but that for many years of my life I needed to discover for myself the essential kernel of the life and art of the people of the world. I always settled down for a more or less lengthy stay, in order to know a new place in all the seasons of the year, and to see past its local surface appearance.

Before starting out for this latest adventure, I stopped to say good-by to Mira and her family. Karli Sohn was burning to come along. For a long time he had wanted to paint in the tropics, but his family had been reluctant to see him go off alone. Now, they agreed to let him accompany me. Mrs. Sohn took me aside before we left and begged me to see that her son came back to her unharmed.

I imagine that Alard and Lili DuBois Reymond were astonished when they received my letter notifying them that Mira's brother would be my traveling companion. In retrospect I see how foolish it was to have Karli with me, since he was so like his sister in every respect. Perhaps in some confused way I thought his presence would help. In any case, in October, 1911, we set off on a journey that was to last until May, 1914, though neither of us had any idea at the time that we would be away so long.

M·S

6

Harry Salpeter in a penetrating analysis of the work of Maurice Sterne wrote of the strong influence his travels had on Sterne's life and art:

The name of Maurice Sterne is neither romantic nor glamorous. It does not suggest magic casements opening on the foam, or the horn of Roland at the pass of Ronscevalles. It is a rather matter-of-fact name. It might be that of a business man or of an engineer. . . . Yet it belongs to one of America's most important modern artists, one whose career trails bright rainbows of reminiscence from the isles of Greece, the plains of Italy, and the pervasive loveliness of the particular isle of Bali. It is the name of the man who discovered Bali for the Western world, who found motives for his art in Egypt, India and Burma, and to whom Italy was . . . a second home. There is the golden dust of far-away places on most of his paintings.[1]

Our first destination was Egypt, and from the moment our ship approached Alexandria, I felt enthralled in some ancient spell. A swarm of boats converged on the ship and vendors of rugs, pictures, and trinkets were suddenly swarming on deck,

[1] Harry Salpeter, "Sterne, the Maestro in Art," *Esquire* (February, 1941).

85

shouting, gesticulating, and forcing their goods upon us. It should have been strange and unfamiliar to me, yet from the very first moment I set foot in the East, everything I saw seemed to have its echo deep in my own past. I felt, quite simply, that it was here I belonged, and I felt it more than I ever had in New York, or Moscow, or even my native Libau.

My emotions were constantly overstimulated by this sensation and there was a steady undertone of perplexity, much like the feeling you have when you see someone on the street who looks familiar, yet whose name you cannot recall, and who does not seem to recognize *you* at all. I felt that I belonged there among a people who looked upon me as a stranger whose presence they tolerated only for exploitation. Coming to the East was for me not a new discovery of an unknown place, but a return to a long forgotten scene. It was as if that face on the street belonged to someone I had known long before who had changed over the years, as I had changed.

The desert also aroused in me feelings which were unique and intense. It was immense, a petrified ocean; yet it did not make me feel dwarfed or isolated as I had expected; rather, my spatial sense was changed. The sky was remote; the distance between the stars and the background beyond seemed far greater than the distance between the stars and the earth. It was as if life and time were suspended in an infinity of space and peace.

Of course, not all of Egypt had this atmosphere. The lewdness, the degeneracy, the sordid poverty, filth, and stench of the Cairo slums, beggars all description. In the doorways sat listless children with swollen bellies and emaciated limbs, their eye-sockets swarming with black flies which obscured whatever was left of their God-given vision. These grim sights were exposed in the brilliant sunlight. Evil lusts were hidden and could be appeased for the price of a pinch of hashish in the dark dives of the Cairo nights.

Egyptian sculpture also was a sharp contrast to the Greek

sculpture I had lived with a few years before. Where the Greeks caught the exultation of the moment in their statues, the Egyptians, in the silence and pathos of their figures, hinted at eternity.

From Egypt, we sailed for India, but my trip was marred by a blatant incident of anti-Semitism, not against me, but against a fellow passenger. The passengers had seemed quite congenial, and I was a rather popular figure aboard ship, because of my profession and my previous travels. In addition to getting to know the people at my own dining table, I struck up an acquaintance with a quiet, though interesting man named Pollock who was an Orthodox Jew. We had long, stimulating conversations, and I took to spending a lot of my time in his company. I noticed at about that time that the attitude of my table companions had distinctly cooled. They no longer sought me out, and seemed to respond very coldly to my greetings. Then one day when I was standing with a British civil servant whom I had gotten to know fairly well, Pollock came up to us. The "colonial" moved very stiffly away, with no explanation. Pollock was quite upset. He said, "I should have warned you before not to stay with me so much. It can't do you any good, and since you expect to spend some time in India, it might interfere with your plans."

I was shocked and outraged. I asked to be transferred to Pollock's table in the dining room, and from then on, spent all my shipboard time in his company. The frigid atmosphere emanating from my former companions did nothing to dispel the scorching heat on that trip and I found myself with another major discomfort. Pollock, because of his observance of Jewish dietary laws, was seated at a table with strict vegetarians. We weren't even permitted eggs!

This was my first lesson in colonialism, but it merely reinforced some of the things I already knew about the British, in particular. They have a dual code of behavior: intimate among themselves, distant to anyone they consider an outsider. They are wrongly accused of being phlegmatic and feeling superior; this attitude is one that has been carefully assumed. The British upper classes are expert at editing their emotions and censoring their outward appearance. At the time I was in India, they were still acting the part of "rulers of the world," and their snobbishness was painful and embarrassing. A well-known British officer had introduced me at his exclusive club in Calcutta and had told me that I might feel free to entertain my friends there. I met Mr. Gegondranath Tagore, nephew of the poet, and a distinguished gentleman and talented painter in his own right. I invited him to join me for a brandy soda at the club, but he said that he could not accept the invitation. When I coaxed him further he added, "You do not understand. Because of my complexion, I am *persona non grata* at the officers' club."

It not only was the English upper class which behaved in this way toward Indians. Once I was on a train traveling to Benares and a Brahman with a most beautiful face was seated opposite me. He was so deeply engrossed in a manuscript that he did not notice the appearance in our compartment of two flushed and tipsy Tommies. One of the soldiers leaned over to the Indian to ask what he was reading. The Brahman did not answer; the soldier repeated the question, but the Brahman continued to ignore him. "Too proud to talk to a British soldier, are you? Well, I'll show you who's boss here!" I was sickened then, when he reached over and pulled hard at the Indian's beard. Without a sound, the Indian got up, took his black brief case off the rack, and left the compartment.

The Brahmans were in a particularly unpleasant position under British rule. For centuries they had occupied the highest level in Indian political and social life and they hated the British for usurping their inherited place. They held their English conquerors responsible for the destitution and ignorance of the masses, when, in reality, these conditions existed long before the British arrived. In a way, there was something more offensive about the Brahman snobbishness than that of the British. The British feelings of superiority were based on a sense of behavior, by personal achievement in India either in the civil service or in the military. The Brahman on the other hand felt that he was better than anyone else merely from a genetic superiority. And this attitude was reflected in the Indian masses who seemed to take pride in, or at any rate take for granted, the gaudy extravagance of the Maharajas. Where there was hostility, it was directed against the foreign "barbarians" and not against the exploiters who were their own countrymen.

Of course, it must be understood that I made these observations in 1911 and 1912 when Asians seemed to be living in some timeless sense of being, almost a hypnotic trance, focused on eternity and not on their temporal lives. This has all changed, for the present state of revolution, of course, could not exist in the old spiritual climate. However, even then, one sensed in many of the people a hidden poison, a controlled venom against their lives and against the hated foreigners, in particular.

This spirit was not typical of all Indians; in fact it coexisted with an exalted otherworldliness in certain of their artists and religious figures. I was invited to visit with the great poet Tagore and spent a long time in earnest conversation with him. He was an admirer of Heinrich Heine yet did not take his position so seriously that we were not, within moments, engaged in a hot dispute over the merits of Heine and *my* favorite poet, Goethe. Tagore felt that Goethe was too self-conscious and self-important to be really great, and when I protested that this was true of Goethe's private life but not of his work, Tagore said, "You are mistaken. A man cannot be one thing in his life, another in his art. Goethe was a conscious superman, arrogant, aggressive, always aware of what he considered his unique place. For this reason, his work never achieves the tenderness and humanity of Heine."

What impressed me most about Tagore when I first saw him in India was his remarkable physical beauty. Tagore's appearance was of a higher physical and spiritual order than that of most men. He was probably the handsomest man I have ever seen—a perfect blending of masculine and feminine features. Unfortunately, my recollections of him are meager, not because my memory is bad, but because I never really benefited very much from intercourse with celebrities. My own drive to make an impression on them, myself, shut me off from any really sensitive perception. I had a tremendous need to be judged "someone to be reckoned with." Even their words of wisdom were to me merely a challenge to say something in response which would be impressive. After these interviews I would remember little that the famous person had said, but every one of my own clever replies. I blush now to admit this.

One thing about Tagore which impressed me powerfully took place several years later in New York. On November 23, 1916, I received the following note at my New York studio:

Dear Sir:

Mr. Tagore asked me if I could arrange a meeting between him and you. I found your address at the Berlin Photographic Studio and gave Mr. Tagore your address. I am writing to request you to get in touch with him tomorrow. . . . He lectures at the Hudson Theater at 3 P.M. Most probably he will be home at 1 P.M. I really do not know his engagements. So please call him up or write to him direct. He wishes to talk to you about Chitra and its staging. Hoping that you will meet Mr. Tagore soon, I am,

Very truly yours,
Basanta Koomar Roy

P.S. If you call him up please insist that you be connected with him or Mr. Pearson his secretary, for you are doing this at Mr. Tagore's request.

I telephoned the next day and asked to speak to Mr. Tagore. I was answered by an unpleasant snicker, and a foolish woman said, "Sir Rabindranath never speaks on the telephone. What do you wish?" Her tone was extremely condescending, typical of the hangers-on of celebrities (including, often, their wives). I gave my name, and, as the note I had received suggested, explained that I had been asked to call. I was given an appointment and cautioned to be prompt.

Tagore had, in the years since I had seen him, been awarded the Nobel Prize and had won world-wide acclaim. He was now an "Eastern sage," fully aware of his own importance, attended by a coterie of mystical ladies who worshipped at his feet and corroded his spirit. When I arrived at his apartment that day in New York, the now-great man was unable even to rise to greet me, since two artists were simultaneously doing his portrait. I had hoped to have a good talk with him, and renew the warm feeling we had had together in India, but now the atmosphere was all wrong. We made light chatter for about an hour, but I was restless to get away. I was relieved when the next visitor was announced and I was able to go. Only when I was leaving did I see for a moment a faint reflection of the old look in his eyes. Now though, their expression was touched with pain and fatigue, and a disillusion that would have hurt anyone who had known him years before in India.

The Indian spirit bewildered me at first with its contradictions: noise, raucous color, and poverty on the one hand; deep spiritual peace on the other. It was not until I got to Benares that I became aware that something new had entered my own spirit, that India was more to me than a mere exotic stimulation of my senses, more than another experience to remember. It had entered my own spirit and altered, by some mysterious process, my inner life and reactions. This, I think, is the greatest difficulty Europeans have in their encounter with India, this bringing into some meaningful inner focus the strange spirit of the place. Perhaps only Hindus can ever really succeed.

These immense spiritual differences also affect our ability to understand Hindu art, which to a Western observer seems overloaded with details. When I first saw a Persian miniature my eyes beat against its lovely surface in vain, like a moth beating its wings against a pane of glass. We must have space for our vision, as we must have oxygen for our lungs.

Hindu sculpture seemed much closer to our artistic ideals than their painting. It also is frequently over-rich in detail, but there is an appreciation of the importance of larger mass, a rhythmic flow of motion, that is sinuous and sensuous. A vulgar elegance, it probably should be classified as "arty" rather than as great art, and yet, when you examine closely the details of their art or their architecture, you are astounded with the meticulous craftsmanship, with the patience and genius of their makers, who must have loved details more than any other people.

Of course, as in any other culture, the art in India is an accurate mirror of the life around it. I have rarely seen a tree there that did not give the impression of overdress, like their rajas whose bodies were completely obscured by elaborate costumes. Only the holy men, seated beside the Benares cremation ghats, suggested a plainer art. They seemed like gaunt gray statues: their bodies smeared with ashes, dressed only in loin cloths, fingering long chains of prayer beads.

While we were in Benares, the ghats were in constant use. All day and all night, the air would be filled with cries of "*Ram, Ram, Sita Ram,*" as the people carried their shrouded dead down to the river for cremation. In a strange way, the city had never seemed so intensely alive. I commented upon this to Karli Sohn, and he said, "Is it possible that you've been so immersed in your work that you don't know what is going on? Don't you know that there are so many cases of plague here in Benares, that it has reached epidemic proportions!" I was astounded, and called our servant in. He confirmed the story, and when I asked them both why they had not discussed any of this with me, they said that they had assumed I knew.

That night we ate our dinner in silence, each of us wondering whether or not he should leave. I saw fear in Karli's eyes, the same fear that he probably saw in mine, yet neither of us spoke—each too proud to be the first to make a move. The next morning we got up, ate our breakfast, and went out as usual to paint the river from the little boat we had rented. The cries of *"Ram, Ram, Sita Ram"* reached us from the shore, and that day we saw another of the horrible corpses of holy men that frequently rise to the surface of the Ganges. Although all castes are cremated, the Sanyasies, or holy men, are placed by their disciples between slabs of stone and, with appropriate ceremony, dropped into the river. That day, while we sketched, a huge, gray-violet mass bumped against the boat and I was horrified to see that it was a bloated corpse. We went back to our quarters, and our private war of nerves continued. This foolish behavior went on for several days, and I almost came to hate my friend. Then, during one night, Karli burst into a terrible scream. A rat had landed on his chest while he slept, and had bitten him. I cleansed his wound and sat down opposite him. Now, I thought, now he will ask that we leave. Karli sat all night with his great eyes staring at the wall. When dawn finally came, our man arrived with our tea and I said, "Vishna, prepare our things. We are leaving here this very day." Karli mumbled, "Thank God," and by noon we were on a train for Calcutta.

While I sat through that terrible night, I had remembered my promise to Mrs. Sohn that I would bring her son back to her, and it was because of that promise that I was able to bring myself to speak. It was lucky that the rat had bitten Karli and not me, for then neither of us would have had the rationalization to break our silence and put aside our foolish pride.

When we left Benares, in May, 1912, we went to Burma, and there had a wonderful holiday. The people were dressed in all the bright and delicate colors of the spectrum, in iridescent silks that made them seem always ready for a party. I had been told that in Burma I would find ancient Buddhism in its purest form, but it was certainly a religion far removed

93

from the austerity and self-denial I had expected. The Burmese were pleasure-seeking, and very happy in its attainment. How Renoir would have loved the place! Our idyllic visit to Burma came to an abrupt end, however. Quite by accident, from an Englishman who wandered into our courtyard looking for his dog, I learned that the plague had pursued us to Mandalay. The Englishman's advice was that we'd "better get moving on," and so we did, the very next morning. I learned later that our German neighbors who had postponed leaving, because they had paid their rent in advance, had died of the disease.

Sterne went from Burma to Java, and from there to Bali, where he stayed from the fall of 1912 until May, 1914. On March 21, 1915, The New York Times Magazine *published an article in which Joyce Kilmer interviewed Sterne about his travels in the Far East:* [1]

Maurice Sterne had conventionalized and interpreted the spirit of Bali in a way like that in which Gauguin treated Tahiti. He is not a Futurist nor a Cubist; he is, however (I do not think he would object to this label), a barbarian. That is, he has absorbed so much of the spirit of the strange, wild land where he has lived for the past few years, and had developed so strong an affection for its strange, wild people that he now finds himself spiritually a citizen of the Island of Bali rather than of the Island of Manhattan.

But before he went to Bali and really found himself, Mr. Sterne travelled extensively through the Orient. . . . Mr. Sterne is by no means attracted by the European dwellers in

---

[1] Sterne wrote very often during this trip to his patrons, the DuBois Reymond family. He apparently described in great detail everything he saw and did in the Far East, reportedly with special emphasis on his life in Bali. The DuBois Reymonds kept the letters, and sometime during the 1930's, began negotiations for their publication. However, the war intervened, and at the war's end the DuBois Reymond house was sacked and, along with their other possessions, the Sterne letters and paintings were destroyed. This Joyce Kilmer article contains some of the best background material extant on these years.

Asiatic lands, and this little anecdote explained, to a certain extent, his feeling.

"The finest Buddhist temple in the East Indian Archipelago," he said, "is at Baroebolder, in Java. It contains 2,000 seated images of Buddha, and if the reliefs which decorate it were placed side by side in a line they would make eight miles of sculpture. When the Mohammedans conquered Java the Javanese buried it [the temple] to save it from the invasion. They covered it with earth and planted trees above it, and the Mohammedans passed over it unknowingly.

"Well, I attended a great feast at this temple in celebration of the anniversary of the coronation of the Sultan of Dgokjakarta [sic], who is one of the two native rulers of the island. It was a splendid festival; the food was brought in by a force of 2,000 men. Eight Princesses danced a beautiful Javanese dance. They were girls of 16 or 18 years; they were painted a bright lemon yellow, and their hair was drawn over their foreheads like lotus leaves and decorated with gold stars. In the back their hair was contained in great veils made of buds and blossoms woven together. As they danced their slow, graceful dances—the Dutch officials and traders who were the Sultan's guests, sat and played poker! That annoyed me more than anything else I saw during my entire stay in the Orient.

". . . I had for a long time been attracted by the Orient. I wanted to see the people of the East, and I particularly wanted to go where I could study the nude human body among people who were not self-conscious when they were nude. When I first went to British India I had no special knowledge of Bali; I reached that island more or less by accident. . . .

"I went to Singapore and to Java. I was disappointed in Java; I had expected too much. Java has the most beautiful landscapes to be seen in the tropics, but the Europeans have been there so long that they have spoiled it. The people are less conservative than the Hindu. A Hindu would rather cut off his head than take off his turban. A Javanese will take off

95

his beautiful turban and put on instead some discarded European sun-helmet that he has found in the street.

"I thought that I could find the conditions I desired in Borneo. So, in spite of the fact that people warned me against the head-hunters, I planned to go to Borneo. But I missed the boat! I am glad that I missed that boat, now.

"I asked the agent what place I should go to since I could not now go at once to Borneo. He suggested Bali, so I got a ticket good for one month's stay. I went to Northern Bali, and did not like it at all.

"But one day in the bazaar I saw the group of strangers—beautifully formed men and women almost nude. I was amazed; they looked like ancient Greeks. I asked the Controlleur who they were. He said, 'They are South Balinese.' I asked, 'Are there any more people like that in South Bali?' He answered, 'Oh, yes! They are all crazy in South Bali; they all go around like that.' So I went to South Bali.

"You see," said Mr. Sterne, filling a large American pipe with American tobacco (there is nothing exotic about the appearance or habits of this painter of exotic subjects), "I went to the East to see the human body as it is created. I do not want to study the human body by having a model come in to my studio and undress; I want to see nature. In South Bali I saw it.

"The nudeness of the Balinese seemed to have a curious effect on the appearance of the landscape. The landscape was satiny, and the bodies of the people looked like velvet. When it rained there was a change in the looks of country and people; the rain made the landscape velvety and the people satiny. The Balinese have great bones; I watched crowds of Balinese in the rain and saw the rain trickle over their collar-bones and breasts, and I seemed to understand the origin of rivers."

Mr. Sterne would not allow me to call his beloved Balinese savages. "They have a wonderful civilization of their own," he said. "They have their own morality, their own conventions. . . . [For example] Balinese men and women never dance together.

"As I crossed over the volcanic mountains to the Southern part of Bali the landscape became more beautiful hour by hour. On the south coast I found an old bamboo hut near the river and there I lived. There were two or three white people in Den-Passar, the nearest town, but I did not go to the town. At first the natives resented my going into the temples; but when they saw that I respected their religion—as I respect every religion—they became kind and would always tell me when anything interesting was to take place.

"They are a brave, silent, proud people, these South Balinese. Eight years ago Holland decided to annex Bali. The 8,000 of the highest caste of the population, having arrayed themselves as for a Temple festival, with precious golden bowls, silk brocades, lances and spears, went to meet the conquering Dutch troops. At a given signal the men, women and children drew their flame-shaped krisses and killed themselves.

"People have said of my pictures that my subjects never seem to smile. The Balinese do not smile; neither do the wild beasts! I never saw a smile in Bali, but sometimes I heard laughter like a volley of shot.

"In Bali the men do most of the playing, flying kites and attending cock fights. The men and women are built alike physically to a great extent. They do much the same sort of work. The women do the buying and selling at retail. There are as many priestesses as priests."

In his talk with me Mr. Sterne dwelt on the fact that he felt more at home at Bali than in any other part of the Orient. "When I left Europe," he said, "I felt that my energy was all gone; I could not work. But in Bali I could not stop work, I felt that it was a crime to sleep.

"There is a difference between the religion of Bali and that of any other island of the archipelago. The Balinese have retained the Hindu religion, they have a passionate, fiery religion, in which the gentler gods of Hindustan are almost forgotten. The religious rites are for the most part hysterical trances or frenzies. The elements are symbolically expressed in the sacred dances at the temple festivals. The coffins are shaped partly like fishes; they have the heads of beasts and flame-shaped wings, thus symbolizing earth, air, fire and water. The art of Bali is a religious expression.". . .

Mr. Sterne . . . [told] me some reminiscences of the days he spent in his tropical studio of bamboo. He made during his three years in the East some ten thousand studies, many of which he destroyed. But he found that he must be discreet in destroying sketches that he did not like. Once he tore up a drawing before the girl who had been posing for it. Instantly she screamed and brought an angry crowd around her. She thought that he had put an evil spell upon her by destroying her image. The only other time that he aroused the enmity of his neighbors was when he idly sketched an old woman's likeness on the ground with a stick. . . .

Although there is violent action in some of Mr. Sterne's canvases, the quality which he chiefly admires in Bali is re-pose. . . . "The East is static; Bali is static; even in the crowded bazaar in Bali I never witnessed a loud quarrel. . . . The European idea of deity is force, the Eastern idea is re-pose."

Bali was a completely satisfying artistic experience. The landscape, the beauty of the people, their exquisite aesthetic sense contributed to a greater whole, a completeness that one finds only in the greatest art. To find this quality in "real life" changed my concept, not only of art, but of what life itself might be. From the very beginning I found in South Bali beauty that moved my soul. Karli Sohn and I had begun traveling south and had got about midway across the island, to Bangli. It was the most beautiful place either of us had ever seen. Karli was all for settling down but something urged me on. I convinced him that we should first go to Den-Passar, the capital of South Bali.

We set out at dawn and by mid-afternoon we had entered a small wood of shimmering, gray trees with rich, dense foliage that hid the sky. We seemed to be within some fantastic Gothic cathedral, with hundreds of columns—some a foot in diameter, some but a fraction of an inch, but all exactly vertical. What gave the grove its ghostly appearance were the myriads of stringlike creepers that grew straight down from the branches above, and took root in the earth.

The "woods" turned out to be a single banyan tree, whose complex growth we were in the midst of. The natives apparently appreciated the beauty of this remarkable grove, for at its center was a rough stone altar, on which had recently been placed yellow camellias and a lovely white flower I had never seen before. I too wished to pay my respects to the god who dwelled in that place and though no flowers grew on the shaded earth, I found a cluster of orchids wound round a nearby branch. It made a handsome and fitting offering to put with the other flowers on the altar.

D. H. Lawrence has said that humanity is too much alike externally, and that internally there are insuperable differences. I found quite the reverse in Bali. There are many different physical types on the island, but their actions and their responses to stimuli are almost identical. It is as if they have a very strong, well-defined group consciousness, with few personal variations; a harmony that functions person to person, and also between man and his land. They are truly a part of their island.

This harmony is tangible in their every movement. They have the freedom of limb of animals, and particularly in groups, this coordination results in perfect patterns of changing compositions.

Their dance is a woven scheme of staccato motions and sinuous fluidity, as angular knees and elbows move in counterpoint to the swaying torso and arms. It is not a sexual thing, like the Arabic harem dances which accentuate the pelvis, but a chaste and modest religious ritual. The dancers often seem to move in a trance and they are, in fact, frequently in a kind of religious fervor when they dance. When the music stops they fall to the ground in a sobbing collapse.

I was fascinated by their art and bought whatever old pieces I could afford. There were no antique dealers, as such, in Bali, but people who heard that I was buying would bring me their things. It was always the women who came, sacrificing in their family's need cherished belongings, heirlooms, even household gods. My pleasure in those lovely pieces was always underlaid with a sadness for their owners' tragedy. Once, a woman came with her little girl to sell me an exquisite old wooden doll, beautifully dressed in gold and purple brocade. The woman wanted a *ringit* (about one dollar) for it and I gladly paid. She took the money, but as she started to leave, the child grabbed the doll from my hand and clutched it violently to her small body. The embarrassed mother wrenched the doll out of the child's arms and handed it back to me with an apology. As they walked away, I could hear the girl's wild sobbing and I knew that I could never enjoy the doll. I called them back and returned the toy to its owner. A short time later the woman returned. She told me that she could not accept my money for nothing and she pushed a magnificent bowl into my hands. It was worth a lot more than a single *ringit*, and although I paid her a fair price by Bali standards, I knew that she was sacrificing a part of her own past for a very brief financial reprieve.

I got involved in a less serious commercial venture in the bazaar one day. I would go there every morning to sketch the wonderful colors and patterns of the place. One morning my attention was caught by a small boy who was absorbed in a ghastly game. He had caught a bright blue bird and had tied its leg to a twig. Every few minutes he would jerk the twig sharply and the startled bird would leave its perch and take flight, only to find itself caught by the string a few inches away. It would end each flight hanging helplessly from the twig, fluttering its lovely wings. The boy was apparently having a fine time. He was not really cruel; he simply had not thought of his game's consequences. I called him over and asked to buy the bird. He was quite reluctant to part with it, and agreed only when my price rose from coppers to a silver coin. I took the bird and noticed that the boy and a few men from the market stood watching curiously to see what I would do with my purchase. A shocked gasp went up as I took my penknife out of my pocket; but when I used it to cut the string and release the bird, they were even more surprised.

The following morning, my little friend was back, with another bird. I grinned at his cleverness and he grinned back, but our understanding did not prevent him from playing his awful game. I tried to ignore him, but the bird's bright color and the boy's clever maneuvering to stay in my line of vision were too much. I paid him off again and released the latest victim. The next day I sat waiting nervously for my new "business associate" to appear. The hours passed but he did not come. I was convinced that I had escaped, when from every side of the bazaar came small boys, each armed with twig, string, and bright blue bird. I buried my head in my sketch pad, gritted my teeth, and determined to ignore them. They came closer and closer, jerking their twigs with greater and greater violence. I had started a new industry in Den-Passar, and I cursed myself for my stupidity! After a very long and very nerve-racking morning, the boys gave up. I had won, but I fear for the psychological health of that particular flock of Bali birds.

One day my *yongos* (servants) told me that the widow of one of the island's rajas was visiting and that she would like to pose for me. I sent them to invite her to come the next day and when the appointed hour arrived an elaborate procession made its way to my bungalow. The princess was carried on a litter by two burly attendants. Half a dozen lovely young girls surrounded her, each carrying a silver bowl filled with fruit or cakes. The Maharani was middle-aged, I guessed, with pale ivory skin, a delicately chiseled nose, and very thin lips which she augmented with liberally applied lipstick. There was something almost unpleasantly feline about her, although she moved with uncanny grace. I did two drawings of her and presented her with the one she liked as a gift. The procession departed as silently and elaborately as it had come.

Later that night, I was dozing on my porch on a chaise longue I had brought from Java. I heard a slight noise and there appeared before me two of the exotic widow's attendants. The lady herself came up the steps and went through my open door, beckoning me to follow. Inside, still without a word, she dropped her sarong and stood before me, exquisite, but somehow sinister, for although she had the body of a twenty-year-old girl, her hands were like claws, with long crimson nails. In particular, the nail of her little finger had been sharpened like a knife and measured about three-quarters of an inch. I moved to embrace her, although I felt very uneasy about this encounter. The Maharani could not fail to notice my inadequate ardor and was furious, probably because she knew that I had spent many other passionate hours on the island. She dug that claw of hers into my thigh, summoned her servants, and swiftly left my house. She left me with a bad wound on my leg. I cleansed it that night, but it later became infected. Perhaps she had come armed with some strange poison in that weapon she carried—in any case it was a night of love I was glad to forgo.

In spite of its surface harmony, Bali eventually became a place of enormous emotional strain for me. By the beginning of 1914 I was working feverishly almost eighteen hours a day especially during the season of religious festivals. I could not seem to stop painting the singularly beautiful Balinese rituals. Many of these events took place at night, so that I seldom had enough sleep. I was becoming tense and irritated with a surfeit of aesthetic caviar as well as a lack of sleep. I even snarled at my *yongo* and threatened to fire him one day when he came to tell me about still another temple feast.

Late that same afternoon, I took a walk in a direction I had never gone before, through rice fields and thickets of bamboo. About three miles from Den-Passar I came upon an abandoned temple. It had an ornate, well-preserved entrance, but the courtyard within contained only the crumbling ruins of several altars, whose statues lay where they had fallen on the ground. Huge trees had overgrown the place and it had an airless, utterly still feeling about it. It was a restful contrast to the life I had been leading, and I slumped beneath one of the altars to rest.

While I sat there, a man came through the entrance gate, followed by a group of sixteen teen-age boys. They carried bows with them and silently filed into two rows, in places they apparently knew. The older man struck a pose with drawn bow, and the boys imitated his gestures. I realized that this was a class rehearsing for some martial dance. They practiced in absolute silence. If a boy made an error, he would be corrected by example. Patiently, inexorably each movement was being transmuted into a frieze, a decorative pattern created out of the identical gestures of human beings. It was attractive enough, but I felt that these sixteen boys were being transformed into some monstrous mechanism. It evoked in my heart the image of what men dread most: death and the loss of individuality. I could never forget my horror when I first saw German troops in Potsdam marching in goose-step. I had almost cried like a scared child, and now watching the Bali boys move like puppets on a string, I was frightened again. One could hardly imagine a greater contrast than between these golden boys in their long sarongs and long waving hair and the heavy-booted, gray-uniformed Potsdam marchers. Yet, on that strange day they seemed alike to me, for they too had expressionless masks instead of human faces.

When the rehearsal was over, the group of dancers left the temple as silently as they had come. Night was falling. I felt singularly suspended and outside myself. All nature seemed to have come to a stop and in my heightened emotional state the afternoon had become a revelation, a warning that I must go back before it was too late to save myself, that I ought to go home. I realized, there in that dimly lit ruin, that I was an exile; more, an exile surrounded by a way of life that would eventually destroy me. The silence, even the great, wondering eyes of the island women I made love to, now seemed vacuous, and unsatisfying. I felt a great urgency and with a sudden movement, I flung myself from beneath the altar. As I did so, I must have frightened from its hiding place the huge coiled python that moved toward me. I am deadly afraid of snakes and I leaped for the door in utter terror of that beautiful monster.

I stumbled through the dark country until I reached my porch, and when I got there, I took down from a shelf a bottle of brandy I'd had for a year and drank a good deal of it, hoping it would calm me. Before I'd left that afternoon, I'd begun a letter to a friend in Italy in which I had written, "I doubt if I will ever leave this Garden of Eden, the West has faded from my memory *senza rancori*." Now, I added a postscript: "This evening I have at last met the Serpent of Paradise. I, too, will probably be expelled from the Garden, not because I have disobeyed the Lord (for I have had my fill of the fruit of the tree and He has not seemed to mind it) but because I have discovered that our Western world is not merely a memory that cannot be effaced. It is something infinitely more than that; I am a part of it and it is part of me. So, don't be surprised if I suddenly appear at your villa."

I drank my brandy and had many sentimental thoughts about the joys of Western life: the theater, fresh bread, spring at a Roman café, and other foolish trivialities. I knew that a compelling reason for my return would be my continued love of Mira, that in this respect, the kind DuBois Reymonds had not realized their intentions. I knew, also, that I must return in order to keep my hold on the reality of the kind of person I was. I fell into a drugged sleep and woke ten hours later to find my friend Karli standing over my bed. He had been living north of Den-Passar, in Bangli, and I had not seen him for about three months. He told me that he was ill, that he suffered from excruciating stomach-aches, nausea, and fits of dizziness. He had consulted a doctor in Bangli, who did not seem to know what was wrong. I took a good look at Karli and was frightened by what I saw. He had lost a lot of weight, his sunburnt skin was a pasty gray, there was physical pain in his tightly drawn lips and a fearful spiritual pain in his eyes. I said, "Karli, we've been here two years. It is time we went home!"

Karli agreed that it would be better if he returned, but did not want me to leave because of his poor health. I laughed and told him of the previous night's crisis and added that his indisposition made it seem certain that the gods wanted us to go. Ten days later we were headed for Naples on a Dutch steamer that sailed from Surabaya, the southern port of Java.

I never saw Bali again. In my mind it has remained a paradise, although I know that in later years it changed, became "westernized" in the worst sense of that word. The pure innocence of Balinese sexual freedom had been turned into exhibitionism by foreign exploiters. Even before I left there were warnings of the ugliness that would overwhelm the island. The governor had ordered that the beautiful open markets be covered with ugly, red tin roofs. When I first came, goods in the bazaar were wrapped in lovely brown and green banana leaves. Later, they were taken home in my own discarded sketches. Still later old newspaper was used, so that ugly pieces of the *Dublin Herald* could be found all over the island.

But the Bali I remember made of every phase of daily life a ritual in which all the people participated. Life was an undulating spectrum of colors which played against the most lush and fecund background, which moved to the constant, exotic pulsing of the Balinese music.

When we returned to Europe, Karli and I went directly to Rome where Karli joined Mrs. Sohn, and Mira and her husband. The DuBois Reymonds came down to spend the holidays with me, and that Christmas season, back with my old friends, remains one of my most cherished memories. I was anxious to pay my debt to Alard DuBois Reymond and I showed them all the work I had done during the time I was away. I urged them to take whatever they wanted. They liked what they saw and showed excellent judgment in their selections, taking about six small paintings, six drawings, and the "Bali Festival" that is now at the Phillips Academy at Andover. It was their generosity alone which had allowed me the opportunity to get to Bali and to paint there but they firmly refused any more canvases—still another occasion to be grateful to them. In the introduction to the catalogue of my New York exhibit of the Bali paintings, I wrote a public acknowledgment of my debt to the DuBois Reymond family, although by then the war had begun and I was advised to conceal my German connections.

While he was in Rome, Sterne's English friend, John Marshall, invited him to stay in his apartment. After Sterne had been there for about two months, Marshall told him that Auguste Rodin was coming to Rome and asked whether Sterne would mind if Rodin, also, stayed with them. Sterne was, of course, delighted.

Rodin asked me for a pail of clay soon after he arrived. While talking, he would take out a chunk, and with his huge hands squeeze it into all sorts of fantastic shapes. Sometimes one of these forms would suggest something to him and he would put it aside and allow it to dry in the sun. He told me that he often got usable ideas from these casual accidents.

He had the hands of a maker of things, not of a creative artist. They were huge, square, large-boned and muscular. Watching him I thought that with those hands his touch would necessarily be coarse. His vision, was, however, very fine. His works were like the forms of the earth because he, more than anybody else, was the incarnation of the *Erdgeist*.

I noticed that for the first few days he looked unhappy at mealtime, whenever the fine-grained sliced bread was passed to him. I suggested to Marshall that Rodin might enjoy a long crusty bread, and the next night when we sat down to dinner a thirty-centimeter, golden loaf was at Rodin's place. He grinned, and broke it in two pieces. By the end of the meal, only a small morsel remained. I never saw anyone eat as much bread as Rodin did, nor comment so frequently on how much he loved a crust of bread. It was an equal pleasure for me to watch his enjoyment of that simple food.

Rodin and I spent hours talking about art and its problems. I asked him if he was familiar with the work of Matisse. He replied, "I have seen it, but it gave me no desire to become familiar with it. When Matisse first showed me his things I asked him how old he was, and when he told me, I said it was time he grew up and took a look at nature."

Rodin added that Matisse had no talent, only "unmitigated cheek." I asked him if his opinion was based on the drawings, since Matisse was considered a master colorist. Rodin did not know the paintings at all. Apparently Matisse had brought him a bronze of a resting woman for the master's judgment. Rodin told me, "It looked like a poorly modeled nude that had been broken in three parts and put back together by someone who was blind or trying to be funny—in any case, who didn't know what he was doing."

I protested that Matisse really did know what he was doing, that there were good reasons for his distortions. Rodin snapped, "That's no excuse for what he does. We do not forgive a murderer for killing his wife, *especially* if he knows very well what he is doing." Rodin was growing increasingly impatient as the conversation continued. He said about Matisse's drawing that it is "easy to draw when one has no respect for the truth," and with a brusque, "*C'est assez maintenant*," he turned to Johnny Marshall to ask what his plans were for the following day.

Those spring days in Rome passed like an idyll. I spent stimulating hours with Rodin and Johnny Marshall, but the greater part of every day I stayed with Karli . . . and Mira. Our love had reached a feverish intensity, if anything, heightened by my long absence. Swept along, we no longer worried about ultimate goals, and indeed, it would have been useless, because on a sunny July day, fate made the decision for us. I was walking on the Via Condotti, about to enter a café, when I heard a friend calling to me from a passing carriage. He asked me to come to his house and spend the afternoon with him and some mutual friends.

I got in, and as our carriage approached the Corso, we saw little knots of people gathered and newsboys running with their papers and shouting. I bought a paper and stared at the headlines: "Archduke Franz Ferdinand and Archduchess Assassinated in Sarajevo."

I wondered, "Where the devil is Sarajevo?" and when I saw my friend's serious face, I innocently asked, "Why are you so upset? The Archduke was unpopular anyhow. One less Archduke will hardly upset anyone."

My friend carefully explained to me that the world was now almost certainly at the brink of war. His ominous tone convinced me and I rushed to Mira and Karli to tell them what had happened. Both Karli and Mira's husband were of military age; it was serious news indeed for them. Within a week, they left Rome, together with all German nationals. I was desperate with frustration and anxiety. I tried to persuade them that their child would be safer with me in America, but they thought I was mad to make such a suggestion. I probably was, for a few days after they left, I decided that the way to convince Mira of my devotion and to be near her was to volunteer for the German Army. I went to the German Consulate and tried to enlist. Luckily I was turned down flat, but what an irresponsible, insane impulse that had been!

I stayed on with Marshall and Rodin in Rome. It became
known in the city that I was close to Rodin, and I was besieged
with requests to meet him. The correspondent of the *Frankfurter Zeitung* begged me to arrange an interview and I agreed
to try on the condition that Rodin not be disturbed by
questions about the war. He agreed, I consulted with Johnny,
and the meeting was arranged.

A few days later a messenger from the French embassy
arrived at the apartment and said that the Ambassador wanted
to speak to Rodin immediately about an urgent matter. We all
wondered what was up, especially when we saw Rodin's
flushed face when he returned from his talk. He told us that
the Ambassador had been furious, that he had never even
asked Rodin to sit down. Rodin had been warned that he was,
in the future, to keep his mouth shut in public, that artists, like
children, "should be seen and not heard." The Ambassador
had shown the bewildered sculptor a clipping from the
Frankfurter Zeitung in which the correspondent asked Rodin
whether he believed the reports of German atrocities in
Belgium. Rodin was quoted as replying, "After all, the
Belgians are no saints either. I recall the inhuman atrocities
they perpetrated in the Congo. Life is sacred, you know,
whether black or white, yellow or red."

Rodin told the Consul that he had probably made that
statement during the interview. He added, "It's true, isn't
it?"

The Consul had explained to Rodin that since the war had
been declared, the only "truth" was that the enemy had to be
destroyed.

My own affairs, vis-à-vis the war, were progressing badly. I
noticed a distinct cooling in the attitude of John Marshall and
eventually he confronted me with the current rumor that I
was a German sympathizer. He added, "Why, I've even heard
the ridiculous exaggeration that you tried to enlist in the
German Army!"

I poured my heart out to Johnny then. I told him of the

despair I'd been in because of my hopeless love, the madness which had prompted me to go to the German embassy that day. I grew quite hysterical and told Johnny that he was the only friend I had left in Rome, that I needed his help badly.

My confession was a mistake. Marshall, though a generous companion, had never permitted our relationship to touch upon personal matters, and now, his English reticence was as much offended by my outburst as by my attempted enlistment. After a few minutes he reassured me that he understood, but I could see that he found my behavior repugnant. I began immediately to make plans to return to America. By good fortune there was a last-minute cancellation on the SS *Rotterdam*, and I sailed for New York the very next day.

"Italian Beggar Woman"
(*Owned by Professor &
Mrs. C. A. Robinson, Jr.,
Providence, Rhode Island*)

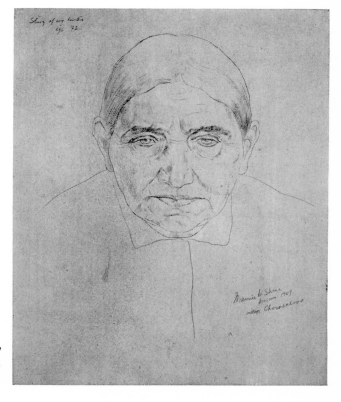

"Study of My Mother"
*ourtesy, Museum of Fine
Arts, Boston*)

"Study of Nude" (*Courtesy, The Berlin Photographic Company*)

7

It was almost a year since I had left Bali. The war, the painful separation from Mira, and the tiring trip to the Far East had drained my energy and made me apathetic to my surroundings. I was exhausted when I reached New York, uninterested in renewing old friendships.

The spring of 1915, however, brought back a certain kind of memory of Bali which did arouse my interest in the present, and caused me to go out and seek feminine companionship. I had been in this condition before and had learned to regret an imprudent tendency to pounce on the first woman who passed my way, who, all too often, confused my starvation with true love.

Although it was in this state that I met Mabel Dodge, it was much more than sex that attracted me to her. I was amazed with Mabel. For the first time in my life I could relax, rest my will, and do what someone else decided was best. It was a period when my own self-confidence had shrunk to zero. I was tired and diffident, and I found relief in Mabel's super-confidence.

My usual instinct was to be intolerant of anyone who tried to impose authority upon me, but, to be honest, Mabel had no way of knowing this during our first meetings. However, it did not take me long to resent being a chattel, and whenever I insisted upon my own ways, she was puzzled. Thus, we muddled into a misalliance for which I was as much to blame as anyone, though I was to suffer terribly and my masculine pride was to sustain a great blow.

In Movers and Shakers,[1] *Mabel Dodge writes of her first impression of Sterne:*

"Well," I thought, "who might *that* be? He really has a face!" His straight, fine black hair, fine almost as feathers, fell back in long locks in the manner of Liszt, and his broad forehead had a pale, innocent look, especially at the temples where people show for good or bad. His long-lashed brown eyes were nothing more or less than *orbs*, there was such a splendor in their liquid regard. The nose, of a Biblical dignity, had a good bone ridge; but below it, oh, dear! his mouth, when he forgot to arrange it, was not so good—more or less a thin, straight line, without curve or meaning. . . .

What I liked about him was his handsome look of suffering. A dark torture ennobled him and added a great deal of dignity to that countenance that would in later years become decidedly patriarchal. He was positively enveloped in a cloud of secrecy and caution. The man might have been in a jungle, so watchful he was, so studied every glance and motion. That interested me. I wondered what it was all about. . . .[2]

I always loved the slightest appearance of masterfulness in a man, because it hinted at an opportunity for me to exercise my strength.[3]

Mabel purchased a drawing of mine and invited me to visit her in the country. When I arrived at Croton, New York, there was no conveyance to take me to the Sharkey Cottage, which Mabel had rented, but I knew the way from having

[1] Mabel Dodge Luhan, *Movers and Shakers* (Harcourt, Brace, 1936).
[2] Ibid., p. 350.
[3] Ibid., p. 351.

visited the Duncan School, just up the road, about a month before. It was late in the afternoon of a rainy April day. As I walked from the station, the rain turned to a light drizzle and finally stopped. I went hesitantly up Mt. Airy Road, wondering how I would find Mabel's cottage.

Suddenly, at a bend in the narrow lane appeared the most eerie sight I had ever seen: in a weird, silent funeral procession moved a line of about twenty people in double file, led by six men carrying a plain black coffin on their shoulders. The single figure of a tall, gaunt middle-aged woman, dressed in a white bridal gown and veil, followed behind them. She was hatchet-faced, wore spectacles, and walked stiffly, leaning backward as she moved. She carried a nosegay of lilies of the valley like some ancient votive offering in her extended and rigid right hand.

The mourners, clad in black, ill-fitting clothes, walked slowly and stiffly, hesitating at each step. I was horrified when I realized that they were moving in the march of a bridal procession, as if down the aisle of a church. All that was lacking was a skeleton dancing in front, piping a gay wedding march on his flute.

It all had the strange immediacy and queer lack of reality that early American primitive painting has—uncouth, and in dead earnest. I stood spellbound. What made me doubt that I was really seeing was their utter disregard of my presence. They did not even give me a passing glance. It seemed like an ominous mirage. Or was it a warning, a glimpse through some magic telescope focused not on the stars, but on my future?

When at last I got to Mabel's and told her about my encounter, she laughed and said, "You have quite an imagination! Of course you either imagined the whole thing, or what you saw was just some poor man's funeral."

I was to recall this macabre procession whenever I doubted my relationship with Mabel. Even that day the woman I was then to visit puzzled and intrigued me, attracted and repelled me. She was entirely different from the kind of women I had always been attracted to before—robust, rather than tall and slender, without the fine bone structure in which I had always taken such pleasure. (I'm afraid Mabel's bone structure didn't show at all.) She was one of the first to bob her hair and wore it in a bang on her forehead. However, her most amazing feature was her eyes. They were cool, dark gray pools, shaded with long black lashes. They reflected her complex emotions spontaneously and honestly, could flare up with fury, be lucid with pleasure, or glow with rapture. But I loathed their flashes of cruelty. There was something inhuman in that particular look of hers! In contrast, her voice was like a viola, soft, caressing, mellow, with confidential overtones.

Mabel Dodge recalls her feelings at the beginning of this relationship:

My long struggle with Maurice was already under way. I unhesitatingly did all I could to strengthen my influence over him, and to bind him to me. I invited him to Provincetown for the summer and told him he could have the life-saving station to work in. . . .[1]

He bustled around and bought pounds of different-colored papers in huge rolls, and tubes of new paint. I was determined not to let him have more than one tube at a time.[2]

Mabel and I spent that summer together in Provincetown, although most of my time was devoted to my work. One day Bobby [Robert Edmond] Jones was visiting me at the abandoned Coast Guard Station on the ocean side of Provincetown. He went swimming, got caught in the undertow, and began to yell for help. I plunged in after him and I was soon bobbing helplessly up and down with him in the wide Atlantic. We kept shouting until a few Coast Guard men on the shore heard us. They quickly launched their dory. After a few unsuccessful tries they brought us both up—rather down and out, I'm afraid.

[1] Luhan, *Movers and Shakers*, p. 372.
[2] Ibid., p. 375.

A few hours later, Hutch Hapgood brought Eugene O'Neill round to visit. O'Neill, whom I'd never met before, said, "I envy you. Why do all these exciting things happen to you? I understand you recently returned from a lengthy stay on an island in the Pacific. Jig Cook [1] tells me that you lived about a year in a Mt. Hymettus monastery. You are about to marry Mabel Dodge, and, today, you experienced the thrill of drowning!"

Hutch laughed. "I wonder if there is any connection between those last two events?"

O'Neill admired my house and said that any time I got tired of the place to let him know. That day had been more than enough for me and I answered, "You can have it. I am through with it."

I moved out and he moved in and stayed for a number of years. He wrote some of his best plays in that old Coast Guard Station. When he was through with the place he sold it at a profit, and it was just in time, for soon after, at a high tide, the house disappeared into the sea.

In the fall of 1915 Mabel and I returned from Provincetown to Finney Farm in Croton, where we hoped to live together in amorous and pastoral bliss. I suggested to Mabel that to have a real farm we needed more animals, and she agreed. She went to town and returned with a pair of turtledoves in a beautiful bamboo cage. Their constant cooing and cuddling was quite touching. I wondered whether they were intended as a symbol of domestic felicity. If they were, their fate proved prophetic!

Mabel had also purchased two magnificent Persian cats, a blonde female I called Chiara, and a smoky gray male I named Scuro, in the hope, I suppose, that our farm would soon be enriched with small chiarascuros. But the cats did not seem to have the least attraction for each other and their original animosity eventually turned into Platonic tolerance.

They were exquisite, especially Chiara, with her long,

[1] George Cram Cook.

pinkish gold fur, her blue eyes, and her majestic sweep as she moved slowly from room to room. Scuro had an unnerving appetite for bird flesh and I put a little bell around his neck to warn birds of his approach. Furious at the noise, he shifted his interest from out-of-doors to the turtledoves on our porch. Chiara joined him and nothing could thereafter compete with the irresistible attraction of the bamboo cage. They constantly lay in front of it, their great round eyes fixed on the loving couple huddled fearfully in the farthest corner.

One morning we found the cage on the floor, the door wide open, the inhabitants gone. A few white feathers and a dark stain on the rug were all that remained of the birds. Outside, in the bright morning sunlight, the cats were dozing peacefully, full of contentment. They had good reason—had they not had their fill of the doves of peace?

A belligerent red and green parrot who easily outglared the cats was Mabel's next attempt at a bucolic setting. She hated talking birds and bought this one because he was dumb. But he very soon began trying to imitate human speech. The sounds that came out were like human belching and what is now called the "Bronx cheer." It was the sort of joke that always disgusted Mabel. She very quickly gave the parrot to our butcher, who was delighted with so gifted a bird.

The next ill-starred pair were monkeys. The male was a cruel and ugly brute, who promptly broke the female's neck, sulked in his cage for a few days, and died himself a short time after. Dr. Brill [1] pronounced the beast to have died of suppressed desires, but I preferred to think he died of a broken heart.

At one point during this period, Sterne and Mabel Dodge apparently agreed to spend less time together and he rented a room in Pottsville, Pennsylvania, where he hoped to get some

[1] Abraham Arden Brill (1874–1948), Austrian-born American psychiatrist. Studied with Jung, practiced psychoanalysis in New York, translated works of Freud and Jung. Wrote *Psychoanalysis: Its Theories and Practical Applications* and *Fundamental Conceptions of Psychoanalysis.*

*work done. He wrote Mabel from Pottsville on February 13,
1916:*

> It is no use Mabel. I *can't* stay away from you. . . .
> What hurts me more than anything is the suspicion that
> you don't want me to come back so soon. . . . I long for
> you all the time. Only you I love. You are the undercur-
> rent in me— Even when I don't think of you, you are
> there— Tell me dearest is it because you know that with
> each day that I am away from you my love grows stronger
> that you want me to stay away? But *I don't want* to be
> possessed by you or anyone else. I must plant myself body
> and soul, heart and mind and nerves in my work.[1]

*A short time later Sterne returned to New York and went
again to live with Mabel Dodge in Croton:*

Evidently couples did not thrive at Finney Farm, whether
they were animal *or* human. Mabel was jealous of every
attractive woman, and when I moved in with her, she broke
with all her female friends except Mary Foote. Mary was
lovable and sensitive and quite a gifted painter, but she was
safe because she was a rather shriveled-looking New England
spinster. She later spent about twenty years in Zurich being
analyzed by Dr. Jung. Mabel quite wisely preferred the more
realistic Freudian analysis. She believed that her own spirit had
reached the freedom to soar in the higher regions, where she
could breathe a sort of fourth-dimensional chemical far superior to the oxygen required by grosser spirits.

I definitely did not belong in this astral sphere nor in her
entourage. Her closest souls were Bobby Jones, who had
recently come from Germany, where he studied the new
theatrical techniques of Max Reinhardt, and who eventually
became quite a prominent stage designer; Andrew Dasburg, a
painter very much under the influence of the Bauhaus;
Marsden Hartley, another well-known painter who had

[1] Letters of Mabel Dodge Luhan. Yale University Library collection.

brought with him from Germany certain painting techniques and also certain hypersensitive emotional reactions. There was also the writer, Bayard Boyesen, who looked like a Nordic late Hellenistic plaster cast and who had an inordinate thirst for old Scotch. He used to absorb a quart of whiskey a day. Although he was still young he seemed to have too much he needed to forget and the Scotch helped him.

Even from a professional point of view, it was strange that I, who loathed German transcendentalism and worshipped French realism in art, should have found myself in this atmosphere. I did not belong at all, in any sense, and all of them, including Mabel, looked upon me as an intruder. But Mabel felt she needed me for her "center," and was convinced that I needed her for my "center," which she considered physically alive but spiritually unformed. By virtue of contrast, since she believed I had very little other virtue, she thought we would both derive a great deal from an intimate association. Indeed, Mabel had always believed that if she had a physical relationship with a talented writer or artist, she would somehow absorb some of their power.

She really disliked intensely what I was, but she believed that, with effort, she might carve me into a being nearer her heart's desire. She might have succeeded had she been content with enriching and cultivating me, but this was not her purpose. Mabel was bent on first destroying completely, and then creating a new, synthetic being—especially in her dealings with men.

In the fall of 1916, for propriety's sake, to somewhat cover up our sexual relationship, we decided that I ought to move into the Green House at Finney Farm with Bayard Boyesen. I settled down to a strenuous painting schedule, but Bayard sat staring at the few lines he was able to put to paper. I had grown very fond of him and tried to help him during that time we lived together to write rather than drink, but it was to no avail.

I often thought, also, about Bayard's violent anti-German

feelings during the war. I was, myself, greatly saddened by conflicting loyalties. How could I hate either of the belligerents when in a way I was a synthesis of them both? Perhaps the German influence was the more powerful because I had been steeped in its culture from early childhood. As the war progressed, I worried about my German friends (and most of all about beloved Mira), surrounded by enemies bent on their destruction.

I reacted to the war like the chameleon who changed color according to where he was placed until the day he landed on an early painting by Matisse—and burst. Although I had previously been confused, on the day America entered the war, I realized without any doubt at all that my loyalty must lie with the United States. I loved this country, had pledged it my allegiance, and owed it gratitude for my liberty and for the opportunity it had given me to become what I was. However, that the bond with my own past could suddenly snap at the signing of a declaration of war in Washington was out of the question. The conflict remained. I knew who our enemies were, but I could not hate them. I hoped we would be victorious, but I was skeptical about our stated goal of making the world safe for democracy, and I quite openly opposed our intention to fight until Germany unconditionally surrendered. I knew the Germans too well. Their pride, their arrogance, and their efficiency would sooner or later impel them to try to blot out the stigma of utter defeat. My opinions sometimes got me into difficulty even before we entered the war.

Mabel wrote Sterne about this problem:

> *Finney Farm*
> *October, 1916*

You *must* keep out of that [pro-German] current if you want to sell. Walter [Lippmann] says that feelings never ran so high. It is desperately "fashionable" to be pro-Ally—dear Maurice—I know all this is against your deepest feeling, and I understand and know how that feels. I am not saying this *meanly*—only to tell you to *realize* it and know about it and be politic *if* you want to make money, which is a horrid consideration, anyway. One German thing after another has gone to pieces here. *You must not* get called German or a German sympathiser if you *care* to succeed in a worldly way. But you needn't care if you trust to me.

At Finney Farm, life continued in its doomed way. The kind of person I was constantly irritating Mabel, her false refinement seeming absurd to me. One night Bayard, Mabel, and I were chatting after dinner. Scuro, the gray male cat, had died and Chiara was sitting contentedly on my lap while I stroked her. Suddenly I noticed something incredible and I shouted, "A miracle has happened! Mabel, what did you say this cat's name was?"

"What's the matter with you? You know her name is Chiara."

"No, Mabel, *his* name is Chiar*o*. If you don't believe me, take one glance under this long coat."

The evidence was indisputable and I could hardly control my laughter at our longtime misapprehension. But Mabel did not laugh. She kept staring at me and suddenly hissed, "Put down that cat."

Bayard got up and left us and I said, "Why, Mabel, you're actually jealous of a cat, and an unmistakably male one at that."

"You disgust me," she hissed, and she hurried up the stairs.

This is the humorous incident she turned into a secret and evil ritual years later in *Movers and Shakers*.

> Maurice pouring his hot magnetism into the cat, the cat passing his electricity up to Maurice. It seemed terribly dark and evil. Perhaps this is "bestiality," I thought.[1]

[1] Luhan, *Movers and Shakers*, p. 428.

What a distortion of fact! It was another example of what Mabel considered her fine perceptions, her "center," turning out to be quicksand. Yet, had she not had so much money, she might have been a fortuneteller. She looked like one, dressed like one, and created that kind of atmosphere.

On another night, Mabel, Bobby Jones, Bayard Boyesen, and I were silently gathered around a bridge table waiting for the ouija board we all touched to perform. I began to get tired of the long wait and I solemnly announced, "I feel something."

"What?" Mabel gasped.

"The table is trying to lift its hind leg. Evidently it takes *my* leg for a tree trunk."

Mabel jumped from her seat and switched on the light, while Bobby and Bayard exchanged a long, meaningful look.

"I guess we need a breath of fresh air," I said. As I flung the window open, a bat swooped into the room. Mabel grew panicky. She shrieked, "Take it away, take it away," and she ran from the room. I am convinced that to her overwrought nerves it seemed that a spirit, outraged by my disrespect, had returned to torment us in the form of a bat.

I often wondered if Mabel would have had the courage to live her life as she pleased had she been poor. As it was, she was attracted by the bizarre and the unique, and not being very intelligent, could not distinguish between the good and the bad in things that were unusual. She always had "hunches" and courageously followed her impulses, as she did when she promoted Gertrude Stein in this country. Gertrude's portrait of Mabel turned out to be the cornerstone of her own *gloire*. The door that Mabel had pried open, Gertrude managed to force in with her own bulk. As soon as she felt that she needed Mabel no more, she cast her aside like an outgrown glove. Mabel, of course, claimed that she never missed people anyhow, only their "chemical," though what she really missed was an outlet for her own flow.

Mabel Dodge wrote to Sterne in Maine:

> Provincetown,
> Monday, July 30, 1916

Dearest, I have been feeling depressed all the whole day. I think of *us* all the time and want a solution and I want to see you and be near you again. I was bitterly disappointed that you didn't come this way because you wrote that if you couldn't "stick it out at Croton" you would "be glad to do as I say and come to the place I said," so of course I was counting on it. I wish I could feel you care as deeply as I do—that you need me and our relation vitally—that you couldn't replace me with another. . . .

> Provincetown,
> August, 1916

Now you old darling—you just stop having indecisions about coming here—cause you're coming—next Wednesday. The place is all engaged and everything. You will like "my life here" all right—and I can change anything you might not like. . . . You can sleep in your bungalow if you prefer—and eat here. You will have plenty to do with a head of me like an early Greek thing—and a picture of Elizabeth and her boat—and perhaps a painting of me. I mean you to do one of the best things you have ever done—in the wooden head. I have always believed I was like those archaic heads of the early Greek things—the base like a tree trunk. Do you remember the ones I mean? I think the expression is more that than any modern woman type I know of. Perhaps it will serve to interpret me to the world so people won't say any more "Mabel Dodge can't be done. No one knows what she looks like or what her *looks mean*." . . .

I am sure we can't go home till Oct. 1st on account of the plague [influenza epidemic]. I am eager to stand up to an experiment—of how you get on in real work with me—and I have the feeling I will show you you'll do much better.

I don't want us to break up this—too many things are disintergrating around for me to feel it anything but commonplace to fail in human things. . . . The *idea* of your saying you "don't know if you like this arrangement." You will like it. Unless you meet me in Boston I will come to Ogonquit [Maine] and snatch you away, so be prepared! . . . All my love darling—MD

When Mabel, as she did from time to time, said, "Let's get married," I asked, "Do you really mean it? If we don't make a go of it, it would be more serious for you than for me, since it would be my first venture, but your third." I wrote that I mistrusted our relationship because of two tendencies of my own—a certain sexual adventuresomeness and a craving for material security. I frankly told her that if we married, it would not be only because she attracted me sexually but also because she was wealthy.

I explained that she should not assume that I was marrying her for her money, but, on the other hand, that I doubted that I would have married her if she were poor. I had never been a fortune-hunter. There were at least three women much richer than Mabel who had also been my mistresses and who were interested in making the affair legal, but they each had personal characteristics I could not tolerate.

In spite of its problems, the kind of life I had been living with Mabel had many subtle temptations. For example, at the very beginning of our relationship we traveled from Croton to Cape Cod in her car. It reminded me of my first ride in a horse-drawn carriage on the day of my father's funeral, though now I was no longer the child of a virile father, but a man with his own physical needs. I know this physical factor was basic in our relationship, but I have a suspicion that the long ride in the spacious chauffeured Pierce-Arrow touring car added much to my attraction to Mabel Dodge. At that moment, it was only an adventure, but the adventure soon developed into a love affair, and I began to prefer the ride in a touring car to the New York Central train. These material comforts did much to undermine my deep-rooted aversion to marriage.

I did not think of it at the time, but now I wonder whether my frank confessions to Mabel of these considerations were not prompted by my own semi-conscious realization that she suspected my motives. I probably thought that, by being honest, I might put myself in a more favorable light. However, that was only part of the story. As I see it now, there was a far stronger reason for these confessions—my unconscious conviction that it would be a mistake to marry her. I unconsciously hoped that honesty about my motives would make Mabel give up the idea of her own accord.

On the other hand, my own self-respect had suffered. I did not cherish the idea of being a "lover," reducing a man to the status of mistress, of kept woman. I had always been contemptuous of fortune-hunters, but to be an illegitimate one was even worse. I thought marriage might restore my *amour propre* by giving me the authority of a husband, which rested on a prestige built by tradition and custom. The marriage vows would bring the two of us on a par irrespective of our former social or financial status in society.

On her side, Mabel, deep down, was a very respectable bourgeoise, though like an impulsive adolescent in rebellion against custom mainly because of exhibitionism. However, when the initial impetus was spent, she always had middle-class scruples about her misdemeanors *against convention*. This is why her love affairs eventually had to be sanctified. She felt she had to pay her debt to society by marriage, like a good Buffalo Christian. Only when she had sexual gratification was she really alive, and since she was a Christian and not a pagan, she hated the sexual act for that very reason, and required a legal union.

We had so many warnings against the marriage, and we

each had conflicting feelings about whether we were making the right choice. In a letter on July 30, 1916, Mabel wrote:

Could we marry and be all in all to each other, do you think? When I write of getting over it or not being with you again it is on account of my suspicion that you don't love me truly and deeply. Brill thinks it should be worked at sensibly. I think that we can do a great deal for each other—that it is a practical arrangement. But that doesn't satisfy the heart and spirit. I want to know that we truly love each other and always will. If I knew that—I believe if I knew it by conviction, I wouldn't mind our being separated sometimes, and I could leave you free to work away from me if you wanted to. . . . Write me openly. When do you want to go to Boston? Yrs, Mabel

On October 12, 1916, she wrote:

Walter [Lippmann] looks American—unalluring—sound—and all the things I should cultivate. He has absolutely no charm—or grace— You have ruined me for the every day sort!

In January, 1917:

I really think we must call our relationship a failure since there can be no trust between us. You have your own suspicions of me and my faith in you is practically negative. I suspect you—and in each case I wait until you will tell me the truth.

My own friends were doubtful about the marriage. Shortly after he had introduced us, Hutch Hapgood warned me: "Watch out for that witch. In order to remake you, she will try to destroy you first." He was rather drunk, and I laughed at his words. When I got home I painted a nocturne of Mabel astride a broomstick riding through a tempest while I, dangling precariously in space, clung to her sturdy legs.

When I showed the picture to Hutch he said, "You must

send it to her." I agreed, but I added that I would have to tell her who inspired this *chef d'oeuvre*, and taking out my pen I wrote on the margin, "Suggested by her friend, Hutchins Hapgood, as a tribute to the bewitching Mabel Dodge." Hutch, of course, begged me to forget all about it, but the subject came up between us again and again. I was always humming or whistling a tune suggestive of my mood. One day I unconsciously began to whistle the famous aria from *Samson and Delilah*. I jokingly remarked to Hutch, "Perhaps Mabel, since she is a witch, might also be the reincarnation of Delilah."

Hutch was quite frank. He said, "I wouldn't be a bit surprised. But I tell you, Maurice, she really *is* a witch. That woman has supernatural powers. She is insanely jealous. The only way she can be sure of a man is by castrating him. Since she must be the sole possessor and cannot make him impotent toward others only, she makes him impotent toward all."

My mother showed me her feelings about the match in quite a different way. When I was born she had insisted on giving me the middle name of Jesus—which must be close to an unprecedented choice for an old-fashioned Jewish mother. I suppose she considered that if the Almighty should fail me, Jesus might save the situation. The only time she ever called me by that name, however, was when I told her of my marriage to Mabel. "A Gentile!" she exclaimed. "I hope, *Jesus*, you know what you did. But let me advise you. If Mabel should slap you on one cheek, slap her back—on both. Remember that you are also named Moses."

With all this, Mabel was in many ways an admirable woman. What I loved best was her utter disregard of material possessions. When a maid dropped a magnificent and valuable Chatham glass which Mabel was particularly fond of, she kicked it aside and just told her maid to be sure to take away all the small pieces.

But we were never really in accord, married or not. We were in the midst of one of our frequent crises when, one

DANCE OF THE ELEMENTS (1913)

Friday in August, 1917, my good friend, Stephan Bourgeois, the art dealer, informed me that he was going to a ranch in Wyoming with another friend. He invited me to come along for the riding and fishing and simple rest. My only reply was, "When are you leaving?"

Bourgeois answered, "On the Monday-morning train," and I told him to get accommodations for me. Then I went back to Croton to tell Mabel of my decision. She agreed to the plan and wired a Mr. Rumsey, whom she knew from Buffalo, that three of her friends would arrive in a few days. He had a huge ranch on the Blackwater River between Cody and Yellowstone Park, where Mabel's son, John Evans, was already visiting. The next morning Mabel appeared in my room while I was packing my suitcase. She quietly watched me for some time, and then suddenly said, "You think you are through with me—but you'll be back. Let us finish this impossible impasse and get married."

"That's an excellent idea." I laughed. "We'll take the plunge when I get back."

"Why wait? You know you'll be fretting about it and worrying. It will spoil your trip. Let's get married today!"

"And what about Wyoming?"

"There's no reason why you shouldn't go there on Monday."

"And do you plan to come along?"

"Of course not! You'll go alone with your friends."

I said it would be a rather novel honeymoon, but that it might be fun. Mabel told the chauffeur to bring the car at once, and we were soon driving to Peekskill with Bobby Jones and Agnes Pelton, a house guest we scarcely knew.

Bobby asked, "Why are we going to Peekskill?"

"To get married," said Mabel.

"To me?" grinned Bobby.

"No, to Maurice. You and Agnes are to be our witnesses."

When we reached city hall, the mayor informed us that there was no time for a wedding since it was almost noon and he had to leave in ten minutes. But Mabel implored him, until he agreed. He asked if I had a ring. I was, of course, unprepared. I ran to a store across the street, bought a simple gold wedding ring, and on the stroke of noon Mabel and I walked out of the mayor's office, man and wife.

I went back to my room and finished packing.

Bourgeois and his friend could not get away on Monday because of some business, but they promised to meet me at the ranch at the end of the week. I was glad of the chance to take the long journey west by myself. I was dazed by recent events and at such times I always have liked to be alone.

All the way to Wyoming I kept wondering how it had happened. I was sure that I had not wanted to marry Mabel and that Mabel had not wanted to marry me. I feared it was a shotgun marriage in the hands of some perverse fate.

Mabel wrote often. In one letter she informed me that she had a surprise for me. Nothing, I wrote her, could surprise me after our trip to Peekskill!

When I returned east I found that she had taken a lovely apartment on a top floor on Washington Square North and that she planned that we spend weekends at Finney Farm. Mabel was surprised when I told her that I must also have a studio. She had imagined that I could work in our living room! I found a studio in the old Benedick apartment house, designed by Stanford White, on Washington Square East. It was a dismal place. Something died in me the minute I entered that studio. The large north window faced an air shaft which was surrounded by sweatshops. Soon after I rented the place I heard that the last tenant had committed suicide and the previous one had found a new home in the Bloomingdale Asylum!

My nerves were on edge. At home one evening I lit my usual after-dinner cigar and Mabel said, "Please don't smoke that filthy weed. I can't stand the nauseating smell!"

"You didn't seem to mind it before we got married."

"I have always minded."

I sat seething for a while. Then I got up and went to the Brevoort where no one objected to my smoking.

The next night, as soon as we had dined, I got up to leave. Mabel asked where I was going and I told her that I was off to the Brevoort to smoke my cigar.

"You must have smoked at least half a dozen last night. You didn't come home until midnight," she said icily. "I wonder what or who kept you."

I went out and when I returned Mabel was in bed with a headache. After dinner the following night our Japanese cook with a wide grin on his face set before me a box of Corona-Corona cigars. Mabel said, "I really don't mind the smell of a *good* cigar. These were recommended by Arthur Brisbane."

I laughed. "I didn't know he smoked Havanas. I thought he chewed domestic tobacco."

This trite foolishness was my only victory since our marriage. We settled into a harmonious relationship that lasted several months. Then a new crisis, like a dark ominous cloud, suddenly appeared. I was telling Mabel that her hunch that we get married had been truly constructive. My feeling for her, which had formerly been centered on sexual attraction, had developed into love and affection, and a sense of well-being in her presence. This was far more than mere compensation for the loss of freedom which had at first interfered with our relationship.

Mabel disliked what she called my "Russian confessions." She snapped, "Don't fool yourself! The moment sex is over between us, all will be finished."

"You certainly can't mean that."

"I certainly do," and rising from the couch, she added, "I don't want to hear any more about it. I am going to bed."

"Good night," I said. "I hope you'll sleep well, and don't worry."

"Worry? Why should I?" With great contempt she swept from the room.

I soon discovered that it was I who had reason to worry.

What she had said had a paralyzing effect upon my senses, upon my ability to perform in the very sphere she so stressed. I perceived that the edifice I had considered safe and sound had a feeble foundation.

The next morning, when I went to her room, she was having breakfast in bed and seemed quite rested and cheerful. I said, "Mabel, you really shocked me badly last night."

She was quite casual about the whole thing. "I don't see why you were shocked. I thought you knew all that."

"Knew it!" I shouted. "What about the spiritual IT which you always boast of. Had I known that all I could give you was the service of a bull, I never would have taken that phony trip to Peekskill."

She did not answer. She just stared at me in silence as I rushed out of her room. I went to my studio where a model was waiting, and I tried to work, but I had to send the girl away. I felt as if I were on the edge of a precipice.

When I married I had hoped it would lead to a lifelong companionship, to love and affection. What I longed for most was to love someone so close that I might share my innermost thoughts, never feel shame in confessing what one hardly dares confess to oneself. However, like termites, Mabel's fatal words began their attack on the foundation of our marriage. Her talk about sex and marriage was a declaration of war between mind and matter—I was soon convinced that in my case the physical had no chance. She challenged a man's potency, and most of the men she knew were defeated in the very early rounds. Mabel wrote about our marriage and her relationships with other men:

> But why I should choose men too immature to satisfy me, or too lacking in essential qualities,—ah! that question must be answered later on.[1]

I knew some of the men she wrote about, and they were far more mature than she was ever aware of. Such callousness is

[1] Luhan, *Movers and Shakers*, p. 263.

incredible! She accuses me, in the same book, of having forced her to burn her love letters from John Reed, as some sort of human sacrifice she says I require. I remember very well the incident to which she evidently refers. She never showed or read to me a single letter from Reed, but that night she did show me a long letter from the painter, Andrew Dasburg. She wrote in her autobiography:

> When he came to the expression of my admiration for and interest in Andrew, Maurice leapt up and crushed the papers into his pocket. "I can't read this with you. I will read it when I am in town!"[1]

That is a damn lie! I liked Andrew, his looks, clear mind, and his talent. It is true that when reading the letter while she watched, I had suddenly jumped up and put it in my pocket and said, "I will finish it alone." It was unbelievable that anyone but a craven exhibitionist could allow another person to read it at all. I took the letter to my room but, after a few more lines, it became too painful to go on, and I decided not to read any more of it. It was the outpouring of a sensitive and perceptive soul, describing his suffering and frustration when at last his ardent desire was about to be consummated, and he was alone with Mabel.

She should have destroyed this letter as soon as she had read it, but her vanity and exhibitionism made her treasure it, as proof of the depth of human suffering on the deprivation of MD. (Ironically, Andrew, when he first fell in love with Mabel, had painted a picture entitled, "The Absence of MD.") This was the letter I had handed her and, pointing to the fireplace, had urged her to burn.

Now our own relationship was in a similar state. I began to suspect that our marriage was a mistake and I was also having trouble with my work. I spoke to Brill and he advised a temporary separation. My friend, Joe Asch, a New York

---

[1] Ibid., p. 435.

physician, had some friends in New Mexico. I decided to go to Santa Fe where I might get some fresh perspective on my personal problems and where, I had been told, the Pueblo Indians would awaken the same sort of creative outburst I had experienced in Bali.

I COULD not face the knowledge that all was finished between Mabel and me. I told myself that after a few months of asceticism our former perfect physical adjustment would be resumed. Therefore, although there was sufficient temptation, I did not encourage the women of the West, not even a very attractive young sculptress I met in Santa Fe.

Mabel and I corresponded regularly, as if I had gone on an ordinary trip:

> *23 North Washington Square*
> *November 13*

Dearest Maurice—

It seems awfully queer here without you. I don't like it much. But I have people in a good deal. . . . I haven't seen anyone who was at the sale [Bourgeois Art Gallery] but Bourgeois telephoned me. J. Quinn bought 15 or 20 pictures. Pascin went for $111 and Dasburg for $5.00! I haven't heard how I went! [1] Picasso went for $31.00. Your painting went for $70.00 with spirited bidding and Bourgeois bought the drawing for $50.00. . . .

I found that I could not paint in Santa Fe and I went to live with the Indians in San Ildefonso, seeking some inspiration

---

[1] Presumably she is referring to a painting of herself by Andrew Dasburg that was the object of much gossip.

that would free my mind for work. I had expected to feel about them as I had about the people of the East, where I had a real sense of belonging. However, the American Indians did not attract me at all, rather they repelled me. They were not only strangers, they were decidedly antagonistic; and yet there was something about them I found compelling. It was the fascination that opposites have for each other and I suddenly realized that it was much the way I had felt about Mabel. I would speculate about Mabel's ancestors and I became convinced that she had some Indian blood, and that part of her interest in me was based on the fact that I too was evolving from the somewhat exotic and complementary civilization of the Mediterranean. She had long been fascinated with that area in spite of her total lack of understanding and the fact that her years in Italy had no real effect on her soul, nor on her manners.

I tried to coax her in my letters to come to the Southwest and forget our past problems. Mabel, of course, saw our failure in terms of my inadequacies in "giving" to her. However, she seemed, in spite of her sadness and her jealousies, to be living a full life in New York and was reluctant to come to New Mexico. She wrote to me on November 13, 1917:

Dearest old Maurice—

It is possible that we can live together in a rich and happy relation if ever you come to the place where you want it more than anything else, and if you have the power to protect it. Otherwise we can not be happy together. If I came out [to New Mexico] it would be because you make me feel that we are one and you want nothing else. Otherwise it would be the old hell over again. . . .

I am lonely and depressed but I love you and such love must be good in the end. . . .

I have Pascin coming to dinner. I want to explore him a little.

Jo Davidson was in this morning and is in a kind of despair. One of the best things I ever did was to get you out of here. Every one is weakening here. . . .

Later in November another letter arrived:

Dearest old Maurice—

I went this morning to see the Birnbaum Show so I could report it to you. I found it pitiful and him idiotic. He says it's going beautifully. I will send you clippings. Your lilies look very well I must say.

Birnbaum laughed in a horrid way and said to me that Nazimova [the Russian actress] is going to Arizona too. He was horrid in his suggestion. You will let me know the truth of this—won't you? . . . I am in a kind of agony all the time. Truly only the belief in your love and in your art seem worth anything to me. If I lose faith in you as a husband *and* an artist it would be *serious* with me. . . .

I continued to write Mabel about Indian life, about the dances, etc. I called her my squaw, and tried to minimize our problems. Finally I wrote her that the Indians needed saving, and that did the trick:

Wednesday,
November 27

Dearest Maurice,

I am now waiting like a soldier—for orders. I wired you I'd come if you wanted me really.

However, at that time, Mabel became ill with a bad throat infection, and her trip was postponed. She also continued to be doubtful as to the wisdom of coming, torn between her worry about our marriage, her wanting us to be together, and a "pull" toward the West.

On December 4, during her convalescence, she wrote:

Dearest,—Bobby [Jones] has gone to town and Fay and Walter [Lippmann] are out to walk—so I am all alone. I

135

am missing you more all the time though I don't feel any place for me with you yet. . . . You must feel the same affiliation with the Indians as you did with the East. They *are* the same blood and the same culture—totally unmixed with our own known civilization. . . . When they mix they die, the ancient part of them dies. In their unconscious lie things that neither they nor we can fathom. Perhaps I too would feel this curious affinity with them that you do. Certainly the live heart of me—the inner life, is a life that finds no counterpart in Western civilization and culture. Only now and then do I find one of my *own*.

December 12, 1917

Dr. Brill told me I was not to go West—not being well enough. "Stay here until he comes back," he said. "He cannot stay away from his best good forever—he knows it himself." I said, "But he doesn't like New York." "It doesn't matter—he will like it, or Croton later." So, I obey him and the others, and stay.

Finally, on December 17, 1917, Mabel wrote:

The plain truth is I am just dying of loneliness without you and I have to come to you. I can't struggle along like this any more. I can't get over my grippe and have always a sore throat and some fever. I am going to start the first of the week as I wire you today and when I get there we can arrange something. . . . I don't know what you have written about my coming—letter hasn't come yet. But my mother has given me some extra money for going and I am going to pay bills here and leave Monday or Tuesday. . . . I'm no good away from you. We must learn the secret of being together. Mabel

Mabel appeared in New Mexico after a trying journey by train and car. I met her at the train, we spent the night together, and I was overjoyed to find that my former physical debility had been only temporary.

136

Mabel had heard somewhere of a town in the hills of New Mexico called Taos, and insisted soon after she arrived that we drive up to see it. She was fascinated when we got to Taos and said that this was where we must settle down. I, on the other hand, did not like Taos from the moment I set foot there. I felt its void, a primeval space before concrete form began to take shape. It not only failed to stimulate my own powerful sense of form, the absence was like an ache that made me feel empty myself. There was a loneliness about the place under which I physically suffered.

Our attitudes toward the Indians differed also. One day we decided to have a picnic lunch. We reached a remote spot with a magnificent view of the mountains and unwrapped the cold roast chicken we'd brought. One after another, Indians began to appear. I had the distinct impression that they had not accidentally come upon us, but had followed us there from town.

They all had a lean and hungry look and eagerly joined us when Mabel invited them. The chicken disappeared very quickly, although we had meant to keep part of it for dinner so that we could stay and picnic in the moonlight. I was disappointed but took it good-naturedly, believing that since the white man had taken their land away, it was only proper that we should feed them. When our new friends saw that all the food was gone, they left, without a word of thanks. I commented to Mabel about their rudeness, but she defended them, saying that the Indians are proud, and that it was we who were the ungrateful intruders. Unfortunately, our fame as benefactors quickly spread. Mabel hardly said anything those first few days at Taos, but I could see that she was deeply stirred. I was therefore not surprised when she announced, "Here I belong, and here I want to stay." I replied that I had known she would love it, that I had somehow sensed that she belonged. To myself, I recalled my theory that she must have had some wayward Buffalo in her ancestry.

We found quite a large house, which belonged to Mr.

Manby, a mean and eccentric old Englishman. It was beautifully situated on the outskirts of the town. We imported servants from New York and soon had a comfortable household—which entertained more and more lean and hungry guests—and always at mealtime.

However, late one afternoon an Indian came all by himself. This one did not look starved at all, but was quite a magnificent man. Mabel said, "Come in, Tony." I was surprised that she seemed to know him so well, although I had never seen him before. She very seriously introduced us and he grunted something unintelligible while we shook hands. I did not like him even at this first meeting. He had an arrogance which, although it was not directed particularly at me, seemed to come from some deep inner feeling. I thought of Kipling's "East is East and West is West" and when he left I mentioned it to Mabel and said, "Kipling must have been referring to New York and New Mexico." Mabel was annoyed with me, and did not seem to be in a joking mood. I am convinced that even then she was determined not only that they meet, but that they be fused.

Mabel's fascination with every aspect of the spiritual life of Taos continued. There was an old abandoned church in the desert about a mile from our house. It was owned by a sect called the Penitentes, who every Good Friday made a pilgrimage to this chapel and used it for their masochistic rites. Mabel had heard about the flagellants and was eager to watch them. Apparently late at night the almost naked worshippers dragged huge crosses over the desert and whipped each other with sharply spiked cactus plants. It sounded like a gory business and I did not want to go. I have always respected the privacy of others, especially in the matter of religious practice, and in this case, to spy on this secret desert ritual would be debasing to ourselves and to those who believed in it.

But Mabel had made up her mind to go, and that was that. On Good Friday night Mabel, Andrew Dasburg, and I went with a local man who claimed to know a good watching place.

There was a full, bright moon that night but it was bitterly cold and windy. As we came near to where the Penitentes were apt to be, we practically crawled along, eyes straining through the night, silently ducking behind trees and rocks like hunters stalking their prey.

After hours of cold, and useless suffering, I had had enough. Mabel tried to persuade me to stay but I was determined to get home to my warm bed. "Go ahead," she said, "you'll never find the way back alone anyhow." I knew she was right and I became quite savage about the foolishness of the whole expedition. I called my companions impotent sadists, and other appropriate names. As I was storming on, we suddenly saw a group of figures emerging from a copse of trees. They were clearly silhouetted against the sky, but in the moonlight they did not seem to be flagellating themselves. We surmised that they must be on their way to some particular place where they would be safe from intruders. I stopped talking at once, we quickly hid ourselves, and the hunt was on again. We followed them breathlessly. At times they seemed to veer in our direction, and we would hurry to move back. Sometimes we thought they had discovered our presence, for they seemed to be deliberately trying to evade us. After several hours, I was shivering again. I whispered threats that I would shout, "For God's sake, begin the show!"

However, nothing helped dissuade my companions, and the chase went on all night. Almost at dawn, chilled and exhausted, they were convinced at last that there would be no performance that night. We guessed that the Penitentes must have known we were watching and postponed their ceremonies. We stood there in the cold gray dawn, trying to decide which would be the quickest way home. Suddenly, the men and women we had been pursuing came out of the morning mist. Face to face, the "Penitentes" turned out to be half a dozen Taos artists, who all through the night had been playing hide-and-seek with their own Penitentes—with us, of course.

* * *

Mabel soon forgot the ignominy of this episode and we settled back into our routine of entertaining dirty, smelly Indians at lunch every day.

They ate their food silently and ravenously, almost drowning in it. But Tony was different. His white sheet was spotless, his long braids were beautifully arranged, intertwined with a white ribbon that made an exquisite pattern. He was well built, though on the portly side, and had an enormous chest. He stood out from the rest like a proud cock amongst a flock of meek chickens, strutting with his head thrown back, with the air of a conquering hero.

I asked one of the other Indians if Tony was a chief. He laughed scornfully. "He's no chief. He's a no-good show Indian." It turned out that Tony's fondness for whites and his familiarity with their "culture" came from a tour he had once made to Coney Island with a Wild West show!

We went one day to visit the nearby pueblo. As we approached the dwellings, an Indian in a gray blanket who had been standing at the door rushed inside. A handsome squaw came out to greet us with a pleasant smile and invited us to come in. We entered a long, dark room, unfurnished except for some mattresses along the wall. The man in gray was now squatting on the floor, beating a drum and murmuring guttural sounds. He did not look up when we entered but seemed to be absorbed in a mystical state—until at last he slowly raised his head. It was, of course, Tony.

Mabel later wrote of this meeting as some instantaneous religious experience between the two of them. But it should have been clear to anyone who was there that his "communing" was merely a show rather hastily put on for the benefit of visiting tourists.

Mabel invited Tony to come to visit us and he turned to me and asked, "Where you live?" I felt like saying, "You know damn well where we live." He had visited us once officially and I had also seen him several times sneaking around Manby's house. Evidently Manby had seen him too, because he came to me and said, "There's been an Indian spying around the place. He's a no-good loafer and you'd better watch out."

I knew Manby was unreasonable in his hatred of Indians, and his words therefore made little impression on me at the time. Now, I too was put on guard, by Tony's question. Mabel was unaware of this undercurrent or indifferent to it, and she asked Tony whether he could bring his drum when he came. He agreed and added that he would also bring some friends to play and sing Indian music for us. It was arranged then that we would have a tom-tom concert. We invited our friends, and on the appointed night, Tony and three other Indians arrived —at dinnertime of course. They ate, rubbed their stomachs in contentment, and went to the other side of the room to prepare for the concert. I told Mabel that I felt a cold coming on and would go to my room rather than stay for the music. I went up to Tony and paid him $25, making it clear to him that $10 was for him and $5 for each of his friends. Then I went miserably to bed, and fell asleep to the droning sound of Tony's drums. Tom-tom music always had disturbed me and that night it seemed more than ever like a relentless marking of the passage of time.

A few days later I ran into one of the performers on the plaza. When I greeted him, he turned away and did not answer. I was surprised and asked him whether he was angry about anything.

He spat out, "Me and my friends come to you when you ask, sing for you, play for you, and then you don't give us a penny!" Greatly embarrassed I explained that I had given Tony money for them all.

"Tony! Tony never gave us anything. Tony no good."

I went home and told Mabel about my encounter, but she did not say a word. When Tony arrived that same afternoon to take Mabel for a ride, I asked him why he had not paid his friends as we had arranged. With great arrogance he mounted his pony and did not deign to answer. I lost my temper at all the silence around me and I shouted, "That's right, you can go now, but you'd better not come back."

Mabel was a witness to the scene. Her only reaction was to hurl a savage look at me and fling herself into the house. I went to my studio to work, but it was impossible to concentrate. I was filled with tension and with a premonition that Mabel's startling reaction to this dispute was a beginning to some other struggle in which we would all become entangled.

A few days later, I had forgotten my fears, and when I saw Tony and Mabel riding off together in the direction of the pueblo, I did not give it much thought. But when Mabel came home hours later I was appalled. Her eyes had the look about them that I had myself seen only after Mabel had been sexually gratified, when something would seem to come to life deep within her.

Years later Mabel was to insist that she and Tony had sexual relations only after I had left. This is another lie that got official publication in her memoirs, in this case in *Edge of the Taos Desert:* [1]

> He [Tony] bent a firm, gentle look upon me and held out his hand, and I took it. "I comin here to this tepee tonight," he said, [*sic*] "When darkness here. That be right." And it was right. [2]

Mabel places this conversation as taking place after my departure, and implies that after long restraint the romantic couple could feel free to do something about "IT." One wonders what was going on with "IT" for the two months before I left. Mabel would hurry out of the house every night to the tepee she'd had set up on our lawn, preferring its "air" to the "stuffy" house. It could not have been that Tony kept coming for nightly tom-tom concerts, for the only sound that ever reached the house where I lay listening was the arrival and departure of a solitary horse and rider, and the creak of

---

[1] Mabel Dodge Luhan, *Edge of the Taos Desert* (Harcourt, Brace, 1937).
[2] Ibid., p. 334.

Mabel Dodge Luhan
(*United Press International Photo*)

Samuel Lewisohn,
patron and friend
tograph by Lusha Nelson)

Vera Sterne

the house hours later when Mabel sneaked back to our bedroom. These nocturnal trysts, so near to the house, filled me with a great disgust.

I would make fantastic plans and sinister schemes. I borrowed a huge revolver from Manby, who handed it to me with a mean grin and said, "I hope you're fast on the draw." He knew! I was humiliated when I realized that it was not possible for me to be the only one in town who heard the horse stop at our place, who saw its rider proceed to our outdoor "annex." Of course I never used the gun, only kept it under my pillow in a childish, rather pitiful attempt to play cowboy to Tony's Indian.

One terrible night, only an hour after Mabel had gone out to the tent, I heard her stealing back to bed. I had not heard the horse, but when the sound of her regular breathing told me she was sleeping, I burst into loud, sneering laughter. Mabel sat up. "What's the matter? Have you suddenly gone crazy?" "Poor Mabel," I laughed, "poor, poor Mabel. Her lover doesn't show up and she has to go to bed without her nightcap."

Mabel was furious. She ordered me to get out of the bed. I shouted, "This is my bed, you go back to your tent." We struggled a few minutes, and I pushed her down, off the bed and onto the floor. Mabel stormed out of the room and her parting words were, "Tomorrow, you get out—do you hear me?"

Never before had I felt so low and humbled. Mabel was within her rights in ordering me out. It was her house, her money, her food. . . . All my instincts told me to run, but I had been working for weeks on two pieces of sculpture that I could not give up. Those two heads kept me chained to that house, miserable, but unable to leave. However, I thought of a solution which I presented to Mabel. I would take Pete, my model, and go off to stay with a friend at his isolated house in the hills. Mabel was enthusiastic about the plan, and I left the Taos house.

At Twining, a deserted mining camp, I worked feverishly

on the busts of the young Indians, Albidia and Pete, with the single aim of getting them done and getting away from that atmosphere of deceit and lies. When both busts were finished, I returned to Taos, but I could not stand it there. I told Mabel that I would leave for New York the next morning, and she replied that she thought it was a good idea. "The change will be good for you. You will come back and everything will be right again." But I knew that when I left, it would be more than just a change.

When I went outside I found that the privy was filled to capacity. I asked, "Mabel, how can you stand that awful stench? Why don't you get one of your Indian friends to clean it out?" Mabel said nothing, just went straight off to the hills with Tony.

I got a wheelbarrow and began the disgusting task of emptying the privy. It took all afternoon, but with each odorous load that I dumped in the arroyo I seemed to be cleansing myself of my life in Taos. When the job was done, I vomited, and went back to the house for a bath. I felt that I had paid my debt in kind, and was now ready to go with a cleansed body and spirit.

When Mabel returned, I proudly showed her my handi-work, and she threw me a look of deep and unique sympathy that I could not forget. I got into the car that was to take me to Santa Fe where I would get a train for New York. Mabel embraced and kissed me, and repeated, "You must not worry. Go east, and have a good time. Then come back and every-thing will again be as it was before."

When the car started, I had the impulse to turn around and wave good-by. Instead, I turned my back upon Taos and its odious associations.

The trip east was a terrible mental and physical ordeal. The heat that summer was awful, particularly during the long hours traveling through Kansas. My worry about the head of

Albidia added to my discomfort. I always built a solid core of Plaster of Paris first, upon which I modeled my sculpture in wax, but I had not been able to get the plaster in Taos. In my impatience, I had constructed the entire bust of wax, without any idea of the infernal heat I would encounter on the train. Now I thought of nothing else.

As soon as I could, I rushed to open the wooden crate, and when finally I was able to get at my work, I saw that the beautiful head, that lovely maiden, had been melted into a grotesque monster.

The eyes which everyone had admired were now two narrow slits; the mouth, a deep, toothless gap; the cheeks were swollen into two bulbous lumps; the subtle, elusive smile was now the leering grin of a gargoyle . . . mocking me.

I stared in shock at what had been my own escape from reality, an idealized image of the past six months. It had been changed to instruct me in irony, to become the true vision of how I had felt. The pain and abasement, the horror and disgust were all there to see.

"This," I hissed, "this you did, you Mabel, you vile, disgusting creature. You tried to destroy me, did you? I'll show you who can destroy." I hacked that monster into a thousand pieces and felt that I was murdering Mabel and our past together.

Now, I realize that it was a mistake to destroy the head, in spite of the emotional deliverance I got from doing it. Had I been able to foresee the art of the future, I would have had that brilliant accident cast in bronze and perpetuated the leering grimace as a spiritual symbol of our era.

It has been a long time since I felt the passionate hate that moved me to smash that sculpture. Now, I see the life that Mabel and I had together with a perspective the passing years have given me. Although our relationship had begun tempestuously, as time passed our attachment deepened. I had really begun to love Mabel very much, to have a feeling of completion and comradeship with her. The break came then. The orchid found another, more attractive tree to attach itself to.

Part of the problem was that Mabel had always been enthralled by the mystical. She thought that she had finally found what she had been searching for in Tony and in the Indian mystique. As soon as she discovered the Pueblo Indians she was like someone under hypnosis. She sat entranced when they beat their tom-toms and chanted their weird music. Most of all, their silence fascinated her, and I must admit that practically the only words I heard them say myself were, "I'll have more chicken." Once, when she was raving on about the eloquence of their silence, of how it revealed their depths, I jokingly reminded her, "Mabel, not all locked closets contain valuables. You can lock up an empty closet too."

And despite my humiliation and pain during that time, I now bear her no grudge. Why should I? When we parted we did what was ultimately right for us both, and Mabel deserves the credit for taking the initiative. I, with my incurable habit of attempting the impossible, might have tried to preserve the marriage, but Mabel's instincts toward Tony were, in a sense, true. In Evans, her first husband, she did not find the true green to complement her own red. Dodge, her second husband, was not the right blue for her orange. I, the wrong red-violet for her yellow-green. A painter's extravagance? Life, too, is fulfilled in complementaries. In Tony, Mabel at last found the perfect rainbow, resplendent with all the nuances of the spectrum. Of course, rainbows are found in oil-slicked puddles in the gutter as well as in the heavens; but, in any case, Tony was what she needed. Mabel had no vitality or creative power of her own. She was a dead battery who needed constantly to recharge with the juice of some man, though she might leave him "dead" in the process.

I had a great deal of my own to struggle with, in my work. When I was exhausted with it, I longed for the soft pillow of tranquillity, where I could relax and recuperate and prepare myself for the next day's fight with the stubborn spirit. Instead of finding the peace I needed, Mabel and I often fought bitterly. At the end of a quarrel I would go off to my studio and forget everything but the task before me. Mabel chafed and fretted and resented my escape. When I returned, calm and happy, she was poisoned with envy and bitterness. This separate life I had, more than anything else in our relationship, aroused her fury.

In Tony she found a mate like a rock in the desert. He could not be hurt by her passionate frustration, and so she did not attempt the hopeless task of hitting him.

She had never before come in intimate contact with primitive people so that she thought that the Pueblo Indians had something unique. As a matter of fact, what she found so abundantly in Tony, she could have found in any primitive place in the world, on any of the five continents, but most especially in the least civilized regions of Australia.

What Mabel needed, although it took her years to consciously act on it, was not someone who bore a cultural, temperamental, or mental resemblance to herself, but rather her antithesis, someone whose physical presence would liberate her from her inner prison. What psychoanalysts, artists, and writers could not accomplish, this Indian medicine man did. He helped her find self-realization just because he was, in the truest sense of the word, her mate . . . because of a complete absence of similarity, her complementary.

Eventually, her ache to be doing something "significant" got out of control but luckily she found an outlet in writing. Her memoirs, of course, also provided a way for her to promote the thing that interested her most in this world, that is, her own *gloire*.

WHEN I got back to New York I was lonely and unhappy and was anxious to see people. Mabel had disapproved of almost all my former friends, particularly of attractive women, but neither did the men escape her disparagement. . . . "Mrs. G. was a moron; Miss L., vulgar; Dorothy, an intellectual snob; Mrs. H., a social parasite; Ben, such a boring bourgeois; and poor Hamilton gave her the creeps." Obviously none of them were worth seeing.

I had chafed under this social tyranny, but I bore it with patience, because I had always sought from my personal life a relaxation from the tensions and conflicts of my creative work. My old friends were sacrificed to this craving for domestic peace, but now that I was not living with Mabel, I hoped in my restored freedom to resume these relationships. What I had forgotten was that New York is a perfect place to leave in July and August. Everyone I had hoped to find was away from the city. After the bitter struggle at Taos, I longed for the solace and affection of a true friend but I was bitterly disappointed.

I would take long walks as if my legs could carry me away from myself and my depression. Once, on a hike from Washington Square to Central Park, I suddenly saw a familiar figure slumped on a bench. Even at a distance I could not mistake him—it was my dear friend, Pascin.[1]

Jules Pascin was the only friend in New York who had been in Paris with me and because of this we had the special intimacy that comes from having shared early struggles and aspirations. Unlike later art students who are taught to "understand" the more recent masters, we had to learn on our own, the hard way, and Pascin and I each developed a mutual respect for what the other was doing.

Now, I was ready to shout with the joy of finding him again after a year and a half; but as I got closer to the bench, I saw that he was dozing. I sat down quietly beside him and had a long sad look at my gifted friend. He was thinner than I had ever seen him, pale and sick-looking.

When finally he opened his eyes he looked at me in silence for at least a minute. Then, I was relieved to see his look of surprise gradually change to one of genuine pleasure. He told me how glad he was to see me, then after another long pause added, "I never expected to see you again." His intense black eyes were moist with tears.

"How foolish, Pascin! What is it, are you ill?" He did not answer my questions, but asked about my work and my affairs. I told him about the failure of my marriage and he did not seem surprised. He said, "I'm glad it's over, I knew it couldn't last! If only that damn war were over, I'd drag you back to Europe where we both belong."

At that moment, a middle-aged man sat down on the bench opposite us and opened his newspaper. Pascin stiffened and whispered, "Watch your step, there he is again."

"Who?" I asked.

"That man with the paper. I am being followed day and night."

I tried to reassure Pascin by pointing out that the man was no one to fear, that he was a harmless stroller who had stopped

[1] Jules Pascin (1885–1930). Painter born to Italian-Serbian and Spanish-Jewish parents. Achieved critical and popular success both in Paris and the United States.

near us to read his paper.

He answered, "He only pretends to be reading. He is watching us, all right. If you knew what was good for you, you'd keep away from me!"

He was panicky and there was a haunted look in his eyes. I realized that Pascin was really sick and tried again to comfort him, but he would not listen. Instead, he got up abruptly, and walked away.

I followed him and said, "Look, Pascin, that man doesn't even know we've left. He's still buried in his paper."

Pascin replied, "Like hell, he is. That's his technique, he is watching us all the time. You must be blind not to see it."

I took him to a French restaurant on Forty-fifth Street, where a good dinner and an excellent Bordeaux cheered him a little. We were walking toward his home when he stopped and said that he had to get some food for his wife, Hermione.

I had completely forgotten about Pascin's wife, and begged him to forgive me. He said, "No, never mind, she never goes out." We went to a delicatessen and Pascin picked out all sorts of things, but before it was time to pay, he looked embarrassed for a moment and sheepishly put almost everything back. I knew he must need money badly, but I knew also that he would never admit it if I should ask.

I was worried about Pascin and saw him constantly for several weeks. He suffered greatly, moped in his dreary room, peering out through dingy curtains at the detectives he imagined were spying on him from an entrance hall across the street. What worried me most was his inertia. He never painted. The colors on his palette were dry lumps, his brushes lay on the table, unwashed.

Pascin's wife, Hermione David, seemed equally disturbed. Although she too was a gifted painter she sat reading silently in a corner of the room for days on end. She had come to look like a cross between Donatello's emaciated John the Baptist and a habitué of the Moulin de la Galette, by Toulouse-Lautrec.

I tried hard to reason with Pascin about his fears and to urge him to resume his work. At last he showed me the work he had done in the past year and a half. I was particularly pleased with the progress he had made in New Orleans and in his Havana paintings, and urged him to have a show. He seemed to feel that he was not ready for this step. He had sometime before given some of his best paintings to a dealer who had apparently sold them, but kept all the proceeds. I was indignant, and urged him to sue, but with that gentle, low voice of his, Pascin asked, "Can you see me suing anyone?"

After spending time with me he would go home and write me sad, formal letters, which broke my heart:

Dear Sterne . . .

The evening we spent together was very agreeable to me. Your suggestion, I should leave some drawings at your studio I apreciat very much, especially coming from you. Although this is probably not a matter of importance to you, I would like to be frank about it with you.

I had an awful trouble destroying hundreds of drawings and several rolls of pictures I did not show to you, that I mad[e] during the disagreable last year and I don't know if I would not, after some time, feel much the same about this last output. You seemed to like some of the things but then it would have been absolut inhuman, knowing the unpleasant conditions I was in most of the time, if you would have told me things that could discourage me. And as I had no occasion since years to show anythings, I would not like things to be seen that I am not more sure about. I am not so sensible about was the [what they] may think about my stuff, but these last things are not satisfactory to me, lacking much in warmth, and so—I hope you don't think this a sentimental letter, I would only like you should not misunderstand me. . . . Sincerely yours Pascin

At my wit's end about Pascin's mental state, I decided to consult my friend, Dr. A. A. Brill, who that year came once a week from Nantucket to his New York office. Dr. Brill told me that Pascin was in a bad state, and that it would be best to get him away to some country place immediately. I trusted Brill's judgment because of my own experience with him. During one of my crises with Mabel, she, as usual, had blamed all our problems on my emotional difficulties and had insisted that I consult Brill. I had no money for stiff consultation fees and Brill agreed to accept a painting in lieu of payment. I am not sure which of us got the better of the bargain. After one session, Brill said to me, "There's nothing wrong with you. All you need is a new cow." —I'd been quite fond of the lilies on that canvas, and indeed the painting had been quite famous for its artistic, rather than exchange values.

Now, with Brill's solemn words in my mind I thought of a plan to help Pascin. I had arranged to move out to the Elizabeth Duncan School at Tarrytown, New York, as soon as I wound up my affairs in New York. There was, for my use, a small house at the end of a pier on the Hudson. I wrote Elizabeth; she gave me permission to bring Pascin with me, and we installed ourselves there for a week. Elizabeth's cheerful company and the lovely young students practicing in their pale blue tunics performed a miracle, for at the end of the week Pascin seemed quite normal again. He actually smiled when I pooh-poohed his fear of those tiresome vestibule detectives.

However, there were some serious and very real problems in the poor man's life. I tried to help him sell his work and since he could not bear the idea of strangers visiting his home I took some of his drawings to my studio. I showed about thirty of them to Dr. A. C. Barnes, the collector, who said, "I have seen his work—he is merely a first-rate illustrator—a bit vulgar!"

I was bitterly disappointed but had some satisfaction two years later, when Pascin had become prominent in the École de Paris. Dr. Barnes then bought every one of those drawings from a dealer on the Right Bank of the Seine, and, of course, paid four times as much for them.

Barnes had two passions: he loved Renoir and he loathed sham. His wealth enabled him to indulge both. He bought all the Renoirs he could get, and he never missed a chance to insult people whose motives he distrusted. I sometimes wondered whether the pleasure he derived from his superb collection was as great as the diabolical delight he took in being the perpetual *enfant terrible*.

His abusive, often vulgar replies to strangers who politely requested permission to see his collection have become collectors' items themselves. I saw one such letter which a distinguished Washington hostess had received and preserved. In it, he asked whether she dared come without a chaperone, since the last lady who had come alone had given him a venereal disease.

I asked the lady if she had answered this impertinent note but she had not. I suggested that since Barnes had made his fortune from the manufacture of the popular drug, she ought to have wired, "Why not try Argyrol?"

I met Barnes for the first time when he came to my studio on Washington Square in 1919. He walked in and without any preliminaries said, "I am Dr. Barnes. Let me see what you're doing."

I told him that my works were either at the Bourgeois Gallery or at the Duncan School in Tarrytown. He replied that he liked neither schools nor dealers and insisted on seeing whatever I had at that moment. I showed him some drawings of cattle, and after studying them, he asked me the prices of a few. I said, "When I tell you how much I want for them you will probably say that you can get live cows for half the price."

Surprisingly, and most graciously, Barnes replied, "Don't forget that live cows have a tendency to die . . . yours will live forever." With that, he handed me a check, said, "Send them to Merion," and left. It was the first sale I had made since Taos, and it made me feel that I could stand on my own legs again. That felt very good indeed.

Although Dr. Barnes did not buy his work that year, we were slowly able to solve some of the other physical problems of Pascin's life and I think this went a long way toward giving him the emotional peace he needed.

His letters are a chronicle of his improvement:

Dear Sterne,

I just received your telegram and thank you very much for the trouble you went in for, searching me for the room. I would be glad to take it and it is much cheaper than I pay in towne.

Only in receiving my bank statement I noticed that I have much less left than I thought, so I would be unable to undertake anything before I get answer to a cable for money I send abroad. . . . Should the people wish on account on the room . . . Please give it. I will return it to you at the first occasion.

A week later I received another note from him:

Dear Sterne,

I came to see you. Reason: I got this morning at last notice that my record of arrival had been received at the Naturalization Bureau. . . . Could you go with me [as a witness] on Monday or Tuesday, at Noon-time perhaps best, or any other time that would suit you, to the Hall of Records, near City Hall? And have another witness to. You would have both to have your naturalization papers or passport. Perhaps you know somebody downtown in business we could get at lunchtime. . . .

All this took a good deal of my free time but when I found that Pascin was quite well again, I realized that my concern over his predicament had eased my apprehensions about myself. As so often happens, helping Pascin had helped me recover my usual tranquillity which had been so shaken in Taos.

I looked up other old friends and tried hard to fill up my life. Mary Foote [1] was also having difficulties making a living and trying to find the time to paint as she liked. In 1918 she wrote:

Dear Maurice—

Your note and your paint have been forwarded to me and I am much touched at your efforts in my behalf. It will make all the difference when I get at painting flowers again to have colors at hand that are dark and rich enough. I am going through my usual agonies trying to paint a scrubby little wriggling boy of six with fifty expressions a minute, and I can't fix any of them. By lying awake nights, and because I have always pulled out somehow so far, I suppose I shall live through this one.

I had dinner with Djuna Barnes, the avant-garde writer, occasionally. She ordinarily spoke very little, being more interested in observing the people she was with. One night at Polly's Restaurant in Greenwich Village, Djuna suddenly exclaimed that she saw someone she knew. She took me over to a table where a mousy girl was dining with some friends. Djuna began hissing, "I hate you, I hate you, I hate you" over and over again. The tan mouse smiled sweetly but there was an electric spark in her smile and they had an ominously quiet, violent fight before Djuna stalked out with that long stride of hers.

Djuna's most intimate friend was the loveliest young woman in the village, a Titian-haired beauty who was fatally ill. When Mary Pyne died I found Djuna sobbing painfully, her head buried in her arms, saying over and over that she would

[1] Mary Hallock Foote (1847–1938), American author and illustrator.

155

never get over the loss. These were the only times I had even a glimpse of the true intensity her controlled façade covered.

Leo Stein came in and out of my life for all of my life and his, until his sad death. In New York that year, he dropped in on me, with a sleeping bag, and no roof under which to put it. I, of course, invited him to stay with me, and offered to buy another couch for him to sleep on, but Leo preferred the sleeping bag. When I asked him why he liked it better than a nice soft mattress, he said that when he crawled inside and was cozily tucked in, he felt that he was back in his mother's womb.

The top of the bag had quite a complicated opening, which depended on a gadget which must have been the forerunner of the modern zipper. One morning I watched him struggling to emerge from the womb, but the thing had stuck fast. I got up to help him, but it seemed impossible.

I said, "Don't you think I'd better call an ambulance? Obviously this is not merely a case for an *accoucheur*. You probably need the help of a surgeon who can perform a Caesarean operation."

His remark about the womblike aspects of his sleeping bag amused me because only a few days before he had held forth at great length about *my* mother complex. When I brought this to his attention, he admitted that in the past he had been handicapped by such feelings, but that self-analysis had freed him from this and all other complexes and inhibitions. I had never known anyone so honest with others, so subjective about himself. I did not feel at that time that he had rid himself of many of his neuroses. I think that in his last years he did at long last achieve a great degree of freedom from his complexes. What a pity that he did not live another dozen years to fulfill the promise of his later years!

Although I managed to occupy myself with old acquaintances, I grieved over my broken marriage, and found it very difficult to work. The air was filled with rumors and scandal about Taos that pained and humiliated me. I worked and worried about the head of Pete, I suppose in some unconscious effort to make up for the scupture I had lost. Mabel wrote to me as if our separation were only temporary, talking about the house she and Tony were building and chastising me for my lack of interest in it! She wrote:

You must have some curiosity about it for probably we will pass our old age here together!

I began to panic at the nasty stories in which my name was involved and angrily wrote Mabel that her behavior in New Mexico was ruining my reputation as well as her own. She seemed to resist the idea of a divorce at first, and to make threats in answer to my own hysteria:

March 21

I don't quite understand the tone of your letter. It is new from you. I cannot come East at the moment. If you de-cide after a little more thought that you want a divorce I can get one here. I think you exaggerate the talk. People always chatter. . . . Of course if you want a divorce it will mean a cessation of the maybe small but anyway par-tial income you have been getting. I am sorry for this for I hoped it would help to set you free to work. I do *not* con-sider myself to blame for your lapses in work. Nor do you.

Later in the year she wrote:

Aug. 23

But I do not believe any irrevocable final separation is for us. We have meant and do mean a lot to each other spirit-ually. You know that. Of course I can send you $200 a month and probably more when you need it and I will do so—though not thro' lawyers. . . . So long as you are loyal and do not dramatize our situation to others at my expense I will be loyal to you and as helpful as I can be. But if you continue to feel meanly towards me and talk so to others—it may make me feel like cutting away alto-gether.

My financial dependence on Mabel was a terrible thing for me. However, an important reason for it was that during the short period we were together, she had antagonized not only my friends, but also those acquaintances who were potential buyers of my work. In America, far more than in Europe, personal contact is imperative for the artist's survival. With Mabel, I had hoped that freed from the imperative need to earn a living, I could devote myself exclusively to my work. Now I felt as if my physical foundation had crumbled. I also feared that that short period of material comfort had undermined my former technical skill in the art of survival, like a domesticated animal, suddenly set free, who perishes because he can no longer get his own food or take care of himself in the wilderness.

This dependence hurt me, expecially after our marriage had reached so critical a state, and I was eager to feed myself through my own efforts. However, Mabel and I discussed my financial dilemma and she arranged to have her bank send me one hundred dollars a month until I got back on my own. This lasted a couple of years, and it was a happy moment when I informed the bank to discontinue those monthly allowances for services rendered in the past. I was too young to be pensioned, and in any case had not served "in arms" long enough to be entitled to a pension.

It was partly at Mabel's urging that I decided to move out to the Duncan School that year to try to work. New York seemed to have no room or time for the dreams that are necessary in an artist's life, and I hoped that Tarrytown would give me the peace I required. I found when I got there that the school was a haven from the cares of World War I as well as from my own problems. The beautiful children in their flannel dancing frocks were a great solace to everyone who watched them.

The slow tempo of life at the school also helped me in my perennial creative problem to slow down the tempo of my own output. I hardly ever stopped long enough while I was working, to create in the midst of that rushing stream some islands for contemplation, or recapitulation, or even transcription. What I needed was a point of arrival, where I could get down to the arrested movement of the static canvas or panel. Instead I swiftly dashed off tens of drawings. The tempo of my progression from day to day was too rapid, so that it was a torture for me to stop long enough to concentrate upon a single work that would fully demonstrate some present thing. As a result, I have ruined many more paintings than the comparative few that I have carried out successfully. I painted and repainted and painted again according to my constant changes of mood, and in the end, each separate painting became a battlefield, or a cemetery, in which were buried literally dozens of excellent things, in layers, each destroyed by its successor.

The Duncan School also gave me time to think and write about painting and about the relationship of the artist to life. Looking now at my notes of those days, I find that I am curiously sympathetic to the man who wrote them:

> The relation of art to life is not founded in a conscious necessity. We have certain essential needs; some luxuries, even, have become indispensable. But our attitude toward art is rooted in love or in interest. . . .
>
> Unfortunately instead of serious concern for the artist, there exists only a certain curiosity, with a smack of gossip and a seasoning of the scandalous. There is no attempt to define his place in society, and no effort to better it. He, with the criminal, embodies our deep craving for difficult adventures, a craving rooted in the remote Past, when there was no sharp distinction between war and peace, when life was uncertain and full of dangers. . . .
>
> What caused the unrelatedness of the artist to life? First the critics; they are the priests, judges, and interpreters. . . . Curiously there has ever been endless speculation about the meaning, value, and function of art. There is no

harm in that, but there is in being taught by dogmatic critics which artists should hang in our homes and museums, and which should hang themselves in their garrets.

We are told that "art is long and life is short," and that it does the artist good to suffer. It does not, especially not when he is present at artistic gatherings in $5000 "studio apartments" with wonderful view and light, where he hears the latest "artistic success" explained and exploited, whilst he and his colleagues work in miserable rooms by poor light, and buy a tube of cadmium with the money that should be spent for a decent meal. . . .

When one considers these great obstacles and the fact that, as a rule, the worthiest gain fame when they are old, and a market when they are dead, one wonders that the artist manages to exist at all. . . . He survives because he must, because his art demands it. For the privilege of doing what God meant him to do, he will serve the Devil himself. This, I believe, is mainly responsible for the decadence of art as a moral factor, for art always has been and always will be a perfect mirror of the artist's soul.

In order to live decently, to support himself and often a family, the artist confuses issues; he strives for success as an end in itself, though he knows that such strife is against the nature of art and the artist's high endeavors.

That there does not seem to be a relation between art and life is not the fault of the critic and dealer alone. It is also the fault of the artists themselves. They have no constructive policy, are ignorant of life and modern conditions, vie with the critics in belittling the achievements of one another. Theirs is neither a trade nor a profession, for these derive their strength and dignity from a conscious human need. The perception of this strength is a source of prestige and power, which through organization has become a potent factor in our social system. But there is no apparent human need or demand for what the artist has to give; there never has been. At best this function was decorative; he made an existing need more palatable and more beautiful.

Modern science has revolutionized every phase of life. Her astounding discoveries displaced both art and religion as a creative evolutionary force. . . .

Science has become a pragmatic religion, and it will continue to minister to our material welfare. But that it can add much spiritually is questionable, although our great imaginative reactions were evoked by its first discoveries. At present there are indications that the greatest future discoveries will fail to stir us profoundly. The element of the incredible, the miraculous, will be lacking. We have begun to feel that nothing is impossible, and are learning to accept scientific disclosures as a matter of course.

But life is dynamic; it must grow, develop, change. Which known or still unexplored faculty will be called upon to perform so essential a function? For ages, art expressed life, not as it is, but as it ought to be, as an ideal. Now we are growing impatient with ideals. The artist's new mission will not be merely to make life appear more beautiful and attractive, but to show that life *is* beautiful, attractive, and significant. . . .

The crying problem is not what the artists should express. It is rather to devise a working plan which would encourage him to become an artist and not a caterer to the rich or sophisticated few; to shape him to express the unconscious needs of humanity; not to demoralize him through the struggle for existence, assigning him to a stratum lower than that of the day laborer, but to encourage him to become what he should be, a sensitive instrument vibrating to and reflecting nature's mysteries. Assuring the artist a decent living would encourage him to experiment. Our scholars and scientists are given this opportunity; they carry on their experiments and research in laboratories and endowed institutions. Astronomers are encouraged to gaze at the stars, and we ask of them only that they tell us what they see. Why not extend this privilege to artists? For they also minister to our potential needs. If this were done, we should have a vital art, a rich spiritual adventure in the realm of the unknown, and not just a bad habit of repeating salable failures . . .

Then art would be pure, honest, and moral, untainted by hypocrisy, opportunism, cheap sentimentality, or charity.

The opportunity to think and work at the Duncan School seemed an artist's dream. Elizabeth Duncan kindly gave me the use of the cottage on the Hudson to which I later took Pascin. I was touched by her cheerful welcome, but I soon discovered that one of the functions I was expected to perform was that of the resident bull. My services were not required for the young "Isadorables," but rather for the one or two middle-aged cows who were to be milked to feed these younger calves. To serve Miss Duncan's financial needs with this kind of service of my own was definitely not for me. I found it far more enjoyable to hold drawing classes for the teen-aged girls who were eager and enthusiastic students. They posed tirelessly for each other and for me, and I made innumerable drawings at the school.

It was at the Duncan School that I met Vera, the woman with whom I have lived so happily ever after. She was just a girl then, but she has retained the strange quality which attracted me to her from the first. It was her innocence and simplicity, her lack of worldliness that made me turn from the intellectual and sensuous, the sophisticated and factual, the egotistical and domineering that I had found in Mabel. Vera was most real in her unreality—like air and space. In her, I found neither the past nor the present, but nature in the process of formation.

Vera Segal Sterne tells of her experiences in the Duncan School:

Elizabeth Duncan had had a school in Europe where she trained young girls in the method of dance and movement used by her sister Isadora. When the Duncans came to this country, Elizabeth established a school in Croton, New York, and went on with her work. However, Isadora, after some time, claimed those original girls for her dance troupe, and Elizabeth began again, this time at Tarrytown on the Frank Vanderbilt estate. Funds for the school came from wealthy patrons (one of whom was Mabel Dodge).

Although my father was a physician, my family was very interested in the theater and would consider no other career for my two sisters and me. My mother had been on the stage under her maiden name, Paula Seldes, and had been a famous beauty as well as a singer. Vivienne Segal, my older sister, of course did very well in musical comedy, was a successful star for years in such shows as *Pal Joey*, *Bird of Paradise*, etc. My parents expected that I would follow in her footsteps, and Mother, in particular, was unhappy about my somewhat faltering way of doing so. She thought my carriage was dreadful, that I was round-shouldered and had weak ankles. Really, Mother and Vivienne were stately voluptuous dark beauties who instinctively knew how to enter a room with glamour and poise. As much as anything else I think my mother was confused by the fact that I did not look like them at all, being very slim and blonde, rather than dark. At any rate, she was determined to get me ready for the career they saw for me, and having heard about the work that the Duncans did, decided to send me to Tarrytown for a summer of corrective exercise. And although my father objected, I did not leave Elizabeth for three years. I had a fairly good voice but since both my mother and Vivienne were singers, I was determined to do something else. After the first weeks at Tarrytown, that something became dancing.

Elizabeth Duncan was very easy to live with, and although she undoubtedly had love affairs in Tarrytown, and did not discourage the other adults from doing so, this sexual freedom did not carry over to the young girls. We lived in the clouds, lived only for beauty. When I try to explain what it was we learned from the Duncans, I can only say again what they all said: "It was moving like Greek statues." In a way, the only harm that the school did to the children was that it made them somewhat unfitted for life in the ordinary world.

There were about 12 or 15 permanent girls in Tarrytown at the time I was there. Elizabeth had brought six German girls from Europe, there were 4 or 5 full-time American students, other people would come and go. Mabel Dodge supported a young, dull-witted girl named Elizabeth at the school, and her son, John Evans, joined the class for a time.

Maurice and I met at the Duncan School, when I was 15. I was a very serious and precocious young girl, worked hard at my dancing, read Schopenhauer and Nietzsche, and had no use for boys my own age. Perhaps the Freudians would say that I was looking for a father whose interest I would not have to share in an uneven competition with Vivienne, Louise, and my beautiful mother. I fell in love almost at once with the magnetic older man who sketched us while we danced.

My family was quite upset when they heard of my relationship with Maurice. They thought he was much too old for me, and although he was by then an art celebrity, they knew only about the theater world and considered Maurice an unpromising nobody. Mother was finally won by Maurice's charm. He told her that if he'd met her first, he'd probably have married her—which did not help his cause with my jealous father.

———

I was fond of Vera's father, Dr. Segal. He was a self-sacrificing Philadelphia physician who loved children and devoted his life to his work. With blond hair, modest, delicate features, and a boyish figure, he conveyed the impression of a rather vague introvert who was destined for a life of serenity. Instead, he fell violently in love with his precise opposite: a beautiful, full-blooded, full-breasted woman of unbridled passions, a person who had a strong intolerance of the very idea of self-control.

They had three daughters. The oldest, Vivienne, inherited neither her father's honesty with himself nor her mother's impetuosity. She was ambitious, and had extraordinary good looks, with a crafty, intelligent face and an exquisite figure. Her appearance, combined with a pretty voice, soon made her a prima donna.

The youngest daughter, Louise, was cool, beautiful, and impersonal. I have never seen a more perfect body, nor a less committed face.

Both Louise and Vivienne resembled their mother, but Vera, the second child, had a style that was her own. She inherited her father's fair good looks and his love of music. From her mother, she got her magnificent figure, broad-chested and slim-hipped. Unlike her mother, she had powerful thighs and the legs of a Michelangelo Sistine youth. It was a body free and innocent, yet with Rubens breasts; a strange combination of the masculine, feminine, and child.

But in spite of her fully developed body, Vera had hardly any psychic form at all. She was, instead, made of reflections of a Cellini sky, responses to some gentle breeze.

I WAS still restless and reluctant to settle into a routine life even with Vera. I left the Duncan School and went back to Paris to seek the happiness and excitement I had known there. I could hardly control my agitation during the last hour of the train trip. I did not stop at the hotel long enough to wash but rushed off to my old haunts. I went first to the Café du Dôme where for three years I had taken my apéritif before dinner, my cognac and café noir after dinner. There were only a few people on the terrace that chilly, gray day I arrived and they did not even bother to glance up when I entered. One man did stare at me for a minute, then went back to his *Figaro* with a look that plainly asked, "What's eating you?"

I realized then the sadness of returning to a large city after many years' absence, and how important people are in our memory of a place. All my friends were gone. Leo Stein was in Settignano, Purrmann and Levi in Berlin, Kellermann off somewhere else. Gertrude Stein was of course still in Paris, but I had written her what I now realized was an insolent letter about *Three Lives*. She had answered me with a savage letter of her own, and I thought it imprudent to try to renew our friendship.

Even the waiters saddened me. One had lost an arm in the war, another was absent—killed in action. I could not bear all the ghosts. I jumped in a taxi and headed for the Louvre where I hoped that the Mantegna Crucifixion, the Giotto, the Delacroix, the Avignon Entombment would be the constant friends I remembered.

However, my own mood was so black that even these paintings which had meant so much to me in my student days seemed cold strangers. In those first hours, I regretted having come back to Paris. I had never been close to the native Parisians; my French was primitive, as was their patience. It seemed that Paris was a hostile hostess, unwelcoming and disdainful.

I went back to the Left Bank, sat at the Dôme, and ordered a Pernod. The sun came out, the terrace filled with gay chatting Americans, and only I must drink alone. Suddenly, in his old way, Pascin popped up before me, and, in his old way, whispered, "I can't," when I joyously invited him to join me.

He took me to the Rotonde, but when he was greeted with friendly shouts from a nearby table, Pascin felt the need to move again, and off we went to a quiet little Bistro on the "Boul Mich." I was thrilled to see him and chatted on about my activities. I had heard that Pascin was doing well, painting and selling, and I asked if I might come to his studio the following morning to see his work. He replied, "I have nothing to show you. The dealers carry my stuff away, sometimes before it is finished. Anyway, you won't be interested. I am just producing, producing, producing—like a machine. Sometimes I feel seasick when I look at some of the things the dealers rave about."

Pascin said that he had recently seen one of his "failures" at a dealer's on the Quay Voltaire. The dealer would not tell him how he got hold of it but he wanted 5000 francs for the painting. Pascin paid the price, then kicked a hole through the canvas. He said, "I was sorry immediately after because it was such a cheap melodramatic thing to do, but I had lost my temper."

He remained silent for some moments after telling this story and I saw, with great concern, the familiar tears streaming down his face. When I asked him what was wrong and whether I could help him, he answered in his unemotional, quiet voice, "I am very glad to see you. I always wanted to tell you what you did for me during those terrible years in America. You saved my life, for you were the only person I could trust. Do you remember the time you picked me up on Sixth Avenue and took me with you to Tarrytown? I had decided to make an end to it all."

I felt very embarrassed by his gratitude and very saddened that my friend had always suffered so. He now began a long explanation of why we could not dine at the Duomo. He had apparently separated from Hermione David and had fallen in love with Louise, the wife of a famous Scandinavian painter. Her husband told Pascin that since it was known that his wife had left him, it would be very embarrassing if she and Pascin continued to come to the Duomo. They made a pact. Pascin and Louise would switch over to the Rotonde; the Scandinavian could continue to patronize the Duomo.

I asked where Louise was and Pascin launched into a complicated tale about a huge party he had given two nights before at a restaurant in the Montmartre for all his artist friends and models. While coffee and liqueur were being served, Pascin had gone off to a *chambre séparée* with a lovely Negro girl who was one of the guests. Louise discovered them and left Pascin, who now piteously complained, "I thought she knew that I loved only her. Why should she object to my having a little fun? I thought she loved me." He said it so sweetly and so innocently that I burst out laughing and he was hurt at my lack of feelings. Pascin was often roguish and naughty, but never coarse or vulgar. This characteristic was strangely combined with an intense vulnerability and sensitivity. He had frequent attacks of despair, and in 1931 my old friend committed suicide. It was a great sadness to me.

Pascin was as much tormented by his creative problems as

by anything else in his life, and this torment is characteristic of the artist, rather than the mere producer. In painting, the "maker" knows exactly what he wants to produce; before starting he visualizes the finished product. Year after year he is content to repeat this process, although he may use slight variations in color, dimension, or form. He has learned to paint the picture he has in mind as well as he knows how, and there is no need to strive for better. It fits his own requirement, is good to look at, and very often, in the latest style.

The creative artist, on the other hand, cannot foresee the finished product because he grows, not merely from year to year or week to week, but during the very performance of his work. This concept was brought forcibly to my mind one evening after I had left Paris and gone to Rome. I went to see Eleonora Duse performing as Ibsen's Mrs. Alving. The last scene was completely stunning and the audience was quite carried away. A friend took me backstage to meet Duse, and we found her in her dressing room, moaning and swaying gently, her arms hanging helplessly at her sides. She kept repeating, "*Che disgracia, che disgracia.*" We asked her what possible disgrace she could be referring to and she said it was the last scene. "But it was perfect," her friend assured her. "You have never done it so well."

"I know," Duse replied, "but while I was doing it, I suddenly realized how it should really be done. Let me show you." And, jumping from her chair, she showed us. "You see what I mean?" she asked when she finished. She turned her radiant face to us, and in the harsh light of the dressing room, tears traced a brilliant pattern on her cheeks. We could not suppress our own tears, and thanking her deeply, we withdrew.

The same sort of experience was related to me by Chaliapin who at breakfast one morning greeted me with, "Did you see *the* performance of *Boris* last night? I was wonderful. No, what am I saying? I was a dunce, but what happened to *Me*—that was wonderful." Chaliapin then told me that he had played Boris hundreds of times, with slight variations, some nights for the better, some nights worse. At this performance he had suddenly found himself on the wrong side of the stage having walked there unconsciously while singing an aria. This seemingly small detail of staging had fired him with inspiration. He shouted at me, "When I saw where I was I panicked, but then I realized that this was the better way. What a fool I was not to have realized it long ago, a fool, an idiot, but Thank God, no more." And I added quietly, "Until you find another new way."

Rome was very gay and charged with emotional excitement. I would work, see old friends like Leo Stein, Berenson, and others, and also a Roman woman I found fascinating. Then, I heard that Vera had left Elizabeth Duncan's group and was in Vienna, and I went there for a visit.

Vera Sterne continues:

Elizabeth had been having great financial problems and certain personal difficulties which were making it hard to continue with the Tarrytown School. When the war was over, the German government offered her the use of Wildparke, the Kaiser's summer palace near Potsdam. In return, she was to take into the school about thirty German girls orphaned in the war. There were about fifty girls in all at Wildparke, and although it was a beautiful place, one remembers vividly that all fifty of us shared one bathroom!

We would go on tours and give recitals and happily practice in the palace. I had been feeling for some time, however, that I had learned from Elizabeth most of what she had to teach, and that although my own dancing conveyed feeling and expression, it lacked technical strength. We left Potsdam to go on tour, and after our Vienna performance, I decided to remain and study there.

Vienna was gay and lovely, filled with suitors and

beaux. I saw Carl Loesser in Potsdam, then in Vienna, dashed down to Italy where I gave a recital, dined with Berenson, went back to Vienna and enjoyed the company of Joe Asch, who had come to study with Freud.

Maurice heard about all the charming gentlemen pressing for my hand and very quickly left Rome and joined me in Vienna.

When I got to Vienna I found that the sophisticated Viennese could not believe that so naïve and simple a woman as Vera still existed. They were charmed with her. For myself, right before we got married I had been in the midst of a very intense and passionate love affair in Rome. I believed that my main reason for rushing off to Vienna was that my Roman attachment was growing very serious, and I was determined to honor my promise to Vera, that if ever I married, it would be to her.

I really did not understand at all, at the time, why I felt compelled toward Vera. My Roman friend, although she did not particularly interest me intellectually, was the most erotically stimulating woman. I was utterly blind to the fact that there must have been spiritual motives pushing me then, which after many years of affectionate companionship, I consciously discovered.

None of this was easy for me. When we got married I felt self-satisfied at having done the right thing, but I soon found that it was almost impossible for me to give up my old, free ways. I am afraid that my poor Vera suffered greatly for a time. Eventually her patience and devotion taught me that there is such a thing as perfect harmony and happiness, and many years later I learned to look upon women as friends and companions, rather than mistresses. I weighed Vera against all the other women in the world, and learned fidelity.

Perhaps in contrast to purely sensual attraction, spiritual affinity is at first a blind impulse that evolves slowly into a greater and more permanent maturity.

Vera Sterne describes her wedding:

After Maurice's unfortunate experiences in his first marriage, I believe he was very hesitant about marrying again. Mabel had been very aggressive in their marriage, and Maurice now just wouldn't be "caught," although there were several serious attempts. I, on the other hand, never pressed Maurice or seemed anxious to marry, and, really, I was too absorbed in my own work and in trying to be a great dancer to give the matter much attention.

As an added difficulty, Mabel was at first very reluctant to divorce Maurice. I don't really know why, but I imagine that she wanted to protect herself from having to marry her Indian lover Tony, or perhaps she just was reluctant to give Maurice up entirely. Finally she did agree and she was granted a divorce for non-support.

When we decided to get married that year in Vienna we found that the mechanics of the thing were very complicated. I had to write for my birth certificate, and Maurice was told that he had to have at least three months' residence in Vienna. Since he was terribly absorbed in a large canvas he was working on in Anticoli, it seemed impossible to fulfill these requirements.

While all these negotiations were going on, we went one day to a Vienna Museum with Joe Asch. After climbing the long stairway to the entrance we discovered a big placard on the door stating that the museum was closed for a religious holiday. We were quite disappointed but as we came down the steps a Rolls-Royce drew up and we met its distinguished passenger halfway down the steps. Joe stopped him to tell him that the museum was closed, but he replied, "I know, I'm the Director." Joe introduced himself and presented Maurice as "America's finest artist." They were all soon engaged in enthusiastic German conversation which ended with the Director inviting us to his home to show us his private collection of paintings.

It was an exquisitely furnished house with marvelous works

of art. Maurice was very excited with the masterpieces he had never before seen and I could see how impressed our host was with his appreciation and knowledge. Eventually the talk got around to our difficulties in getting married. The Director asked whether we were both Jewish, went to the phone, and arranged with the rabbi of a large Vienna synagogue to have the ceremony take place on Sunday of the following week. Maurice had to pay the equivalent of about one hundred and fifty American dollars for the necessary papers.

Late Saturday afternoon he realized that he had forgotten to buy a ring. We caught a jeweler on the Kärntnerstrasse just as he was closing for the weekend, and Maurice picked a lovely pale gold antique ring. The next morning, on June 3, 1923, my eighteenth birthday, we were married under the "huppa," the traditional Jewish marriage bower.

The Baron von Strakosch gave a wedding lunch for us. All sorts of famous Viennese were present, all sorts of famous Viennese dishes were served, but I am afraid that I noticed little but my own excitement.

We spent our honeymoon in Venice, primarily with Gustav Mahler's widow, Alma, and Franz Werfel with whom she was staying at the time. Maurice and Werfel had so much to talk about, the days weren't long enough for them. Alma and Werfel were later married, but I think that on that visit Alma was quite smitten with my fascinating husband, although on our honeymoon he had eyes only for me.

We left Venice for Rome, and then proceeded down to Anticoli.

Although Anticoli Corrado is only 60 kilometers from Rome, on our honeymoon trip in 1923 it took us three hours to get there, what with the slow puffing up the hills, and the fact that we had to change at Mandela, where the Roman train ended its trip. The Anticoli train looked like an old-fashioned American trolley car. It was crowded with peasants carrying corn flour, potatoes, and other produce wrapped in large rough gray cloths. The men slung their parcels over their shoulders; the women carried them on their heads. The young girls wore modern dress with high-heeled shoes which gave them a strange staccato gait, launched from the hips, and a most unaccustomed and uncomfortable way of perambulating. The older women wore four or five huge wide skirts, one on top of the other, and laced worn dark corsets over them. Both men and women wore *ciocce*, shoes made of goatskins, brought around the soles of the foot to fold over at the toes. They were laced down the front of the foot and tied at the ankles with thick cord.

We arrived at the foot of the hill at Anticoli at about seven o'clock in the evening. There to greet us was the Anticoli musical band, Ned and Peggy Bruce, and a group of Maurice's local friends. As we came up the hill the band played a recognizable, if somewhat off-key version of the Wedding March and of The Star-Spangled Banner. The peasants swarmed around Maurice embracing him and congratulating him. Then they turned to me and looked me over, with small cries of *"Carina, carina! Bionde como miele!"* Then the formal hand-shaking began, and continued until mine was quite numb.

Ned, Peggy, Maurice, and I drove up the long and winding dirt road in a cart pulled by two old nags. The peasants followed after us singing, in shrill, nasal voices, the *Stornelli Romani*. These were very old folk songs about love and remorse. At that time I didn't know any Italian and did not understand the meaning of the songs at all, but I was impressed with the strange beauty of the music, with its half, quarter, and eighth-tone endings. I had never heard this form before, but it reminded me then of the Orient.

After a half-hour climb we arrived at the Piazza della Villa—a large open space surrounded by houses, with a fountain in the middle. This was the center of town and was the scene of many of Maurice's paintings. We got down from the cart and walked away from the piazza through narrow muddy alleys. These winding passages were, for the most part,

Vera Sterne and another model, posing in the studio in Anticoli
for a work of sculpture

The jury of award for the 28th Carnegie Institute International Exhibition of Paintings, Pittsburgh, 1929. Seated, left to right: André Dunoyer de Segonzac, Charles Hopkinson, Vivian Forbes; standing: Wladyslaw Jarocki, Homer Saint-Gauder Maurice Sterne, Leon Kroll (*Museum of Art, Carnegie Institute*)

the only streets in Anticoli. We followed them that evening to a steep flight of stone steps which led to the Castello on top of the hill. This was to be our home for the next few years.

Ned and Peggy had arranged a wedding party and had invited the three or four American painters who were then working in Anticoli. Also at the party were four attractive women who had been Maurice's students at the Art Students' League in New York. They had followed him to Rome, where he also held a class, and were now in Anticoli to be with him. I realize now how attractive they were, although at first I considered that because they were all between the ages of 28 and 35, they were too old to be pretty or taken seriously.

The table was a wonderful sight, for the Bruces had gone all the way to Rome for delicacies. In the center there was a white-frosted wedding cake of enormous proportions, topped by a miniature painter, palette in hand, and a dancer poised for flight. There were many bottles of champagne and the party seems to have gone on most of the night, but I wasn't used to anything stronger than ice-cream sodas and I fell asleep very early in the celebration.

The next morning I explored the "castle" which was my first married home. The kitchen was to the left of the wide stone stairway. Its dark walls were hung with a collection of gleaming and beautiful copper pots. Cooking was done on an open brick stove with squares cut out at the top in which one placed the charcoal. It was quite an ordeal to fan the charcoal into a brilliant flame, and at night the burning coals were carefully bedded down with ashes to preserve fire for breakfast.

There was an open square space in the center of the room for washing dishes, but there was no drainage, and no running water. Dirty water was thrown out the window but every fresh drop had to be fetched by the women from the fountain on the piazza. Delicious, clear cold water came down from the hills above the town. They carried it on their heads in large brass or copper *concas*. The rhythmic, swaying passage of the women of Anticoli as they went about this work was beautiful to watch, and a part of the life there.

There was a huge room to the right of the stairwell which probably had served as a reception hall for Don Giovanni, our landlord, and the Count of Anticoli. (He was a burly, mustached man, who loved liquor and dancing, and I heard later from the peasant women that his name was appropriate because he was always chasing them.)

The ceiling of the hall was covered with painted panels and frescoes of angels, saints, and flowers, but the floor, as in all of the Castello, was made of rough red bricks. The room had grand proportions, about 60 feet long and 30 feet high, but I cannot remember that there was a single piece of furniture in it. Later, I put in a piano and a victrola, and a few pieces of comfortable furniture.

My pride and joy was a soft gray felt rug which Maurice had bought me as a wedding present. It covered the length of the rough brick floor and changed the huge old room into my dancing studio. Without the rug I could not have used the room, since I had been taught by the Duncans to dance barefoot. From then on, I spent most of my time there.

Near the outside door there was a smaller room with a wonderful view, which Maurice and Ned Bruce used as a studio. It overlooked the rolling hills, the olive trees, the rock-hewn houses clustered on the side of the hill, the village of Roviano on top of the opposite mountain, the Agnene River at the bottom of the valley.

The house had an interior garden, like a medieval planting, with an open loggia surrounding it. How can I describe what it was like that first June I saw it? There were raucously blooming rhododendrons, fig trees with tiny, silvery figs, vines bending over with clusters of young grapes, olive trees, silver-green in the sunlight with trunks like gnarled old men struggling for life. The air was light, the sky a soft blue, like the skies in the Piero della Francescas that Maurice had taught me to love.

The house was, I suppose, quite primitive—for sanitation there was a dimly lit outhouse, or the bedside *vasa di notte;* the straw mattresses and iron beds were not very comfortable. But none of these things made much impression on me, or seemed to matter.

On the day after my arrival, many of Maurice's Anticoli friends came calling. They brought gifts for the bride and groom of eggs fresh from their nests; huge light sponge cakes; a delicious cake made from ricotta cheese, eggs and sugar; trout from the Agnene; freshly killed chickens. All these things were great delicacies, reserved for special occasions. The peasants' usual fare was very frugal—a large red onion and dry bread for lunch with wine when the harvest was good. Even spaghetti was a delicacy for them.

I was greatly impressed with the beauty of the Anticoli peasants. The men were very virile, with noble bearing, some of their heads strongly suggesting sculpture of ancient Roman senators. The young girls were exquisite. They had large eyes, black, brown, or amber-colored, beautifully proportioned faces, huge masses of black or dark brown hair. The more mature men and women, even the very old people, had a look that was full of character, their heads very strong and magnificently constructed. They looked like what they were —descendants of the Saracens, pure African types who had come down from Saracinesco to Cervara and Anticoli, where the Italians finally defeated them in the Sabine Hills.

Because of the great beauty of its people, Anticoli had become famous for its extraordinary models. It had been a haven for artists from all over the world for many years, and when I first came, many of them were living in local pensiones, where food, lodging, and wine could be had for one dollar a day. As a matter of fact, I have heard that in the Vatican there is a document which shows that Michelangelo had used the natives of Cervara, Vicovaro, and Anticoli Corrado as models for the frescoes in the Sistine Chapel.

To the people of Anticoli, whose life was a difficult struggle with arid soil and lack of work, a child was a sacred being. It was considered a sort of dishonor not to have children, the *raison d'être* for marriage. They had a very touching, though sensible custom. Whenever a woman lost a child at birth (and as there were no doctors or antiseptics, this happened too frequently) they immediately went to a Roman orphanage and adopted a baby. That they were desperately poor and their clothes were ragged did not stop them. They believed it was a sin to waste their God-given milk.

Though the peasants, with few exceptions, could not read or write, they were sensitive and fine-mannered, with an innate culture and wisdom that was perhaps born of the tragedy in their lives. Maurice had spoken often to me of his affection for them, and when I arrived in Anticoli, I, too, loved them at once.

There was only one store in town at that time, a sort of hole in the wall on the piazza, where the charming, but sharp-faced Agata sold salt and tobacco to the peasants. Salt was a precious commodity and the peasants only bought a few centissimi a week. Several times Maurice saw Agata press her thumb on the back of the scales when she weighed salt out, but when he accused her of cheating, she laughingly replied, "*Che vuole*, Signor Sterne? A grain of salt more or less won't be missed by them, but by the end of the month, I will have enough extra lires to buy my coffee in Rome."

We had to go to Rome ourselves every ten days or two weeks to buy all the food staples. Peggy Bruce and I would start at dawn walking about four miles down the steep hill. In the soft, hazy light the countryside took on an eerie beauty. The familiar hills were strange shadows, the olive trees a misty silver, like dawn on the water. As we passed through the village, it, too, was slowly awakening. Here, a woman fed her big black pigs, an old man loaded his donkey with a huge bag of straw, others pulled their burdened animals up the long hill. There is a painting of Maurice's at the Metropolitan Museum in New York called "Winding Path" that expresses all this so

178

much better than I can.

Another painting, "American in Anticoli," is of an aspect of Anticoli life that was a private pleasure of mine. It shows me standing in the round metal tub we used to bathe in, with the two little maids, Laura and Peppina, in attendance. There was a wonderful luxury about being scrubbed with the rough fibrous cloth they used, and sitting quietly while they poured hot water over my back. The background of the painting shows the rhythmic symmetry of the Anticoli piazza, through the open loggia.

Less inspiring, perhaps, but equally vivid in my memory, were the smells of the village and its people. One day Maurice and I were standing in the piazza, talking to a toothless old crone Maurice had known for many years. She was nibbling at some pieces of "baccala," dried and salted codfish, which she would pull out of her bosom from time to time. She stood telling Maurice a long, involved story in the Roman dialect they used in Anticoli, and when she left there remained in the charming plaza a strong aura of fish and of several human bodily functions. She was a model for Maurice's drawing called "Old Woman" which the critics and art historians compared with the drawings of Dürer.

The people of Anticoli were very garrulous. In the evening you would hear all the family and marital problems of the villagers loudly aired through their open windows or on the piazza itself. Maurice told the story of one of these public arguments to Franz Werfel when we were on a trip to Venice. Werfel was very impressed and asked Maurice's permission to use the little tale. He later sent us a copy of his book, *Verdi*, in which the story appeared and although Maurice greatly enjoyed Werfel's version, he went on telling it in his own lovely way:

———————

Caterina had worked for me on and off for many years, and was to be my cook and servant for fifteen years in all. She must have been in her mid-thirties when she came to work for me.

No one knew who her father was, and her mother, a thirteen-year-old girl, had died in childbirth, at the San Spiritu Hospital in Rome. With the same clumsiness, the midwife who had failed to save the young mother's life also ruined the child's. Poor Caterina was torn from the womb in such a way that half her face and body was crushed by instruments, as if some bungling artisan had taken a lovely Etruscan statue and dropped it while the clay was wet, then fired the half-beautiful, half-grotesque figure.

Probably because of her deformity, Caterina seemed set apart from the rest of the community. I often wondered how her frail, maimed body could sustain the enormous passions that seemed to consume her, that would spill out in her heated soliloquies in the kitchen. It was only when the kitchen was silent that I worried about the tempers of that well-disciplined soul. One day she served breakfast in absolute, impenetrable silence, then went back to the kitchen where the only sound was the fierce clatter of her pots and pans. I had never seen Caterina in such a state and felt uneasy about her all day.

The storm broke in all its fury while I was working in my studio. I heard shrieking and rushed out to find a neighbor, Augusta, out on the stoop of her house, arms crossed on her chest, eyes flashing, spitting her mocking, poisonous anger out at Caterina. She was fury let loose, in a kind of overwhelming and vicious beauty. Caterina had herself in better control, carefully formed her words and pauses, and at just the right moment shot her arrows up the stoop, then leaned back to watch their effect.

At one point, one of Augusta's nine children began to cry and Caterina surprised me with her venom. "Better look after your kids! Isn't that Carlicino who's crying? Are you afraid we'll get a good look at him if you pick him up? Do you think we're really so stupid that we don't know where he got that blond hair and blue eyes and pug nose? We all saw that same face two years ago. By the way, what language does he speak?"

It was too much for Augusta to take. She in turn began to shout comments upon Caterina's legitimacy until a man on the street told her to be still.

At that, Augusta shouted even louder. "You vicious old hag! If you were not a poor cripple, I would—" That was as far as she got. Caterina dropped her arms, grew deadly pale, and turning her back on the silent and victorious Augusta, she began to walk away. Then she turned, fumbled in her jacket, and drew out a few coins which she flung at Augusta's feet. "Here, take some money and go buy goat's milk for your baby. Everyone knows that you are a dried up *bestia*. You have to feed your baby goat's milk not fit for a Christian because your breasts are all withered up."

Augusta howled. "What, my breasts are shrunk? I lack milk for my bambino?" She tore open her blouse, grabbed a round full breast in each hand, and with deadly accuracy, aimed two streams of gray-white milk straight at Caterina's face.

A thousand years of elocution lessons could not teach a Nordic orator this sort of power—that the Italian has as his birthright, a body not only the home of the spirit, but its messenger. I wonder if that extraordinarily developed sense of touch in Italian art, which Bernard Berenson has aptly called "the tactile," finds its complementary in the Italian's eloquent speech of gesture?

And how long it took me to see this beauty! All those years I wasted, when I was blind to the loveliness of my immediate surroundings, irritated when I might have been stimulated. I even read a book at all my meals so that I would not have to listen to Caterina's chatter! I talked and wrote a good deal about Anticoli in those years, but I missed more than I saw.

In an introduction to his show at the Bourgeois Gallery in April, 1922, Sterne recorded his impressions of Anticoli:

The paintings and drawings shown at this present exhibition were made during my last sojourn at Anticoli Corrado. I have lived twelve summers at this small village in the Sabine Hills and my interest grows with each return. Elsewhere life changes; here it is ever the same; elsewhere life vanishes before one's eyes; here there is leisure to observe it, to contemplate its meaning, to feel it. Here the grain is threshed by the feet of oxen as it was in the days of Methuselah; the ripe grape is squashed by the stamping feet of youths as in the bygone days of Dyonisius.

The ancient houses seem to grow from the rocks and foliage of the mountain side. There is no dividing line between architecture and landscape. The people and animals live together—no dividing line between man and beast. Unity. Harmony.

The peasants resisted any changes in their old ways of doing things. Carboni, a well-to-do landowner, decided one year to introduce more modern agricultural methods and, at harvest time, brought a mechanical threshing machine from Rome. The peasants stood around skeptically watching the monster do its work. As luck would have it, there was some minor mechanical problem, and the thresher broke down. This set the spectators off in wild laughter. There was no one in town who could repair the machine and Carboni had to send to Rome for the mechanic who was off somewhere else repairing another broken machine. The rains began, the harvest was ruined, and the next year they went back to their biblical traditions.

Years later Carboni induced them to try the thresher again with the assurance that a mechanic would always be available. Everything went smoothly and the harvest was taken in quickly and efficiently. However, when I returned to Anticoli after a three-year absence, I found that they were again threshing with oxen.

I asked Gigi, a farmer friend, why they had given up the thresher and he spat out, "Why? Ask the cattle why! Only God and the *bestia* know why. The animals would not touch the straw that came from that infernal machine! Some of them actually starved to death, others were so weak they were good for nothing at all. We finally had to go to the neighboring villages and, at ridiculous prices, *buy* the straw."

Vera Sterne continues:

Ned and Peggy Bruce had come to Anticoli shortly before our marriage. Ned was a very successful lawyer and business executive who had been a Sunday painter for years. When he was forty he decided to chuck it all and spend his life doing what he really wanted to. He sent a telegram to Maurice in Anticoli saying, "Can you help me become a painter in a year?" Maurice immediately wired back, "Come along." He moved from his little house on the piazza and rented the Castello where we all eventually lived together, although after the Bruces built their own modern house, Maurice and I went back to live on the piazza.

Maurice was having some financial problems at the time, partly because one-half the proceeds from the last Bourgeois sale were being held in New York. Ned was of great help in getting this money to Maurice more quickly. However, more importantly, until the successful shows later in the Twenties, Ned gave Maurice four thousand dollars a year to live on, although he himself was then getting some financial help from Galen Stone.

As a matter of fact, the finances of American artists and writers living in Europe at the time were terribly complicated. For example, the Bruces later bought a house at Settignano which they let Nina and Leo Stein use. They also sent Leo money for his support. Years later, after Ned's death, when Peggy really needed some help, Maurice got this money returned from Howard Gans, the financial executor of the Stein affairs.

Ned was a creatively stimulating influence on Maurice. He woke at dawn and worked through until dark and this application also kept Maurice at his easel. Peggy was a wonderful cook, and although she had Domenica to help her, the responsibility for the house was hers. We three others were free of ordinary cares. Ned and Maurice worked constantly and I developed new dance techniques and experimented to my heart's content. During these four or five years, working with Ned at his side, Maurice did some of his finest, best-known Anticoli paintings.

M·S

II

A few Anticoli paintings appeared at the 1924 annual exhibition of the "New Society," the newly formed Society of American Painters, Sculptors, and Gravers. Art critic Henry McBride reviewed the show and criticized Sterne for his poor characterization of Italians, and his excessive intellectualism. In particular, he pointed to a still-life of eggs as not having the "rhythm of placement that Cézanne so frequently managed to achieve."

Sterne's reply to this review follows:

> Villa Strohlfern
> fuori Porta del Popolo
> Rome, Jan. 27, '24

Dear McBride:

I was interested in your review of the New Society exhibition, and wish to thank you for the notice of my work. I never used to pay attention to what the critics wrote about my own or others' work. But now I see my mistake. The critic, speaking through the most powerful medium in the world, undoubtedly exercises a strong influence upon the opinion of his time. He either helps shape opinions in the making, or creates them for the ignorant. Since the number of the latter is large, the artist who believes that art should be related to life

185

must concern himself with the critic's doings because the ignorant constitute a much graver danger to us than the enlightened. But aside from my interest in the critic's activities, I am also interested in him—in his personality.

Does it ever occur to you that just as the artist reveals himself in his work to you critics, you reveal yourselves to him in yours? I doubt it. If it did you would either be more careful in your statements or you would hesitate to make them. I don't mean to be rude—I only wish to take up certain statements you made about me and my work.

You ask, "how can an American interpret Italians?" I ask, "how could a Greek interpret Spaniards, or a Spaniard Parisians?" If this contention were valid, we might ask, "how can a man interpret a woman, a puppy, a cabbage?" Perhaps in order to get the very essence of an onion, it ought to be painted by an onion. Then you continue: "Interpret is the word I should like to use and will be most happy to use some day when this artist deserves it." So would I! But I am not at all sure that the reason you were unable to apply it to my present work is due to any shortcoming on my part. You hope for my development—I for yours.

I do not like to make a statement unless I am ready to uphold it, so let me tell you why you believe that I do not "interpret" but "record" and what led you to this belief. The prevalent idea among the elite, of whom you are a distinguished example, has been the absurd notion that pictorial art, like music, can be independent of nature; hence, if the subject matter is too easily apparent, it must be deficient in abstract quality and therefore inferior as a work of art. This perversion has done much mischief. When nature, the standard of comparison, was eliminated, judgment too became subjective and speculative. Painting became the medium of those who dispensed with nature entirely and found an easy outlet in the painting of moods, or others, who vaguely felt that nature should be the keynote but had not the necessary patience and stamina to arrive at an abstract vision through objective contemplation, and were content with things which were half-baked visually, by using camouflage. When the form was pathetically weak, camouflage was a safe guise to hide its defects. In the war, camouflage was used successfully as a ruse to fool the enemy. In art it bewildered the enemy and fooled the friend! Whenever nature is very obvious in a picture, the painter has not "interpreted" but only "recorded."

Do not misunderstand me. I do not defend mere photographic rendering more than you do. I dislike intensely the work of uncreative men, of those who paint from nature like a pianist playing from notes. I believe the painter should be more like the composer: Nature should be a theme upon which he improvises, and no more.

Another statement which I do not challenge, but partly agree with, is this: "He is intensely intellectual and started out in life with the idea that art is something that can be learned." I am not so sure that I am. The little intelligence I possess has been acquired through an intensive study of nature and work. And I never "started out in life with the idea that art is something that can be learned." If I had, and had I known what a hard job was ahead of me—I would never have had the courage. It was urge and nothing else that made me take up art—and it was only after years of struggling, after I had become acquainted with the good work of the past, that I began to realize what painstaking drudgery one must go through before one could but faintly approach it. And now, after having spent more than twenty-five years in the pursuit of learning, I am more than ever convinced of its truth and am happy to tell you that I am still learning and hope to go on learning to the end of my life.

Don't you realize that the kind of art you favor, the variety that was so much in vogue in Europe and hence in America—is dead. The unconscious "naïve" inventions of self-consciously unconscious "masters" is no longer taken seriously in Europe. The foremost painters here are trying to present (I beg your pardon, interpret) nature in all her brutally direct nakedness.

In Italy, in France, in fact wherever art is taken seriously, the conviction has firmly taken root that art is something that should be learned—and learned thoroughly—before one should dare express one's self.

Of course, perfect technique alone is not enough and I admit that the self-critical sense, when developed abnormally, stands in the heart's way, acting as a sort of censor, which eventually stunts spontaneous vision and expression. But did you ever study carefully work by universally accepted masters? As I write, there is before me a drawing by Michelangelo, one of the masterpieces of the Albertina. Every touch reveals profound knowledge coined into wisdom—acquired in lifelong study. Naturally there is more: a powerful passionate impulse. But this unconscious impulse is, when finding expression, born into consciousness.

True art language is probably this: the birth into consciousness of the unconscious; the significance of a work is in no greater degree due to the original impulse than to what we bring to it through lifelong study.

Whether my work is deficient in one of these fundamental qualities, neither you, dear friend, nor I, is capable of judging. This and many other questions of more or less interest to both of us, had better be left to time.

Faithfully yours
Maurice Sterne

Living in Italy, I was unaware that Paris was becoming the clearinghouse for art—that the Parisian dealers could make or break an artist's reputation so far as his international market value was concerned.

On one of my visits to Paris, my friend, Adolph Basler, who was a dealer, informed me that one of the most important galleries, the Barbizange, was interested in my work. He took me to a very large and sumptuous gallery, where the owner proposed that he become my Paris representative. I was to turn over all my work for the following six years and in return I would get an annual allowance. I asked what he intended to do with my paintings and drawings during those years, and he replied that I would have to trust his discretion.

I had heard that the French dealers often kept an artist's works stored away for years before they made any effort to promote him, and I remembered Rodin's warning not to have anything to do with them. I told this dealer that I would have to think his proposal over.

He was polite and very gracious about my work and said that he hoped to be able to help me build up a reputation in France "where," he said, "you are practically unknown."

As soon as Basler and I left I asked Basler to tell Barbizange that I wasn't interested in his offer.

Since then, I have often regretted my hasty decision, but at the time the whole idea didn't appeal to me. It appeared like some scheme and not an honest business transaction. Later I learned that it was quite the custom—that even Matisse had made such an arrangement.

A couple of years later, on my next visit to Paris, Basler, who was adamant that I build a reputation in Paris, told me that the same M. Barbizange would like to give me a one-man exhibition. I was interested in this idea until the question of expense arose. I informed the dealer that most of my paintings and drawings were in my studio in Rome, and quite a number were in America. I thought these things should be shown, but I cautioned him that the expense of packing and transportation would come pretty high. He said, "Of course you will have to pay for all that. I am not going to charge you any rental, although it is quite customary here for shows to be arranged for a pretty stiff price. Even so, there will be other expenses which you will have to assume: printing, advertising —and the press would have to be 'encouraged' to write something enthusiastic." He grinned cynically. "Believe me, it would be a good investment. It certainly would not do you any harm if one of your pictures were purchased by the Luxembourg Gallery."

"Do you mean to tell me that the Paris critics have to be bought?"

He replied, "Not all, but some," and I was shocked.

"You'd be surprised," he added, "but this sort of negotiation is quite an art in itself. It requires the utmost discretion and dexterity, and the dealers have to be masters at it."

I thanked him for his kind interest. I had never spent a penny for the privilege of showing my work, and I didn't intend to. I told him that under those circumstances I was obliged to refuse his offer.

When I was leaving, he said, "You are young and an idealist. It is people like you who most need the help of realists. Some day you will probably find that out. I only hope for your sake that it won't be too late."

In 1925, many Sterne paintings and sculptures were shown at the Biennale exhibit in Rome. A letter to Vera Sterne, who was in Paris at the time, discusses the frustrating problems of public showings:

Hotel Princesse
Friday

Well schnuckel, if I had known what a lot of work is connected with a show—I never would have done it. I was never satisfied with the place I had put the statue [sculpture for which Vera Sterne posed, called "The Awakening"]. First of all the light was abominable and besides, they had put all sorts of odds and ends in drawing, painting, and sculpture in the same room and as I am known as a painter, no one would ever dream that the statue too was mine. Every time I passed her, it gave me a pang—she seemed to choke in her surroundings. So today, I suddenly decided to put her into my rooms—the larger one where the paintings are—and you have no idea what it meant. She came alive and looks fine in her natural surroundings, that is, with my own work as a background. I had finished the hanging yesterday, and today,

THE WINDING PATH (1924)

suddenly, the Paris pictures arrived, practically in the nick of time, for tomorrow morning there will be the press review. I didn't know the opening of the Biennale is such a swell and important function. The King inaugurates the show and all the ambassadors attend in full uniform. In a way I'll be sorry that my little golden flower child wifey will not be here to be presented to that swell bunch for you have suffered with me in the birth of my works, especially the statue, and we ought to get the little pleasure there is possible in the less vital, but rather pleasant way. But I know that sort of thing means as little to you as it does to me. I was surprised to see how well my New York pictures look—everyone is crazy over "Ines" —even more than the "Breadmakers." She is seen just behind the statue and looks like a lovely old tapestry. They assure me that the exhibition will open on Tuesday—I will run out to Anticoli on Sunday (I haven't been there since I left 10 days ago), will arrange my things and get what I need for Paris, and will leave the day following the opening. Leo is anxious to see me about the article for the statue [1] so I may spend a few days in Florence. . . . Miss Gibson descended on me yesterday and took my photograph coming down the steps of the Palazzo de Espasizione for the *New York Times* Supplement.

With all my love and affection—

More than anything else, in those Italian days I was absorbed with the human figure. For three years nude models had posed for me in every imaginable position and I could think of practically nothing else. A Swiss sculptor was visiting in Anticoli that year and he was very interested in modeling animals. Since it was harvest time I thought he would enjoy watching the oxen at work and we went off to the fields late one afternoon. When we got there, the peasants and their animals had already left for the day, and, like good "bourgeois," we lay down to watch the sunset. The sky was filled

[1] Leo Stein, "Tradition and Art," *The Arts*, Vol. VII (May, 1925). An article illustrated with photographs of Sterne's "Awakening."

with huge gray clouds which the wind was pushing about. I was fascinated by the constant change of form. We had our sketch pads and we set to work. I drew the human bodies I saw in the single clouds and the freshly grouping forms—one moment a pleasant pastoral scene, the next a battle of fierce giants. The human images that this light and shade had suggested to me appeared as animals on my friend's pad. A natural Rohrschach test, I suppose.

Another sculptor, David Edstrom, had been in Florence when I visited Leo Stein one year. The Steins had introduced me to Hutchins Hapgood, who was to become my dear friend, and I met Edstrom through him.

In his own autobiography [1] *Hapgood describes these incidents:*

It was in Florence that I first met Maurice Sterne. I was impressed with his concentrated mental force combined with a rich and deep temperament. Soon after I met him, I was browsing around in the Uffizi where I found him copying Leonardo's "Adoration of the Magi." Perhaps because of the unfinished condition of Leonardo's masterpiece, its intellectual form was singularly clear; and this fascinated Sterne so much that he worked over it for months. This concentration on work did not prevent Sterne at that time from being a café companion of the utmost abandon. I remember him and David Edstrom one night in one of the Florence cafés, attempting apparently to murder one another. It would have meant nothing to either to have gouged out the eyes of the other, and any handy object in the café, heavy and blunt enough, was used by both in the service of the gigantic cause in which they were fighting, which was a dispute about the nature of art. This didn't prevent them for a time from being

[1] Hutchins Hapgood, *A Victorian in the Modern World* (Harcourt, Brace, 1939), pp. 219-20.

constant companions; and, under the influence of the surrounding art and of the good wine of Florence, they lived
in the ecstatic heaven of mutual admiration; for each to
the other was the greatest spirit yet. Sterne, of course,
worked from under, for with him it was only a momentary illusion. During this explosive moment I was occasionally admitted to the august association; and I had my
moment of triumph, for they admitted that, on account
of my great diplomacy I was admirably fitted to become
president [sic] of the United States. The occasion of this
remarkable discovery was one night when we were together at Giacosa's, a pastry shop, drinking vermouth.

*Sterne's notes tell us a little about this incident in the pastry
shop:*

David Edstrom had small, triangular gray-blue eyes that
gave him a mean and suspicious look. As he came in the shop
he turned this look on Hutch and snarled, "You are the last
person I want to see."

Hutch answered, "Good, that suits me fine. I hope it
happens soon, but meanwhile, sit down and have a drink."

Edstrom seemed in a savage mood. He spat out some quite
personal poison about Leo and Gertrude Stein, and, as there
were several English-speaking people around, I tried to steer
the conversation to more objective topics. When I mentioned
the powerful Florentine sense of form, he yelled, "The hell
with form! Form is death! Only things in the process of
formation have life. The sculptor should show how he feels
about the things he sees, not how things are." He pulled some
photographs from his pocket. "Here, look at these. They are
the best sculpture of our time—of all time!"

I looked at the photographs and quickly saw in his work
what his looks had shown about his life—a lack of form. It was
the first time I realized that one must *have* form in order to
express it. However, I tried to be "nice" and told him his work

was interesting. He favored me with one of his suspicious looks and said, "You don't like what I am doing, you don't like my work."

I admitted he was right and when he pressed me for an explanation, I said: "You are too damn preoccupied with your innate emotions, and you're obviously blind to intrinsic form."

"I shit on your form!" he shouted.

"I shit on your emotion," I answered.

He grabbed me by the throat and began to choke me but Hutch helped me break away. Edstrom left then and Hutch explained to me that the sculptor was under great strain. His wife had left him, he had become a morphine addict, and he drank heavily. Hutch added that he himself was writing a book about Edstrom.

I said, "Leo told me that you've written a story about a thief, and also the story of a prostitute. Now you seem to be proving the adage: 'All good things come in three's'—You'll have a working trilogy—of bad to worse, to worst!"

The next morning I was still in bed when Edstrom burst into my room on the Lugarno Acciauoli. My throat was sore and I could hardly swallow.

He apologized for attacking me the previous night and explained that he had been drunk. Then he stared at my bruised throat and said, "My God, did I do that?" He burst into tears.

I told him not to feel badly about it but when I looked in the mirror myself, I somewhat ruefully added—"No wonder you are only a sculptor—as a painter you would love this symphony in blue violet, green and yellow, with such a delicate purple border—why it's a superb example of your emotional art!"

He began to grin and I told him that I was glad that he worked in clay and not marble. I added, "I hate to think what might have happened if you had been a stonecutter."

Edstrom told me that he hated all Americans in Florence,

194

that Leo Stein was a vain conceited mummy and his sister
Gertrude an inflated Lady-Buddha. As to Hutch Hapgood,
Edstrom vowed he would kill him. He said that Hutch was a
vampire, a bloodsucker, a leech who pumped him dry, who
dug slimy fingers into Edstrom's sensitive soul.

A few days later, Hutch told me that on the very day of this
violent outburst Edstrom had worked with him on the book
and had made great progress. The book was to be called, "The
Story of a Soul"—a soul that gloried in its own degradation.

I felt that in a certain sense Edstrom was right. People like
Leo, who glorified the intellect, but had no conception of a
soul, because they had no soul themselves, could have little
insight in these matters. Neither could Hutch, who groveled in
inhuman filth, and tried to pull himself from his own quagmire
by exposing the degradation of thieves and whores—thus to
assert his own superiority.

I tried to argue with Hutch about this, but he accused me of
not really "getting" people, especially those I was fond of. He
said that my own approach was too intellectual—that only a
true mystic can perceive the God in things. I said, "You mean
the God within yourself." "Yes," he shouted, "the God in me.
Why not? Because my body is racked with disease? Because I
am ugly? No one, not even you, can remotely perceive the
holiness of my spirit, its sublimity and its grandeur."

I asked him if he approved of the phrase, "Thy will be done
on Earth as it is in Heaven," and he snapped, "What the hell
has that got to do with it?"

He had missed the point again.

There was an ironic end to the Edstrom-Hapgood story.
Edstrom had come to Florence to die, Hutch to record the
death. But although Hutch's book was not complete, Edstrom
suddenly left for Paris. He met a lady Christian Science healer
there, who rid him of TB, morphine, and his other vices, and
then married the resurrected sculptor. He also took up healing
as a profession and they both prospered.

A few years later I ran into Edstrom in Paris and couldn't

believe my eyes. He had grown fat and uninteresting, the round, prosperous Christian Scientist husband of a round, prosperous Christian Scientist wife. Along with the vice had gone the fire we all had admired.

Vera Sterne continues:

We spent the years from 1923 to 1929 in Anticoli Corrado, with winters in Rome and an occasional few months in New York. We rented the small Villa Strohlfern in Rome, an enchanting place outside the Porta del Popolo, next to the Villa Borghese. We had many friends among the Italian and foreign journalists in Rome, and although we knew members of Roman "society" we did not spend much time with them as we found them rather shallow, more interested in clothes, dances, and rather childish love affairs than in ideas or art.

I had had two successful recitals in Rome and my personal friends were primarily musicians, among them Alfredo and Yvonne Cassella. He was then the outstanding pianist in Rome and a fine composer. Yvonne and I were great friends and I spent a lot of time at the Cassellas'. She used to tease me about my "easy" life, and would say that I was "*en pension chez Maurice Sterne.*" We met the Respighis at Yvonne's house and got to know them very well. When Gieseking came to Rome he used to practice all day long in the Cassellas' living room. I would sit for hours listening to his beautiful playing of Scarlatti.

One evening in 1926 Alfredo was to give a concert at the American Academy in Rome and Maurice and I received an invitation from the Academy to attend. Walter Lippmann, his wife Faye, and his young ward Jane were visiting us in Rome then and Maurice phoned the Academy to ask if we might bring the Lippmanns to the concert. The secretary to whom he spoke left the phone to consult with the director and returned with the message, "Neither Jews nor journalists are encouraged to attend the Academy."

196

Maurice was stunned and of course we did not go. We met our neighbor, Tom Morgan, that evening and told him about the incident. Tom was furious, and as he was the head of the United Press in Rome, the next day all the Roman papers as well as the American press carried the story.

Alfredo phoned to find out why we had not turned up. Yvonne, who was a French Jew herself, was enraged at the story and her red-haired temper added to the stir that the affair created in Rome during the following days. Several days later six dignified men in tall silk hats came to call at our villino. They were from the American Academy in Rome and were there to render an official apology.

1926 was a crucial year in my life. My exhibition at the Scott and Fowles Gallery in New York was very successful. Almost all of my paintings were sold to important collections, including that of Duncan Phillips, whom I considered one of the most discriminating collectors in the United States. The bronze "Awakening" was sold to Ralph Pulitzer; Adolph Lewisohn ordered a replica which he presented to the Brooklyn Museum; Galen Stone commissioned a marble copy which was to go to the Boston Museum on his death. On the last day of the exhibition a well-known collector of Italian Renaissance art bought everything that remained unsold—about twelve paintings and twelve drawings in all.

The exhibition had sold out. For the first time in my life I was out of debt. I paid my good friend Edward Bruce what I owed him, and still had one hundred thousand dollars left! This all happened during the Coolidge boom, when securities were skyrocketing, and now that I had the cash, I plunged into the market like everyone else. I took the advice of my barber, my doctor, and my banker friends. The one person I did not listen to was my best friend, Sam Lewisohn. When I asked him to look after my securities, he told me that he would handle my account like he did the affairs of widows and orphans, since artists are apt to be fools in money matters and ought to be carefully protected like other financial dependents.

I did not heed his advice, and when the reckoning came, I was back in debt. My losses in the Crash were in proportion to the social status of my advisors. My barber's advice cost me about fifteen thousand dollars, my doctor's about thirty thousand, and my banker's close to one hundred thousand dollars. That poor fellow felt very badly about getting me involved, but the fact was that his own bank was on the verge of bankruptcy and he had to give his personal fortune to save it.

Those few years of prosperity were the happiest I have ever known. Never before had I been free from financial worries and able to concentrate on my work. I felt lighthearted and independent and I was foolish enough to believe that I had found permanent security.

In 1927, while I was flying so high, Augustus John recommended me as the finest American portrait painter to a rich Chicago family who had asked him to come to America to do their portraits. I always hated commissioned portraits. I felt that I was prostituting myself when I did them, and in 1927 I could afford to refuse, although they offered me thirty thousand dollars for each portrait.

I wrote to them in 1929 after the Crash, and the former millionaire wrote back that if he still had the sixty thousand dollars he would use it to live on.

Besides financial problems during the next years, I was terribly hurt by a quarrel I had with Bernard Berenson, which took years to mend.

Vera Sterne remembers several luncheons and visits at "I Tatti" during the years shortly after she was married. There was apparently at least a close acquaintance between the two families. Evidently, some time during this period Sterne wrote to Berenson asking for an opinion of one of his new paintings

*or of his general progress. Berenson seems to have replied that
he was unwilling to express an opinion in a letter lest he
become known as Sterne's "protector." Sterne here describes
his own answer to this letter:*

I wish I had a copy of my answer. I wrote Berenson that I
had never had a protector, that I loathed the idea, and that I
could not understand what made him think that he was my
superior and therefore eligible to be my protector.

I had to learn when I was very young to be my own
protector. This is how I survived. There is nothing that makes
me so sad and so bitter as to think of the tragic fate of Mozart
or Schubert who tried to "practice virtue" without an income,
and died in their youth of privation. I am made of tougher,
more practical metal.

Of course, what hurt most was that a man of Berenson's
gifts knew how best to strike. Certainly, a struggling young
artist would derive much prestige if he could quote so famous
an authority as B. B. as having praised him. He was a Daniel
come to judgment, demanding his pound of humiliation.

I wonder whether it was because Berenson failed to find
beauty and perfection in people that he was forced to seek it in
art. His own conscious sense of superiority made him a cruel
friend. Not once did I hear him acknowledge the help and
patronage of Ned Warren who put him through Harvard and
made it possible for him to continue his studies abroad
indefinitely.

Much later in life Berenson was equally cruel and thought-
less toward Nina and Leo Stein. During World War II he
found refuge with an Italian nobleman. The Steins, on the
other hand, were close to starving in Settignano. Nina was
helpless in bed with arthritis and Leo burned their furniture to
get some warmth in the house. He had to stand in line for
hours for whatever bread was available and rationed to them.
In his impersonal way, Leo did not complain about B. B.'s
callousness, but never once did Berenson inquire about how

his long-time acquaintance was faring during the war, nor did he try in the least to help. The word "acquaintance" here is crucial; B. B. had no friends.

The most pressing difficulty of our last years there was that I could no longer stand the "new Italy" of Il Duce. The sense of repression that was in the air was even more terrible than the daily rule of the blackshirts. It was unbearable to see a free, spontaneous people, who always did and said what they pleased, suddenly curbed, muzzled, driven by a band of hoodlums. It hurt me to see their graceful walk turned into a German goose step, their eloquent gestures suppressed while black arms shot out in a stiff salute, "Duce, Duce."

These are not Italians, one reasoned. They're putting on a show and tomorrow it will be over. But the reality was all too convincing and terrible, even in Anticoli. At the end of World War I, Cesare, the town's perennial bully, had become a Communist and shouted his maledictions from the steps of the post office. However, when the Duce took over, Cesare became a fiercely raving fascist. When I asked him how a loyal Communist could turn so quickly into a fascist, he looked around furtively and said, *"La camicia e nera, ma il cuore e sempre rossa"*—"The shirt is black, but the heart is always red."

I preferred him as an open Communist, when his outbursts had been purely verbal. The minute he put on his black shirt he felt he had to give proof of his loyalty to the Roman Moloch. One day, during a fascist demonstration he was pushing people out of his way and Agata, who was pregnant at the time, told him to stop; whereupon he kicked her in the belly and the poor woman miscarried a seven-month dead baby.

In Rome, there were more frequent incidents of this kind. One day I saw half a dozen fascist hoodlums attack a teen-age boy right out on the Corso Umberto. They pinned him down and poured a quart of castor oil down his throat.

His crime? He was the son of an anti-fascist deputy who had made an opposition speech the day before. The people went by on the Corso as if nothing was happening, some assuming a mask of indifference, others looking away in horror. One elderly man stood at an open doorway with tears streaming down his cheeks. I was afraid the hoodlums would see him and beat him up too, so I went into his shop and made him follow me. He broke down in tears, "Signore, signore, what will happen to my beloved land?" We cried together and I tried to assure him that we would both live to see the end of these brutal barbarians. At that, he became terribly frightened and begged me to be discreet, lest I get into trouble. The old man's son-in-law had recently been arrested and returned to his family with a broken arm, and his left eye gone!

As Maurice Sterne's work began to be shown in the United States and abroad, his reputation as a serious and important artist grew. After the Third Biennial International Exhibit in Rome in 1925 he was invited to paint a self-portrait for the Uffizi Gallery in Florence, the first American so honored. The 1926 exhibit at the Scott and Fowles Galleries in New York was an enormous financial as well as critical success. After a show at the Reinhardt Galleries in New York in 1928, Sterne was asked to submit an entry to a competition held at the Art Institute of Chicago. There he won the Logan medal and a $750 cash prize. In 1929 he was elected president of the Society of American Painters, Sculptors, and Gravers. In 1930, at the Annual Exhibition of Contemporary American Oil Painting, Corcoran Gallery of Art, Washington, D.C., he won the Corcoran Gold Medal for his painting "After Lunch" and also the first William A. Clark prize of $2,000. That same year he won honorable mention for a painting at the 20th Carnegie Institute International Exhibition in Pittsburgh. Although the Depression seriously affected Sterne's earning power, just as he was gaining recognition, his financial records even for the troubled year of 1930 show a gross income of over $60,000.

Perhaps of the most permanent artistic significance during these years was the award, in 1926, of a commission to do the Rogers-Kennedy War Memorial in Worcester, Massachusetts. Sterne worked on this monumental sculpture in Italy for three years. In a note for an article written in 1928 for the Creative Arts[1] *magazine, he describes his work on this large sculpture group:*

In the spring of 1926 I submitted a model for the Rogers-Kennedy Competition in Worcester, Massachusetts. My model was chosen by the Commission from a group of ten submitted in the competition.

As I had taken great pains with the model and had made many preliminary studies and sketches, I expected the work to take a natural course. I imagined that it was only a question of enlarging my sketch and giving it more finish. I knew that in painting, a sketch can be of use only as a point of departure, never as a goal, since scale is an organic part of the composition; and I ought to have known that if this is true of painting, it is even more relevant to monumental sculpture. Of course, when I made my sketch I constantly would visualize the ultimate scale, but upon closer study I found that the main difficulty was not the question of relative proportions in height or width, but that it was almost impossible to visualize the projection in depth. The elevation of the observer was wrong, the relationships entirely different. In fact, I became convinced that the reason there are so many inferior public monuments is that the artists feel that they must follow the plans they have previously submitted.

I was anxious to get at the modeling but at the same time I realized the futility of doing so before establishing precise proportions. Meanwhile the months passed and I began to doubt whether two years were enough time to complete the difficult task of designing the architecture, modeling sixteen high reliefs containing twenty-four figures, and also sculpting the two large figures at the top. Gradually, my attitude toward

[1] *Creative Arts* (April, 1928).

the job changed. I had always considered my work as something intimate, a personal document, with every touch suggestive of my own momentary emotional state. Now I began to question the importance of this concept in the particular work I was doing. In literature, music, and architecture, the spiritual content, composition, and construction are important. We are satisfied to read a printed copy of a poem; we do not require the original manuscript. . . . As I began the modeling I found that the quality which I have valued most, the individual touch, was relatively unimportant in a work of this nature. . . . I realized that doing a monument was different from painting a picture. I questioned whether the intimate quality, the emotion, so essential in a painting, was really important in a large public monument, or whether it was even possible to sustain any emotion for the years it would take to finish and translate the work. I realized that I would have to adjust myself to leading an orchestra after thirty years of playing solo. I hired assistants, although I hated dealing with people in these circumstances. Gradually, after many problems, we began to work cooperatively together, although it took three years of problems until the work was finally finished, and assembled on the site in Worcester.

Even when the finished statuary was being received in Massachusetts I had almost daily reports of difficulties from Alexander Bullock, the long-suffering Chairman of the Memorial Commission.

On June 25, 1929, he had annoying troubles with the shipping company. On October 28, the base gave problems. Mr. Bullock wrote me:

> I regret to say that the right hand front corner stone was not cut with the same slant as the other three corner stones of the first tier. It will have to be chiselled down on the surface and the next two stones, which had already been layed, [sic] will have to be taken up and relaid.

On October 30, he reported still more trouble:

> I judge from Mr. Cross' man that the bronze's platform
> is three inches longer on one side than on the other. He
> says that it will require some stone cutting, but that the
> difficulty can be overcome. I hate to see these misfits be-
> cause they necessarily add to the cost. I am less mechanical
> even than you and can not explain exactly what must be
> done, but Cross' man says it would be easier to do the
> stone cutting before the top stones are set. Hence, your
> coming on next week would enable you to learn the ex-
> act situation.

On November 26, the landscaping went awry and the grading was too steep. Later the monument was obscured by snow. I thought it would never end.

The following critique of the monument, by Stark Young, was published in The New Republic, *on December 25, 1929.*

On December 6, Maurice Sterne's monument to the pioneer settlers, the gift of one of the citizens of Worcester, was unveiled. It stands in the city park, on a site chosen by the sculptor, a more or less triangular level of ground, at the foot of a slope and surrounded by trees. This setting is a part of the artist's inspiration. The monument has a flat of ground on which to rest and to state its structure and design. It can be seen from various elevations, below, above and around. Its mass, with its two surmounting figures, is seen not as the axis of present-day thoroughfares or the pivot of the surrounding traffic's wheels and eyes, but among trees, its forms against their forms, its constancy against their changing seasons, its pioneer subject against the vista and force of woods.

The monument consists, first, of a sort of base or pediment of Trani stone, a rectangle with a frieze on each of the four sides. The sculptures of the friezes are in high relief, more than half in the round sometimes, against backgrounds of the broken surface of hewn, unpolished stone. These reliefs are so set back into the stone that they do not protrude beyond the single plane of their framing stone; the panels are, therefore, in a sense flat, a flatness broken by these awakening forms within it, and filled with the life of their shadows and textures. These reliefs alternate narrower panels of single figures with groups in which there are three or four. . . .

Surmounting this rectangular base is a stone triangle, on which in turn is a triangle of bronze, and on this stand two bronze figures, a man and a woman, with a plough between them. The height of the whole monument is just under thirty feet. . . .

Mr. Maurice Sterne is the greatest draughtsman among all our artists, and this greatness of drawing pervades and distinguishes these figures of his sculpture. The complete idea of his pioneer monument is admirable: those two strong figures, between them that implement of the hard labor that separates them and binds them together, and makes man the master and child of the earth. They are the dream, the will, the muscle, the waiting, which have brought about the history of this world that has followed them; and beneath them is that mound of stone, which is like that world, peopled with the life and actions that they embodied, and that we see stirring there: the voyagers, tillers of the soil, hewers of wood, sowers, reapers, fishermen, boat builders that they were, with the sea, the land, the harvest, the thanksgiving, the child, the sickle, the pitcher of water, the net, the fire.

The main figures and the partitions of the relief are, as one might expect, unequal in excellence. Of the two, the man is more impressive than the woman; the central panel, the arrival on the sea, has not come so completely to rest in its design as have the other groups. Sometimes a head is a little forced in its position, and the upper part of one or two of the single figures is a trifle tight. But these limitations are less apparent in themselves than in the light of that firm, distinct sculpture everywhere achieved; that grave and tender discernment of

"The Awakening" (*In the Brooklyn Museum Collection,*
photo by Peter A. Juley & Son)

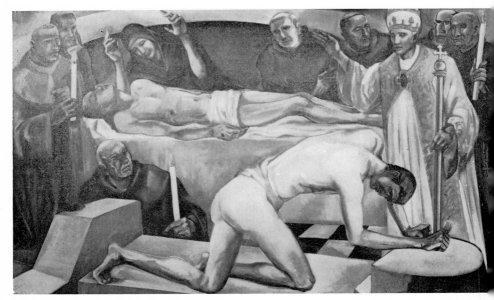

"Ordeal," a controversial panel from the mural "Man's Struggle for Justice" in the Library of the United States Department of Justice (*Photo by Marshall Moxom*)

life; that curiously solid and yet delicate statement; that profound, free intelligence; that humility and goodness by which the ideas are said so that all may understand them, or, at least the main point of them, which is as it should be in a monument, and finally that great piety and purity of emotion throughout the whole work.

Of the panels, the one likely to be most popular is the thanksgiving, the figures of a woman and man standing with bowed heads beside a table on which bread is. It is one of those things in art that run the danger of platitude, but, by this very humanity and plainness with which they apply to life, attain —if the treatment is direct, intense and deep enough—to a beauty all the greater. . . . To me the most moving of the reliefs is that of the fisherman: the bent head and simple contemplation, the rich ornate line of the boat's side, the net, the pouring forward of the whole composition, make it for me the most moving sculpture I have seen in a long time. As composition and superb thought in terms of design, the greatest of the groups is that where the man is working the timbers, and the woman sits with the child on her knees, his little boat in his hand, the fire springing up at their feet. It is genuinely and challengingly modern, and at the same time wholly within the most austere and magificent tradition.

On February 1, 1930, R. R. Tatlock, editor of the Burlington Art Magazine *in London wrote the following much-quoted phrase in* The Art News:

Quite frankly, I should prefer to see the Sterne monument in Hyde Park, London, England, rather than at Newton Hill, Worcester, Massachusetts, U.S.A.

This story was republished in the Worcester, Massachusetts, Telegram, *but the praise did not prevent a sizable outcry from that part of the local population who considered the monu-*

ment "too modern."

On August 14, 1930, Alexander H. Bullock wrote to Sterne in response to an inquiry about his health. He added a comment about the monument's reception locally:

I suppose you will say that it is a bad sign, but nearly everybody in Worcester, and I am speaking of the educated and the uneducated, likes the monument. There are a few of the educated who still look askance, because it does not look like the academic sculpture of the gay nineties.

Sterne's own reactions to the completed monument are noted in a letter to Leo Stein:

Silvermine, Connecticut
January 9, 1930

Dear Leo,

Your suspicions are well founded. We *have* left New York, about a week ago, but I could not write sooner—it took me that long to reassemble my battered and sore remains. . . . But I think you will be more interested in my actions than reactions. Nothing unexpected happened. The monument was unveiled about a month ago and is a really fine work. I was very nervous about it for I had only visualized it during the process of doing it—had never quite been able to verify my visual conception. I was prepared for all sorts of disagreeable surprises— There was only one surprise—the perfection of the thing. There isn't a detail which I would care to change. Sam Lewisohn took our party out on a special train. We had a glorious time; all our friends and many of the N.Y. art critics came out. My only regret was that you were not with us.

I have also been very successful with the few paintings which I did last summer. Everyone asks what has happened. I have suddenly become a painter. It must be because I have been modeling for the past three years—a sort of compensation.

New York is most exhilarating and stupendous—but too exciting, the wrongly directed movement for creative work. One is apt to become a transmitter, not an apparatus which had recorded and upon the pulling of a lever can give out what it has retained.

But New York is not America, at least not all of it. Out here, in Connecticut, life is not only possible, but quite enjoyable. Within the next few months we will decide whether we stay or go back. But *nix* for Rome. It will either be France or America, with an occasional relapse at Anticoli. . . .

Are you painting or drawing or writing or what? And how is your health and how is Nina? Write to me when you have a chance. I am longing for a letter. In America one gets only circulars, invitations, bills, announcements, and clippings.

After leaving Silvermine, Connecticut, the Sternes lived on Columbia Heights, in Brooklyn. Maurice was anxious to paint the view of New York from their apartment and remodeled it for use as a studio. However, he found that the art school he had established in Manhattan was, in its success, absorbing most of his time and energy. On December 28, 1931, in an interview with Louis Sherwin in the New York Evening Post, *he discussed his ideas about teaching art:*

One of the curious things one learns when one undertakes to teach painting is the extraordinary conservatism of [American] youth. . . . In the countries of the oldest culture you find the most extravagant departures and adventures. Futurism, for instance, originated among the Italians, the oldest nation of all . . . in the history of art. . . . Other eccentric movements began in France. Not any of them were born in new countries.

I am trying to teach painting and sculpture not because I have any notion that it is a profitable occupation, . . . but because I have a particular object. I am not trying to teach people to draw and model. Any ass can be taught to draw. I am trying to teach them to see. It is by cultivating not technique but vision that art will escape from conventional channels. . . .

When I was in Benares many years ago I encountered a hermit. He was occupied, apparently, in doing nothing. . . . For four years he had been concentrating on one idea and, he told me, was just beginning to realize new aspects of it that he had never imagined before.

It is that sort of concentration that we must develop in art. . . . The man who has the vision will find his own technique. To one who has seen something that I have not seen I say, "It is not for me to show you how to paint it."

The training of an artist is no specific curriculum. It is a matter of a lifetime. Wherefore I have found it pretty hopeless to try to do anything with those who have taken a course in any art school. For one thing, after they have studied in any academy for a couple of years they consider themselves not pupils but your colleagues and competitors!

When I was a young painter myself, my work was called "ultra-modern"; as I reached maturity, the ultra-moderns called me "old hat." But I have never been popular in either camp, and there was some truth in both accusations. I have always had the greatest respect for tradition, but have refused to be bullied by it. I have revered the old Italian masters, but have also learned a lot from the new masters of the glorious nineteenth-century French Renaissance—a proof also, I suppose, of the supranationalism of great art, though that is a more complicated subject.

On February 23, 1932, at the Whitney Museum of American Art, William Zorach, Joseph Pollet, Richard Lahey, and Maurice Sterne took part in a debate entitled, "Nationalism in Art—Is It an Advantage?" Edward Alden Jewell reviewed

the debate in The New York Times *of Sunday, February 28,*
1932:

Is there something in the Chinese artist and in the Dutch
artist, something deeper than the "symbols" they employ, that
can explain the vital difference? Could it possibly have
anything to do with rice and the Great Wall; with Edam
cheese and dykes; or, if these fail sufficiently to score, then
with Oriental and Occidental culture, with religion—Buddhism and Christianity?

"One must see Umbria in order to fully understand Perugino or Piero della Francesca," observes Maurice Sterne (and,
behold! he, like Mr. Pollet, is loading and booming the guns of
the opposition). In many respects Mr. Sterne's contribution to
the debate seems the most cogent and deeply pondered. Being
oversensitive and having had the grip [*sic*] lately, he confessed
in his preamble, Mr. Sterne was drawn somewhat against his
will into this battle of wits. But once drawn in, he rose nobly to
the occasion. If at times you wondered which side, after all, he
was on, that was because Sterne took, throughout, the long and
broad view. Certainly there was nothing partisan in his
championing of an "open-door" policy for art.

"Throughout the ages," he said, "significant art was not
national in character. It was international. Its language was
universal, understood by all, even if the content was of local
interest. . . . Whether this correlationship was brought about
by direct contact or by subtle infiltration, is hard to discover. . . . The fact remains that archaic Greek sculpture
bears strong resemblance to its neighboring Asiatic and Egyptian; that Byzantine painting descended directly from the
Greek; that early Florentine painting had its roots in Byzantine, &c." [*sic*]

[But] if one must see Umbria to understand Perugino and
Piero della Francesca, it is equally true that "when you have
become familiar with the Tuscan landscape you realize that

Giotto was not only a painter who spoke a language inherited from Cimabue, but also a realist who responded keenly to his native soil."

But if, as Mr. Sterne proposed (despite the fact that he was on the opposition side of the platform), if "we should encourage the growth of a national art," taking care not to confuse the terms nationalism and provincialism, we ought also to bear in mind the fact that "a national art has always been an unconscious growth. We can only encourage the growth and give it direction; we cannot create something from without which must come from within." In that phrase, "unconscious growth," seems epitomized [sic] the full flavor and substance of true expression in any of the arts.

Nationalism, in politics as well as in art, has always been a subject that intrigued me especially, I suppose, because I am a Jew. Nationalism becomes a living "ism" only in times of crisis, when the artistic or political survival of a nation is threatened. The Jews, whose existence has been threatened for centuries, have developed a cohesion fostered by the restrictive conditions of the Ghetto. A Jewish consciousness was created which transcended national boundaries, since the Jews had no occasion to be grateful to the nations in which they happened to be living. This was rather wryly illustrated by a phrase used by all Eastern European Jews of my generation. Whenever anything important happened anywhere in the world, you would hear, "All right, but is it good for the Jews?" They were always on the defensive, without the means of retaliation open to citizens of legally constituted nations. Why should they have loved a country that hated them, where they were deprived of civil rights and yet were forced to take up arms in that country's defense?

They developed a solidarity and internationalism that found its symbol in elaborate religious rites and social customs, in their homes as well as in their places of worship and communities. Perhaps, as some anthropologists tell us, the circumcision of male children in the Jewish tradition is derived from a rite of human sacrifice. But it is also a symbolic warning to humanity in general, to Jews in particular, that a life without suffering is not to be expected.

In 1933, for the first time in its history, the Museum of Modern Art in New York devoted most of its space to a one-man show of a living artist, a retrospective exhibition of the work of Maurice Sterne. The artist wrote a short introductory note to the catalogue in which he tried to describe the goals of his art:

In making the selection for my present retrospective exhibition we were guided by two principles. We wished to show the most characteristic examples of each period and to present a rhythmic and unbroken sequence in order that the whole should become consequential and correlated. When we had made up the list we discovered that we had selected more than twice as many works as could be placed advantageously. . . . It was then decided to show only the most characteristic and successful examples of each period. It is just as well, for even if the opportunity should arise to present a man's work in its entirety, it would be impossible to do so. The records showing years of experimentation and searching, which are the destiny of every serious painter of our time, have often been destroyed by the artist. These cannot be resurrected.

It was different when a living vital tradition was handed down by master to disciple. Then the road was clear and open. It was not necessary to blast one's path through a jungle. Art was not an adventure, as it is today, but a well-planned journey.

Among my memorable experiences during a lengthy sojourn in British India, Burma, Java, and Bali, I often recall frequent visits to the shops where images were produced for the temples. These images were mostly trite and superficial. In the present environment the incentive for art expression is lacking, but those works, nevertheless, show extraordinary precision and craftsmanship. The planning, method, and execution are traditional. The sculptor I watched in Java had undoubtedly inherited his technique from the same sources which created the sublime carvings at the Temple of Boro-Budur. I became convinced that in the East a true art tradition is still alive but for some reason the true instinct is lacking. It is as if one inherited a beautiful language without having anything to say. In the West, on the other hand, there are many who have something significant to communicate but not the adequate means of expression. . . .

In our time we must be guided wholly by our instinct— conquer the limitations of time and space and receive a direct message from the significant works of the past. The revelations of the past should not only be our guide but a test of our accomplishment. The stimulus must come from our environment. . . .

When the works for the present exhibition had been assembled, I realized that the three essentials which have guided me and which I endeavored to fuse in one are instinct, environment, and tradition. The road is a difficult one. But I feel that I have emerged from the *selva oscura* and if I should have the good fortune to live twenty-five years longer I hope to come much nearer to my goal.

In its coverage of the Modern Art Show, The New Republic *continued to be enthusiastic about Sterne as the leading American artist. On March 1, 1933, Stark Young wrote:*

Of all this [Sterne's] career the present exhibition at the Museum of Modern Art constitutes a survey, some 174 numbers, though that represents only half of the pieces now available. . . . It is amusing to see some of these paintings of thirty years ago, twenty-five years ago, and so on, how they

show what Mr. Sterne might have done had he stuck to the
spot, or rather the respective spots, he had arrived at. There
are portraits passable, and portraits, if you like, good. They
are, for example, better than the good Chases and worse than
the bad: in these earlier portraits the disturbing element that
was to drive this artist to importance was sufficiently present
to mar the ease of the painting sum. There is a "Cain and Abel"
with naked young men and proud horses that hints of Géri-
cault, if somewhat thinly, and a girl with a red ribbon in her
hair that has been compared to Whistler. It is more or less
Whistler, with a richer pigment, a texture like certain Cour-
bets, and a charming restraint and tone in its own right. A distinguished taste in things slightly stale ought to find this picture
a comfort in the exhibition's midst. Along with these there is an
admirable painting of a girl with landscape, and there are drawings such as should raise one's hair with wonder and admiration.
It is admitted very often that no living draughtsman rivals
Maurice Sterne. Here we see pure drawings, vibrant life between lines, drawings in a heavier mass, drawings that are
Gothic in intense and delicate emotional precision, drawings
that have great chic, and drawings that lay you low with the
immense imaginative dilation plus an almost immediate concentration and purity in the approach to the subject. . . .

We must note the statue of a girl sitting. It is carved from a
block of Greek marble found in the Tiber. (This should not
be held against this sculptor as un-Americanistic, a crime
already laid on him.) . . . It is a lovely statue, full of this
sculptor's power to isolate a space, for example the triangle
between and below the rib-cage . . . into a unit resting in
volume, so to speak, as well as on the surrounding anatomy.
There is not time to discuss the long since well-known
paintings, such, for instance, as "The Winding Path." . . . It
sees what it sees with the directness of sunlight, but it knows
what it knows with a sort of heavenly communicable mystery.
It is one of the small number of great landscapes. . . .

There is another sort of compliment due Mr. Maurice

Sterne from me. Numerous portraits, so well painted, are to me ugly and tiresome. . . . Such as these Mr. Sterne has rendered not with any photography but with such a truth that my revulsion to the originals is so revived as to kill my pleasure in the pictures. This—with small reservations about taste—is indeed a compliment to the painter. . . . The same is true of some of the still-lifes of fruit. In some of these there is a sudden flash of Caravaggio brilliantly remembered. Detecting that ought to flatter my egotism of culture; but does not do so, so tired am I of these wrinkled table cloths (almost sordid with planes and patterns) that so many painters after Cézanne seem to think essential to pictorial appetite. . . .

One of this painter's gifts is to catch the inner point of the foreign, the Balinese, the moments in Burma, the Indians of the Southwest. He can do the outside, but what he does that really counts must bring the races thus revealed into a pure respect for him that no other painter has received. . . . Only in the painting of the Negro girl in the kitchen has Mr. Sterne failed in this racial vision. . . .

Of the unfinished pictures, and of the Bali pictures, there is one of temple worship that exhibits an almost spectacular secrecy of pattern, not possible without a study of Piero della Francesca, I should think, though the Piero in it is almost indiscernible. It is an unfinished canvas; but, apart from the austere grasp of design, it illustrates one of the best items, in the way of motifs, about Mr. Sterne's work. I mean the figures bowing, the inclination toward reverence bodily indicated. . . . I sometimes think it one of the great signs in art. . . .

Number 57 is the well-known "Bread Makers" poignant with all the truth of simple Italian life, one of the great Sterne paintings. . . . A new piece, of a circus in the Anticoli piazza, . . . is an admirable painting. . . . The mind behind such a picture is alert, brooding and beautiful. . . . The masterpiece of the exhibition [is] the large canvas of "American in Anticoli."

There is not space for a right conveyance of this painting, which I think is the peak of Mr. Sterne's work so far and, it seems to me, the most important painting in American art.

The base of influence in this painting, . . . which there is sure to be in a great guildsman like Maurice Sterne, with his long torment and study, . . . is not discernible to everyone, since there is never quotation but only a form of entrance into another artist's life-tradition, that is, in the final sense. There is an effect of saving the form out of substance. . . . "American in Anticoli" is closer to Giorgione rather than to later Venetian painters, partly through the manner in which it wins us to the central, pure shape—the bather's figure—and partly by an absence of rhetoric in the presentation that removes our resistance—as moderns especially—to it. The landscape is the Anticoli landscape. . . . We know it as Dante knew when he "saw from afar the trembling of the sea." . . .

All three figures have been given the beautiful, living rhythms of unconscious stillness. The central figure . . . has . . . the illusion of deathless form-idea, and the hardness of what will with time decay. Its softness it shares with the soft permanence outside in nature. . . .

As painting this picture seems to me to carry Mr. Maurice Sterne on forward. . . . There is an establishment of relationships that serve for deep symbols of reality. There is a fine balance between paint, which must be a lust, and design, which must be a celestial love. The picture rests on the line-form but dazzles out of it. It has a truly evocative volume. . . . The superb structure of the composition never loses the poem whose bones and posture it is.

In general, the show met with excellent reception, with the notable exception of a review by Lewis Mumford, who felt that Sterne's work did not merit the acclaim the Museum exhibition was affording it. In the May 5, 1934, issue of The New Yorker, *Mumford summarized his objections to Sterne's work, and reviewed a later gallery exhibit presenting hitherto unshown works:*

Did I say last year that the Maurice Sterne show at the Museum of Modern Art was overrated and overpraised? Did I say that the only vital part of that exhibition was the Bali paintings? I take nothing back. But I would like to add that the show of Sterne's paintings and drawings at the Milch Galleries at the moment is one of the finest of an American contemporary put on during the last year, and that it marks Sterne as one of the most distinguished painters of his generation. Do not fancy that a profound change has suddenly come over this artist's work. The fact is that these magnificent little paintings and drawings date from his great period at Bali, between 1911 and 1914; and they have, apparently, been stored in a trunk all these years.

What happened during the Bali period to give Sterne the command he achieved in these pictures is something for biography rather than for art criticism. But some of the elements are plain. One of the most important was a long draught of Cézanne. This comes out in various places: in the sure, economical way he handles the planes of the bodies of the Bali girls, and even in his treatment of the skirt in the "Girl Carrying Child." Then came saturation in an exotic environment: not merely external seeing but internal reception and sympathy, which flow together in the rhythm of his compositions and in his brilliant colors. The sunlight, the deep shadows, the tropical landscape, the statuesque bodies, the alert tingling of all the senses, had their effect on the artist; hence the swiftness and immediacy of his reactions. These oils have the unalterable decisiveness of water color, even in the most complicated compositions, such as "Bazaar Near the River" and "Temple Altar." It is the combination of freshness with a stirring vitality of design, a combination hitherto seemingly the special property of Marin, that one finds in Sterne's Bali paintings. The artist has very modestly called these pictures Bali studies, but the fact is that it is his finished work, such as "American in Anticoli," that one must call his studies, with their labored reminiscences, while it is these studies that one must crown as the very height of Sterne's finished work. And good work it is.

I was often bitterly amused at such conflicting reviews of my own work and, more, at the undue influence of the critics, not only on the buying public, but on the creative direction of the artists themselves. Critics are often like trained bloodhounds who, having been shown some tattered object that belonged to a Picasso or a Braque, follow the scent and pounce on some "new genius." They actually seem to prefer these synthetic and derivative works, I suppose because they are easier and neater to think about. The critic maintains himself one step ahead of the general public, but remains one step behind his creative contemporaries. No sooner has he caught up with the immediate creative past, than he is confronted with some bewildering new problem. His artificial concern with what is "up-to-date" is a natural consequence. In the end, there is no such thing as a good art critic. At best he can be a good literary talent who writes about art, and it is only on this basis that he can be rated.

During those years, I was myself often asked to serve as critic, or rather judge, for various art competitions and the like. The Art Department of the University of Illinois invited me to come to Urbana to act as chairman of the jury at its annual exhibition. After the jury had completed its difficult task, the faculty gave a dinner for us in a local hotel. Everything went well: the Martinis were dry, the beefsteaks tender, and the conversation lively.

While we sat sipping our coffee, and chatting, I felt a few drops of water at the top of my head. I glanced up at the ceiling just as a huge crack appeared and an icy shower poured onto my upturned face. Everyone jumped from his seat, anxious to help. The man on my right solicitously mopped at my head with his pocket handkerchief; someone else delivered an elaborate apology that the guest of honor should have had such an accident. Everyone was very embarrassed and to reassure them that I was not annoyed, I tried to turn the conversation to a more humorous vein. I said, "Don't worry, I know exactly what has happened. John the Baptist, on the floor above, discovered that I was one of few people at the feast who had not been baptized, and he effectively corrected the situation. Now I feel that I really belong!"

I am sorry to say that only a few of the guests seemed amused at my joke. The majority looked at me with barely suppressed indignation, a suspect reaction, I am afraid.

I became involved in a much larger issue of this sort in 1936. A $100,000 gift had been left to the city of Denver for the erection of a public monument to the late Mayor Stapelton, whom the Yugoslav-American donor had greatly admired.

The great Yugoslav sculptor, Ivan Mestrovich, was invited to submit a model. He did a very handsome one, which showed the figure of Moses striking the rock, from whence flowed the life-giving water. Some prominent citizens objected to the statue with the query, "Why *Moses* in Denver's civic center?" Although several newspapers reported that a Federal agency had objected to the Mestrovich award on behalf of starving American artists, I believe the decision was originally made on racial, rather than artistic or economic grounds. Had the prophet been a Celt or an Anglo-Saxon, the design would have been accepted, but the Hebrew Moses who struck the right rock in the Near East seemed to strike the wrong note in the West.

After this provincial decision, a public competition was announced and I was asked to come to Denver as an expert advisor to help the committee select a monument from the sixteen models that had been submitted. Five models were culled out, with a vigorous entry by William Zorach as my first choice. The last choice was a model by a local sculptor which I pointed out was the same banal sort of monument that could be found in hundreds of other cities. When I got back to San Francisco, I read with amazement that this last choice had received the commission. I wired my protest, the newspapers heard of the controversy, and there began months of bitter, prejudiced public debate, a lot of it centered on my head. The Kingdom of Yugoslavia disclaimed any interest in the money or the award; the competing artists, various professional organizations, a few local despots, and many admirable and principled local people hurled themselves into the fight. The poor sculptors found their models being shipped back and forth across the country as each faction tried to get them in or out of the other's way. I was very disturbed over what had been done, and that my name and reputation had been used to sanction it.[1]

[1] The controversy was eventually settled with a compromise that resulted in a very handsome monument. William Zorach's model was used, with the architecture executed by a Denverite, Burnham Hoyt.

M·S

13

From *1934* through *1936* the Sternes lived in San Francisco where Maurice taught at the California School of Fine Arts. In addition to a salary, the college provided two large studios for Sterne's use. In one, he worked on the monument, "Welcoming the Peoples," for Fairmount Park, Philadelphia; the other studio was used for the enormous work involved in Sterne's commission to do the murals for the library of the Department of Justice Building in Washington. The contract for this work was awarded in *1935* by the Section of Fine Arts of the Federal Works Agency, Public Buildings Administration, of which Edward (Ned) Bruce was then chief.

The panels were painted on composition board, with cubes of paint rather than brush. The mural scheme traced the historic tools of justice, such as "Brute Force," "Greed," "Tradition," "Mercy," etc. One triptych illustrated the "Continuity of Law"; a second depicted the "Attributes of Justice." The work took five years to complete but was not installed until *1941*, because of a bitter, behind-the-scenes struggle over the subject of one of the panels, "Ordeal," which showed a victim of the Inquisition, his torturer, and a Church dignitary. Monsignor Ready, of Washington, led the opposition to the mural.

AFTER THE RAIN (1948)

My Department of Justice murals interested me more than any other job I had ever done, probably because of influences in my early childhood. The whole subject of justice had been an obsession with my father, and the cause of many arguments between him and my mother, who considered his adherence to the law as impractical and inhuman. My father would, as a matter of daily practice in our small town Libau, adjudicate community disputes. Eventually the rabbi became very disturbed. An important part of his own income came from settling litigation, and my father's free service cut into his business. The rabbi appealed to the municipal judge, who ruled in Father's favor, since Father only judged cases before they were brought to the rabbi or to the officials, and, in general, specialized in disputes between Christians and Jews. I think that, had circumstances permitted, he would have made a great career in jurisprudence. He disliked business and failed in it, and his greatest joy came from his local name, *Hirshe Zwi der Gerechter*—the Just.

In the case of my murals, their completion caused a stalemate which even the Supreme Court Justices interested in my cause seemed unable to solve. I refused to omit "Ordeal," the offending panel, and the Church apparently knew how to prevent the entire work from being installed. In the meanwhile, all the panels were piled up in the basement of the Department of Justice Building and I was quite desperate, not only because of the years of work that lay there, but because one-third of my fee was not to be paid until the panels were in place.

Ned Bruce was furious. That good man had suffered a serious stroke and was really unable to work, but he stayed on as Chief of the Section of Fine Arts because he knew how important his work for artists was, during the Depression. He labored ceaselessly in my behalf, but I think he came to feel that the placement of the murals was hopeless. On July 18, 1940, he wrote:

Dear Maurice,

I am moving Heaven and Earth, and perhaps going too far, to try to get the modification of the blitzkrieg that the church had placed on your murals. I don't know whether I am making any progress or not but have approached every source I could think of that would take a liberal point of view. If it doesn't work I suppose we are up against it as the political power of the church is so enormous in Washington that it would simply be impossible to put the murals up against its wishes as it could stop our program over night.

I have had your contract modified so that you will receive a payment of $3,000 at once and I hope it will relieve your financial difficulties at least for a while.

Sterne went to Washington and made an appointment to see Monsignor Ready to discuss the matter. However, Bruce and Justice Felix Frankfurter advised against this. Frankfurter also drafted a letter for Sterne to send to the Monsignor:

Supreme Court of the United States
Washington, D.C.

Chambers of
Justice Felix Frankfurter

May 13, 1940

Dear Mr. Sterne:

I return herewith all your documents and trouble you with a proposed draft of a letter to Monsignor Ready. I have read it to Mr. Bruce and he concurs in what I am proposing.

I hope this nuisance will soon be lifted from your concern.

With warm regards,
Very sincerely yours,
Felix Frankfurter

Sterne replied on May 17:

Dear Justice Frankfurter:

I must thank you for your kind note and enclosed draft of letter to the Monsignor which I sent off promptly.

When I submitted to you the draft of my letter, I hadn't realized that it would require much more than just some red pencil marks of censorship. . . .

I think your draft is a masterpiece in content and form and again let me thank you heartily for your kind interest.

Very sincerely yours,
Maurice Sterne

The following is a file copy from among Sterne's papers of the letter to Monsignor Ready:

Monsignor Michael J. Ready
General Secretary
National Catholic Welfare Conference
Washington, D.C.

Dear Monsignor:

It was very kind of you to consent to see me last Friday morning. An urgent matter recalled me to New York. Please accept my apologies. I expected to return to Washington this week in order to discuss with you a complicated situation brought to my attention by Edward Bruce, Chief, Section of Fine Arts. I refer to your letter of April 19th addressed to Mr. John M. Carmody, Administrator, Federal Works Agency. Since it is impossible for me to leave New York just now, I take the liberty of writing to you.

I went to Washington to install the murals in the Library of the Department of Justice. The Section of Fine Arts and the Attorney General had given their approval. Much to my surprise, I learned that an obstacle had arisen—that your Administration Board objects to my panel entitled "Cruelty" [later called "Ordeal"]. This is very upsetting, especially since the criticism directed against the panel is, in my opinion, not justified.

It is not a question of just changing one panel out of twenty. I spent five years on this work and the series of twenty panels are really one organic frieze. I cannot touch a single figure without the danger of having to repaint *all* of the panels—and as I am not a youngster—I am not sure if there is the time.[1] Even if I had the time, I have not the means.

Some of the foremost critics consider these murals a very important contribution to the art of our time, so you will understand that I am very anxious to have them installed and must protest against any attempt to interfere with their prompt installation.

I am not a propagandist. I am a painter—my approach has always been purely objective. Of course I realize that an important work of art is subject to many different interpretations, so I am not surprised to hear that exception has been taken to one or another of my panels. This is quite as it should be—we all have the right to criticize and to disagree. But this right should not give one, whether an individual or a group, the right to tell an artist how and what he should paint, or to interfere with the pursuit of his art which might also have serious consequences in his making a living.

I always believed that this interference is only practised in cases when one has committed a criminal offense—I have not.

You claim that my panel, "Cruelty," "is offensive to citizens who cherish Christian loyalties." I too cherish these loyalties —more—I cherish Christian ideals. As proof, permit me to call your attention to the . . . [several panels which use Christ or Christian precepts as their illustrations].

I trust that these examples should suffice as proof that my loyalties are definitely in sympathy with, and not opposed to the loyalties cherished by the champions of Christianity—even though they have more claim to these loyalties.

I am not a Roman Catholic but during my eighteen years' residence in Rome, it was my good fortune to know intimately

[1] Sterne was then sixty-three.

many loyal Roman Catholics. Some became lifelong friends. I
admire and love them.

And one of my most cherished memories is the hours I spent
with the great predecessor of the present Pontiff. Years ago in
Milan, I was studying the manuscripts of Leonardo da Vinci.
As Leonardo's handwriting is very illegible, a young assistant
said, "The only person who can read it is our Librarian,
Monsignor Ratti."

I was introduced to His Eminence, who showed extraordinary interest and patience, was most simple, friendly and
obliging. He invited me to come again. This I did gladly. Of
course I had a thrill when years later I learned that the
Monsignor had become a Cardinal and that the friendly,
cultured gentleman who showed such extraordinary kindness
to an unknown stranger had been elected Pope Pius XI!

I hope you will pardon my taking so much of your time.
You can understand this is a matter of utmost concern to me
and I would appreciate an early reply.

Very sincerely yours,
Maurice Sterne

I propose to change the present title which is as follows:
"Cruelty. Trial by Ordeal; the accused is forced to carry
red-hot irons, suggesting the cruelty of people. Pope Innocent
III, (at right) abolished this form of trial at the Council of the
Lateran in 1215." To: "TRIAL BY ORDEAL: This primitive
practice, opposed by Christianity, was prohibited by the
Council of the Lateran in 1215."

Ned Bruce continued to work in my behalf, acting as a sort
of chairman of the opposition. In a letter on December 19,
1940, he advised me:

If we can get the murals up, I am perfectly certain that
in due course the recognition of your work will grow and
you will come into your own as a result of it, but for the
time being we must put them up without any fanfare and

I am going to rely on you to play ball with me. . . . Please keep the matter very confidential as any publicity at this time might stir things up.

Yet there were very powerful people on my side. I received encouraging letters from Justice Harlan Stone, from George Biddle, and from Francis Biddle, who was then the Solicitor General. Ned Bruce and Justice Stone wrote me that Robert Jackson, then Attorney General, was present at a luncheon on December 23, 1940, which had been organized by an informal committee of my supporters. The Commission of Fine Arts issued an official report written by Eugene F. Savage, painter-member. It concluded:

In the opinion of the Commission the picture and title impress one as being an unqualified tribute to Christianity and to the Catholic Church.

At about this time Ned happened to meet his friend, Fred Keppel, who was the head of the Carnegie Corporation, and Ned told him about the problem. Apparently, an important Catholic foundation was at that time seeking a large grant from the Carnegie people, and Ned felt that after his conversation with Keppel a few words were quietly murmured in the right ears. In any case, whether through powerful earthly influence or through the prayers and candles of our devout Catholic cook, the murals were finally installed in February, 1941. However, as Ned had intimated would happen, they had a quiet reception. Most of the important criticism had been published in 1939 and 1940, when they were shown in New York.

The murals met with mixed reception, the critics in general agreeing on the intelligence of concept, disagreeing on the success of the artistic rendering. One of the most favorable reviews was by Royal Cortissoz, in the New York Herald Tribune *of December 31, 1939:*

His work as an easel painter has been touched by a certain

high seriousness. This quality, as well as technical strength, has accounted for the distinction he has won as a member of the American school of painting. Sculpture has also engaged him and revealed in him a notable talent. Now he makes a decisive appearance as a mural decorator. . . .

The first impression left by these panels is that in painting them the artist has really mixed brain-stuff with his color. He has ideas about justice and about its antithesis. . . .

The coherence of the scheme is unmistakable. It is unified, and . . . this unity embodies a stimulus to reflection. . . .

It is by the intensely human character of Mr. Sterne's figures that the beholder is primarily arrested. When he symbolized "Ambition," through a picture of Jacob wrestling with the Angel, the latter is conventionally angelic, but Jacob and the striving men on the right and left are creatures drawn from our own time. . . . It is life, to be sure, that supplies the keynote to this entire decorative fabric, and that it is that constitutes the great merit of the artist's work. His purpose, evidently, is to stir one's consciousness of right and wrong, and he succeeds in this to a very definite degree. The visitor to the library at the Department of Justice will not contemplate these decorations unmoved. . . .

By the same token he will observe that while Mr. Sterne has in the substance of his work assumed an essentially modern point of view, he has retained, at bottom, some contact with tradition. As a designer, he is faithful to the immemorial law that a mural decoration should possess a beginning, a middle and an end. . . . In all his panels the painter discloses his wonted grasp upon form. It is a large, vigorous, even heroic type of form that he chiefly celebrates. Many of his figures are nude, representatives of a kind of primitive energy. They underline the force which is Mr. Sterne's predominant trait as an artist. . . . With grace, as the foregoing remarks have sufficiently implied, he is only incidentally concerned—with grace and with that indefinable adjunct known as beauty. It is in these matters that he most drastically parts company with the founders, and I cannot forebear taking a brief backward glance at those sometimes forgotten heroes of our school of mural decorations.

Meanwhile, I crave in his work a livelier sense of beauty than the decorations suggest.

Edward Alden Jewell commented in The New York Times *of December 31, 1939:*

Many of the panels look theatrically "contrived." Some of the devices employed may be deemed superficial or labored or downright tricky. But taken as a whole, the series is anything but an unimaginative rehash of hokus-pokus through the ages. . . .

As for the color scheme used throughout, it is dreary, dead and depressing. It almost never harmonizes with the action, though there are pleasantly sensuous passages.

Horace and Rachel Kallen were long-time friends of both the Sternes. Horace Kallen, writer and eminent teacher of philosophy, recalls Sterne's approach to this work:

Maurice was not deliberate in his art. With him, one had the impression of subconcious vision, of an almost child-like instinctualism (which he frequently intellectualized *after* the work was done). The vital presence of images was the thing that seemed to have counted.

This is not to say he did not work hard at his art. Maurice had had little schooling, but he was an omnivorous reader—especially in the techniques of painting and sculpture. When he received the commission to do the Department of Justice murals, he asked me to send him some material on the subject of mural painting. I sent him innumerable books about murals . . . perhaps, in fact, the murals were less successful than a good deal of his other work, just because they were less instinctual. Maurice had many ideas about the concept of justice which he wanted to express, and his elaborate conceptual plan interfered with his art.

The Milch Gallery continued to handle Sterne's work in New York, with occasional shows of drawings or oils. In March, 1936, the Metropolitan was interested in a large canvas, the "Bali Bazaar with Palms." However, they already owned a small Sterne painting with practically the same subject matter. An exchange was effected by the Gallery whereby the Metropolitan returned the smaller canvas, added some money, and thus bought the bigger, more important painting:

Very little money was involved in the Metropolitan acquisition of "Bali Bazaar with Palms," but of course any sort of sale to that museum was important, especially as fashions changed and all that I knew and had revered in the past came to be ridiculed as old-fashioned, lifeless dross. I suppose that even in the end I owed whatever survival I managed to the few who had faith in my work and did not jump on the bandwagon of the latest fashions in art—or in people.

Even in the late Thirties I began to see the sad decline of my friends, both in health and economically. Ned Bruce was ill, and he, who for years had given generously to anyone who needed help, was himself in greatly reduced circumstances; still longing to paint, but with one arm practically useless because of a stroke; vitally interested in his work for the Fine Arts Section, but not trusting his physical and mental capacity to do a good job. All the gentleness and encouragement that his wife Peggy and his friends could summon could not reassure him during those trying times. To add to his difficulties came a letter from Leo Stein who had sold a group of his Picasso drawings and some other things and wanted to use the proceeds to come to America. He asked Ned to wire his opinion, which was, of course, tantamount to asking to stay with the Bruces. On June 9, 1937, a very tired Ned wrote to me in California:

You spoke in one of your recent letters of the possibility of getting something for Leo to do and I am writing you completely frankly about this. I would love to see Leo and you know how fond I am of him but I confess I dread a little the strain it would be to be with him in long conversations, roaring my head off to make him hear, and I am wondering if you . . . could find something for Leo to do in San Francisco, even if he only had work for a month or two, enough to cover the expenses of his trip. He is . . . very hard up and it would be a very hard thing for me to do to discourage him from coming. . . . I have no doubt that even if nothing else comes up that you can do about it, I will ask him to come along and put him up with us. . . . Let me know if you can take Leo on for part of the time he is here.

Peggy Bruce, in particular, was worried about the added strain which Stein's visit might put on her husband's waning strength, although Leo himself was concerned about Ned's health, and indeed he felt that part of the purpose in his coming was to help the Bruces. Sterne wired Leo to postpone his visit, but Ned Bruce had already regretted his hesitancy, as well as Sterne's message. He set about making contacts for Leo's benefit, and preparing himself for the visit. Leo Stein arrived at the Bruces' home in mid-August, 1937, and on August 20, Peggy wrote Sterne about him:

He [Leo Stein] looks amazingly well, much younger and is gay and witty. When he was in New York he bought himself some remarkable new apparatus which aids his hearing and he now sits among a group of people and is able to enjoy a general conversation. . . . While he seems gay and happy—yet I find he is really a defeated person and has little to give out. The young people are afraid of his philosophy and they do not admire him. He does not appeal to people who are doing things and love the doing. They are so shocked that after all the years of work—and he has accomplished his end, that he doesn't feel up to giving out his message—which of course is defeat. It is really very sad—

Leo went back to Nina in Italy in the winter of 1937 and soon after I received from him a desperate letter about his financial condition. I wrote to Ned about it and Ned later forwarded my comments to Howard Gans, who had always managed the affairs of Gertrude and Leo Stein. I had written:

> Now I am coming to a more painful . . . matter which concerns a friend dear to us both—Leo. I received a very distressing letter from him several weeks ago which sounds like an S.O.S. He mentions in it a plan which had been discussed . . . some time ago . . . a sort of five-year plan to assure Leo an income of $1,000.00 a year. For that purpose we must find ten people who are interested in Leo and his work, who would be willing to give $100 a year for which in return Leo would deliver two paintings a year. . . . Eventually each subscriber would have one painting for which he had, during five years, paid $500. It seems to me a very sensible and dignified plan and would be a wonderful thing for Leo. I believe I can get about four—perhaps five people interested in the project. . . . I don't have to tell you, I consider Leo a very important person, and it is a shame that a man who has never had any money worries should, in his old age, have to face a situation for which he hasn't been equipped. Please let me hear about it as soon as possible because Leo is evidently in a very tight spot.

Eventually, Leo sent some pictures over to me in San Francisco and I managed to get them sold and to send him about $1,000 in profit. Ned himself had sad times during those

233

years, but before he died, some of us subscribed to buy a picture of his for donation to a museum and we also sponsored a testimonial dinner to him to commemorate his achievements as a painter and as a powerful benefactor to the world of art. I could not attend, but Leon Kroll [1] wrote me about the ceremony:

> I am writing this note because I thought you would like to know about the luncheon to Ned. It went off very well and I made the presentation speech which was quite short. . . . You were mentioned as one of the sponsoring committee. We bought a picture of a bridge Ned did in France for presentation to the Smithsonian. . . . Ned was deeply affected by the artists' tribute. I stressed the artist not the administrator.
>
> *Leon*

Other friends were growing old. In 1939 and 1940 I tried very hard to get the Friedsam Medal for service to art awarded to the San Franciscan Albert Bender, a loyal friend and great collector. I invited the head of the award committee for lunch and together we tried to think of ways to bring this about, as it would have been a crowning recognition of a life spent in the service of the artist and the arts.

The chief objection that was publicly raised was that Bender wasn't nationally known, but it seemed to me that there was scarcely anyone at the time who was as internationally known in the art field. The award would have been a way of making him known to the general public.

In America, men achieve national reputation although their sphere of activity is limited to commerce, finance, or industry. Someone who produces a clever gadget in Detroit will quickly become an oracle about war, peace, Art and God! I felt it was time that some of our citizens who had attained distinction in

[1] Well-known American painter. Long-time neighbor of the Sternes in Mt. Kisco, N.Y.

the realm of the spirit should also attain recognition and popular acclaim.

Two years before, the medal had been awarded to Edward Bruce. This award met with universal approval because his years of work had been of the utmost importance to the country as well as to artists. The following year the medal went to John D. Rockefeller, Jr., for his great gift of The Cloisters to the nation. Again, it was well deserved. It is of enormous importance both to artists and to the public to have access to such great treasures of the past.

I felt that it was now time to honor another agency directly connected with the opportunity of the artist to express himself and to survive: the sensitive patron, intuitive, wise—ought to be commemorated. In those Depression days, when the species had almost disappeared, it was important to honor such men. And I did not mean to honor, even then, the collector who buys only the most fashionable products in art, out of vanity, or snobbishness, or economic speculation, but the lover of art and the true friend of the artist.

Albert Bender was then one of the few men in America who embodied that spirit. He had never been really rich, but he practically gave away all he had. I believe there wasn't a single instance where he refused help to a creative artist who appealed to him. I still think of him as a pioneer who went to California and found a rich vein in the expressive spirit of man.

Bender had not been east for years; he spent his money other ways. It would have been grand to get him the trip, to have pinned the medal on his chest, and heard the humorous, scintillating speech he would have made. But our hopes jumped too far; someone else got the medal that year, and Bender died before the next one was given.

For me, another rather bitter sign of the passage of time was the publication in 1936 of Mabel Dodge's *Movers and Shakers*. More recently I have come to understand the reasons for her cruel portrait of me—perhaps in these pages I am also unfair to her—but when I first read her book I was terribly upset. Perhaps the best compensation came in the form of the letters I received from people I hadn't seen in years who wanted to let me know that they disagreed with her portrayal, and to express their loyalty to me. One of the most perceptive and most personally moving of these letters came from Hutchins Hapgood on February 13, 1938. He wrote:

> I have always had an unusual feeling for you, ever since we met so long ago, in Florence. Your mind and your heart go together—you are warm about your ideas, and the perception of form in others arouses your identical passion. . . . But this is not a love letter— . . . as you well know—
>
> When Mabel's *Movers and Shakers* came out, I wanted to write you, but I didn't have your address. . . . I wrote her strongly disapproving of what she wrote about you— of course. I told her it was an insane jealousy that prompted it. She acted in the same way she had in *Lorenzo in Taos* [1]—Lawrence was *always* right, and she *always* wrong. . . . She replied [to my objections] in both cases by admitting the truth of what I wrote!! . . . She didn't get you at all in that book and she knows it—but she had to put it all in [because of] the jealous . . . moments she had with you.

D. H. Lawrence is quoted as stating, after he had seen a typescript of Mabel Dodge's memoirs, that publication would have to be deferred until after the deaths of the people mentioned in the narrative. He apparently added, "But I don't care, so long as she dies before she gets to Frieda and me." [2]

In New York, I resumed my teaching, for financial, rather than any other reasons. I never really liked teaching, since it took me away from my own work. I was, I am afraid, more interested in gaining more knowledge for myself than in

[1] Mabel Dodge Luhan, *Lorenzo in Taos* (Alfred A. Knopf, 1932).
[2] Catherine Carswell, *The Savage Pilgrimage*, rev. ed. (London: Secker & Warburg, 1951).

imparting what I knew to others. I know there are many people whose development is not interrupted by their teaching, who can even be stimulated by it to further personal development. I did not need this stimulant. The truth I was always pursuing could only be discovered by direct contact with nature, with my own inner revelations and struggles with it. However, I suppose I had some success with my teaching. Former students would write me for advice, my classes were popular and attracted public attention, my art "theories" were sought.

The following are excerpts from an interview in American Artist, *December, 1941:*

Q. Mr. Sterne, since more than one critic has called you "the paramount draftsman of our time" I think it is appropriate to start with drawing. What would you say about drawing in the education of the painter?

STERNE: It is axiomatic that a good painter must be a good draftsman. Yet students often ask if I think it is important for the painter to draw well. Evidently they imagine that color in some way is a substitute for drawing, at any rate that it helps out when drawing fails. But must not every touch of color, laid on canvas with brush, have a shape? . . . As the painting develops, a sound knowledge of drawing will make his task much easier . . . for it is the constant struggle with the drawing which destroys all freshness and, in the end, will turn something spontaneous into a tortured battlefield. . . .

Q. There is a lot of confusion about this matter of drawing. What is good drawing to some is very bad drawing to others.

STERNE: Drawing which suggests playing the piano from notes is obviously all wrong. . . . One cannot make a decent drawing while the vision is divided in seeing different parts at different times. Only when the vision is so coordinated that every part is seen in true relationship to the rest has one the right to indulge in drawing. For drawing is not a visual experience in the making. It is a direct simple statement of the experience. . . .

Unlike drawing, [painting] is an experience in the making. . . . In the beginning the painter must assert himself. In projecting something the painter naturally dominates the situation. But when the projection is there, there comes a moment when the painter must cease to assert himself; rather he should endeavor to carry out the potential needs of his painting. At first he must be the master. At the end he becomes a slave. . . .

Q. Would you say that attitude toward painting is characteristic of modern art?

STERNE: Definitely. Centuries ago a painting was a piece of craftsmanship, not unlike that of the cabinetmaker or goldsmith. The old masters were essentially interested in producing a finished object. Today, while there are still good painters who have this traditional art conception, the modern attitude considers painting as a form of self expression. This should be particularly true in America where our reactions are much more immediate, where we are intolerant of obstructions and red tape; we love to come straight to the point. This, by the way, is why we have so many superb watercolorists: the medium is most spontaneous and depends to a great extent on lucky strikes. . . .

[About drawing] Mediocre draftsmen see and draw the body in movement. A Michelangelo or a Daumier did nothing of the sort. To them the body was not a static object swayed by an outer movement, but a living organism moving in its own right. They saw and identified the source and quality and center of the movement. Hence they could draw the movement in the body, instead of drawing the body in movement. . . .

Q. How much preliminary drawing do you do on your canvas before beginning actual painting?

STERNE: A painting should be conceived in paint, not

The painter at work (*Photo by George Yater*)

Sterne in the later years

drawn and then painted-in. What I draw on my canvas would be unintelligible to anyone else. It is a sort of shorthand of drawing, symbols to indicate where certain forms of color are to be placed in the painting.

Q. What about your technical procedure in painting?

STERNE: . . . I like to see a painting develop like a photographic negative. First a few vague gray indefinite spots. Then as the picture develops the forms begin to emerge, take on more shape and more color. That procedure is consistent . . . with what I have already said about a painting being an "experience in the making." As to color, I start with understatement and gradually bring it to greater intensity.

Q. What about your palette?

STERNE: . . . With a few colors you can control your painting and produce better harmony. The more colors the more complicated your painting will be. Rivera had an interesting experience with his palette which at first was simple. His color was admirable. When he added more pigments he went wild as is seen in his Cuernavaca murals. . . . The lack of organic color relationship in bad painting is due to the rather prevalent custom of using certain colors on the palette for certain objects instead of using *all* of them for *all* objects. . . .

Q. You have told me that you have painted nothing but flowers all summer. Is this just an impulse or is there some logical reason for it?

STERNE: I've painted flowers off and on for many years, and they have served a definite purpose in my painting development. When in 1915 I returned from Bali after two years of painting there, I found that after the color and excitement of that enchanted isle my appetite had been jaded; the only subjects that tempted me at all for four years were flowers. Ten years later, after completing the sculpture commission for the Rogers-Kennedy Memorial at Worcester, Mass., I again turned to flowers for refreshment. Now, having finished the murals for the Department of Justice Building in Washington, I am painting flowers—before tackling life in the raw once more.

Flowers are so light and brilliant that it is hard to reproduce their colors with pigments on the palette. I find the effort to do so is very stimulating to my color sense; it seems to strengthen my color in subsequent painting. I used to have a very dark palette. Flower painting has been a real factor in bringing it up to a brighter key.

Q. There are few artists who are both painter and sculptor. I'm curious to know how you happened to take up sculpture and what effect it has had on your painting.

STERNE: My early painting . . . was much more static than my latest canvases. I was so much interested in form and reality that my painting was too sculptural. I insisted too much upon the representation of actual weight and volume. A friend of mine in Italy gave me the idea of turning to sculpture. He said he thought it might serve as an outlet for my preoccupation with sculptural form and release my brush for greater freedom in painting. It proved to be so. I began to work in the round in 1910 and my first sculptured head is now in the Metropolitan Museum. . . .[1]

Q. To get back to painting, we have not touched upon composition.

STERNE: . . . I might say a word about space, which to me is synonymous with composition. Pictorial space . . . is a limited volume in depth, intimately related to the height and width of the painting. This spatial unit has a definite foreground and background limitation. Everything between these extremes is suspended within these spatial limitations and is satisfying only when the different objects move toward and away from each other in an unbroken rhythm. Unconsciously our vision responds to and is swayed by the rhythm in the painting and we have a sense of something alive when the painting stimulates this visual movement. . . . The sky [in a

[1] "The Bomb Thrower."

240

painting] should *enclose* the pictorial space rather than extend it. . . . At any rate the space must be confined or there cannot be pictorial unity.

Q. In your work one is conscious of great expressiveness through emphasis upon simplified form and subordination of anatomy. Will you comment on this?

STERNE: As you probably know my early drawing was characterized by painstaking and patient study of detail—in fact some of those drawings seemed to come from the school of Albrecht Dürer. Gradually and slowly, I came to the realization that detail was of little consequence, in fact it often interferes with the more important fundamentals—direction, movement.

Q. Do you consider simplification essential to good drawing?

STERNE: Definitely. But I must define what I mean by simplicity. There are two kinds—the simplicity which is concerned with what one leaves out—that is taste. The other simplicity, the result of what one puts in—that is art.

M·S
14

O F course, neither teaching nor creative or personal problems had much meaning in the Forties when the people of the world were faced with the horrors of war. Isaiah has said that it is the fate of the innocent to suffer for the guilty, but I wonder whether the sacrifices of those years benefited even the guilty. In the case of the Jews, surely over the centuries their persecutors have been deprived of the Jewish genius in the arts, sciences, and the humanities. The Jews have been hated not because they killed the Christian savior, but because they have given the Christians a God and a standard of human behavior which they have not been able to live up to. The Jews have become a living reproach to the Christian world for its failure to practice the tenets of Christ, that other Jew.

In spite of his efforts to "belong," in times of stress the Jew has always been looked upon with suspicion. The Nazi period was, in reality, a revolt against the entire Mediterranean civilization, and the Jew, as the embodiment of that civilization, was a natural target. More than any other people have they suffered, and been driven close together in their suffering. Certainly Israeli nationalism is a direct result of their longing to find a home where there would be no pogroms.

The Germans were bound to hate the Jews who were so unlike them. The Jews, on the other hand, esteemed in the

Germans what they themselves needed most: ruthlessness, efficiency, arrogance, and contempt for the humble Christian virtues which the Jews were more apt to put into practice than those so-called Christians. Indeed it would seem that the "eye for an eye" doctrine was forced upon the Jews by Moses, their realistic leader. He had been raised in the palace of the Pharaoh, and was keenly aware of the weaknesses of his own people in their struggle for survival.

Anti-Semitism is often indulged in by the Jewish community itself, and I relish it as a delicious example of self-criticism and of longing for perfection. However, it sometimes takes the form of an admiration and envy for the gentile world, and of all the Jews scattered over the globe, the German Jews are, in this respect, the most offensive. It was bad enough that the Germans considered themselves superior to all other people. What was worse was that the German Jews believed it.

In my own childhood I was, for a brief time, completely under the domination of an erratic and bullying neighborhood boy. I was fascinated with Heinrich's physical recklessness and brutality in very much the same way that the German Jewish adults reacted to *their* Aryan neighbors.

As a Jew and as an American I felt helpless during the Second World War. There was almost nothing a man my age [1] seemed to be able to do. A committee, Artists for Victory, was organized to sponsor various good-will and benefit exhibitions, donate posters, etc. One of these exhibits, the American Good Will Exhibition, sent a traveling show to England, and I was very proud when the Tate Gallery acquired my "Mexican Church Interior," the first picture by a living American artist that they had ever purchased.

In August, 1945, I was appointed as a painter member of the National Commission of Fine Arts. My duties included judging all sorts of interesting public aesthetic problems. The one which bothered me most was the type of war memorials which

[1] Sterne was sixty-four years old at this time.

were being proposed even before the fighting of World War II had really stopped. The most awful statuary was designed to honor Coast Guard heroes, Pacific fighters, etc. I wrote a piece for the *Art Digest* of March 15, 1946, in an attempt to influence this trend:

. . . Since war memorials are not hidden away but are exposed to public view we must see to it that these exposures should at least be satisfactory as works of art. We fought, not for conquest, but to defend our form of life—consequently there is a strong opposition to traditional memorials, which, it is claimed, have a tendency to glorify war.

From the Revolutionary War on, the country has been spotted with . . . [traditional figures] and there is hardly a town of any pretension without its cast iron soldier on a pedestal. They often suggest the effigies made by primitive tribes which were burned on the public square. But these soldiers were our friends and benefactors—not our enemies. Surely they deserve better treatment!

That such figures can be of supreme excellence, especially the equestrian, nobody will deny. . . . [However] it is still to be shown that a jeep can figure sculpturally in the place of a horse. Roman and Gothic draperies are much more adaptable to the sculptor's medium than contemporary pants. . . .

I see no reason why we should not venture into new, hitherto little explored fields of expression. . . . We should encourage new forms in harmony with the spirit of our time. Simple geometric forms together with ornamental bas-reliefs in which recent developments in new materials should take part have created infinite possibilities.

[As to] the claims of pure abstractionists, certainly there is no harm in naming a street or a public building in honor of a national hero; but such a name is neither a recollection nor a symbol. Memorials must commemorate and the commemoration cannot but be a permanent visible image, not a single word spoken occasionally between long silences. . . .

Why should not a community of today use its civic center to commemorate its honored dead not just with lists of names, but with portrait busts and murals portraying the heroic events in which its sons figured? . . . We . . . may find victory blunted by war memorials, if our very many excellent architects, sculptors, and painters . . . do not pool their wisdom and skill to devise remembrances which will hold the past alive in the active present.

During the years following the war my own work was devoted almost entirely to easel painting, and although I continued to win awards and certain honors, there was a whole group of new painters and collectors to whom my work was either unfamiliar or old-fashioned. In spite of this, in spite of failing health, I felt very excited about what I was doing.

Sterne apparently wrote to Leo Stein about his enthusiasm for his latest work, and a reply from Stein, dated June 29, 1945, echoes some of this spirit:

Dear Maurice:

. . . You say that you are "doing your best work at long last." Do you remember how you used to be amused at my finishing the analysis and I retorted with your discovery that at last you could paint? Well, the wolf did come at last and perhaps he ate up all your difficulties and all my inhibitions.

The Wildenstein Gallery in New York held an exhibition of new paintings by Maurice Sterne in May, 1947. Sterne wrote the following introduction to the catalogue of this show:

My last one-man show of easel paintings, at the Museum of Modern Art, was held in 1933. Since then we have had an American Renaissance. A new generation has grown up. To those who are not familiar with my work and to those who know only my former work, a few explanatory words are appropriate.

My renaissance took place about three years ago. Up to that time I believed that in order to *paint* significantly all one had to do was to *see* significantly and paint as well as one knew how. Then something happened. I was too ill to work and was admiring my view from the porch; the incoming tide, the crimson and orange and gold of the sunset, the delicate nuances, the spatial volumes, when suddenly, nature ceased to be nature and became a wet painting. This sensation was so real that when a sea gull suddenly soared across my vision, I exclaimed, "The fool! Its lovely white wings will be smeared with paint."

For many, many years I tried to paint as *well* as I knew how. I stopped trying when I realized that one must paint *better* than one knows how.

Bonnard once remarked to a friend, "You can't invent painting." These wise words by one of the greatest painters of our time are particularly apropos at present, when so many of our younger painters not only try to invent paintings, but play the game with wild cards.

Well, I still prefer my poker straight and I get a bigger thrill when I hold a legitimate "three of a kind" than I would with a "full house" with one-eyed jacks and deuces wild.

The Art Digest, *on May 15, 1947, carried an illustrated review of this show as its lead article:*

Since few successful painters have the courage, determination and talent to change style in their mid-60s, a time when less gifted men find it easier to essay tried, familiar themes, it is indeed welcome to report that Maurice Sterne's first one-man show in fourteen years . . . is a handsome winner.

It was in 1933 that the Museum of Modern Art honored Sterne by a retrospective showing of his painting and sculpture, its first such show granted an American. Now to a new generation that is only vaguely familiar with the past work of a pioneering modern, Sterne's current show . . . might have been painted by another artist—so changed . . . [is his work] in entire approach and so absent is any sign of transition.

Best known for his famous paintings of Bali—dark, highly patterned rhythmic canvases that were first shown in 1915—Sterne now devotes himself to earnest studies of the changing moods of the New England sea with special emphasis on light. Freshness is the word that comes again and again to characterize nearly all the paintings in the large assemblage, for it applies not only to his new palette but to his overall vision as well. . . .

Sterne's old adversary, the critic Henry McBride, wrote of the exhibit in the New York Sun, *May 9, 1947:*

Mr. Sterne, during this retreat of his, has had . . . a freshening of vision. . . . Of obvious picture-making in the display there is very little. All his old formulas for that sort of thing he has cast aside. What is new with him is a worshipful feeling for the shimmering, iridescent texture of the sea on a bright day. . . . His approach to it could be called realism, except that it is more than that. It has a dancing jubilant quality that does to the eye what ozone does to the lungs. The blue lights sparkle at every splash in the water so that the small boats at a distance seem like jewels in Cartier settings.

It is a real pleasure in all these pictures to see the ocean so consistently well-behaved, and when the sea is so good as all that, it can readily be understood why the artist didn't care to waste time and energy in doing impeccably the houses and piers that in some instances interfered with the view. The sea's the thing, he says, and what principally matters.

Although I remained out of fashion, for that moment in 1947, the critics were friendly enough. But how ironic it is that our aesthetic judgments are so influenced by accidents of fashion and by the ravages of time! The academicians' failure was due mainly to their inability to comprehend what were the important factors in their predecessor's art. They saw only what was obvious in the compositions, and confused accidents of time with original purpose. For example, they did not understand that the brown, golden color they slavishly copied was due entirely to chemical changes in the old oils or varnish. Can one imagine Botticelli painting his "Primavera" in blacks, dull greens, and dirty whites?—in Tuscany of all places— where the spring glows in light and tender color! Or can you imagine how the much-copied Roman or Etruscan sculptor would feel if he could see his bronze work today, with holes instead of eyes, stripped of all decoration? Why he would quickly move to restore his work!

Tradition, by itself, is harmful as a dictum. It can have constructive value only as a principle. Its influence should help form the artist, but not determine the form of his art. Tradition can cultivate his vision, but it must not deprive him of his right to use his own inner sight in the pursuit of the truth in nature. The usual practice today is to give a new dress to old ideas by endowing them with some original small touch. I find less objectionable those who can put an old dress on new ideas, because the content underneath is more important than the outer garment. People without inner form suffer from the claustrophobia imposed by freedom's boundaries. They crave for unlimited license to pour out their amorphous subconscious.

These lost souls have found an outlet in non-objective art, where their aberrations are formless, because only people who have intellectual and spiritual form themselves can endow their creations with form. I deny what many of the twentieth-century avant-garde aesthetes proclaim: that the present chaotic condition of art is an inevitable development from the nineteenth century. Rather, the "new art" is a gesture of frustration and ineptitude in carrying on from where the masters left off. Those who see it as an inevitable sequence mistakenly believe that the leaders of nineteenth-century art had moved away from reality, when, as a matter of fact, they had come closer to it. Failure to perceive this essential precept is responsible for the current alienation of art from nature. Because they could not see nature with the insight of Cézanne, they deduced that he had advocated art isolation. The late nineteenth-century painters were revolting not against nature, but against the contented mediocrity of a stagnant academicism, which was not developing from the past, but aping it.

However, having freed themselves from the disciplinary influence of nature, the non-objective painters labor under the delusion that they are their own masters. To them, nature appears commonplace, but when they turn their vision inward, then indeed are they incapable of producing anything that is not commonplace. What seems trite to mediocre talents can be an object of veneration to a larger mind, a challenge to clarify its mystery.

On the other hand, it may be better not to lament over the revolt of the abstractionists against objective reality. They are the very people who, had they not found this easy outlet, would have gone on painting "Nature" in the academic style. Today their feeble experiments are hailed by the critics and bought by the public. No longer are trials subject to possible error. Every art experiment is now crowned with success although aesthetic accidents are generally sad casualties, and in the art world there are few Drs. Curie or Fleming.

America has become the dumping ground of every innovator abroad, not because we are more progressive, but because we are more ignorant. Painters who aroused only brief interest in Europe are able to sell their discarded wares easily in this country. Convictions, both artistic and spiritual, have their roots in traditions, and are developed through education. Unfortunately, education in the United States accentuates what is "up-to-date" rather than using more basic criteria. Nowhere else have applied science, patent medicine, and the interior decorator gained such popularity. We "adopt" our convictions and passionately defend them—until some new authority speaks, whereupon we tear our paintings off the wall, discard the furnishings of last year's decorator, and buy in the taste of the current masculine-female or feminine-male advisor. Our homes no longer mirror the lives or personalities of their owners; indeed, neither the guests nor the hosts seem to belong. Only the ghosts of the decorators are at home.

I admit the possibility that I am intellectually incapable of appreciating abstract art and I have this feeling most strongly when I see the adulation that the world pays to Pablo Picasso. About fifty years ago, when I first met Bernard Berenson, I told him that I had just come from Paris and he asked what was "new on the Rialto." I told him that Picasso seemed to have stolen the limelight from everyone else and Berenson replied that he found Picasso boring. When I pressed him to admit that Picasso had talent, he replied, "I don't admit anything of the kind."

At that time, I disagreed with Berenson. I thought that although he might be the greatest authority on the art of the past, we lived in a new age which required new authorities. I did not foresee the blind alleys in which art would get stuck. Now, I believe that Berenson was right in his judgment of Picasso, that he is one of the very few art appreciators whose taste and judgment is not local to any place or time. I have seen Picasso's innovations for the past fifty years, and each time I, too, have liked them less. Picasso has never really tried to find his own depths, not even in his well-exploited Blue Period. It had charm, pathos, and sentiment, but it was extremely weak in significant form. The work that followed was either derivative variation upon fifth-century B.C. vase paintings, or on African sculptures, or, more recently, distortion of Poussin. But Picasso is never an honest disciple, nor, for that matter, a vulgar imitator. He is a challenger with a colossal ego, always trying to prove his own superiority to himself and to the world.

I recall an incident at Leo Stein's one night during my early years in Paris. We had all dined together and after dinner Leo took us into the large studio-living room to see his latest acquisition, a superb Cézanne portrait of his wife. Leo anxiously awaited Picasso's reaction, and at last, we heard the master's voice. He jumped up from his chair and, pointing toward the face of the subject, shouted, "This is no nose. It's a shapeless blob." Then he feverishly drew a cubistic nose, obviously influenced by the African sculpture he was then obsessed with. He held up his drawing and said, "This is a nose—not that other one."

Leo said nothing nor did Gertrude who, as a matter of fact, looked rather blank after this outburst. It was still 1906, when she would frankly admit that she knew nothing about painting. I felt that I must defend Cézanne, and in my halting French I told Picasso, "Thank God the nose you just drew is not in the Cézanne portrait. It looks like a bull's eye—and would be shot at."

Only a year or two earlier, Picasso had been one of Cézanne's most ardent admirers. Suddenly he became Cézanne's rival. For his own satisfaction, for *la gloire* he became a monotheist, who believed in no other God but himself.

I think Picasso's outstanding technical weakness is his feeble tactile response. It is the reason he indulges in heavy black outline, hoping to hide an inherent shortcoming. I have often discussed this with Leo Stein who said that, although he had the highest admiration for Picasso as an illustrator, he considered his sense of form very weak, his color tolerable only when limited to monochrome as in the Blue Period, or the Black Cubistic Period of "Guernica." He is essentially a graphic draftsman who uses color for melodramatic effect, unlike, for example, Matisse, a born colorist, whose color sense is so immaculate, so inevitable.

M·S
15

I N spite of my disagreement with most of what takes place in the art world today, I have not participated very much in the struggle. Conflict has never appealed to me. As for physical arguments, I have always avoided them, because I hate inflicting pain as much as being obliged to bear it. I was too timid to fight as a child, and since then I have been too busy to bother. (Now, of course, I am too feeble to even think of it.)

The pursuit of perfection makes all other struggles seem of little importance. During my own chase after this artistic ideal, I would sometimes find that life itself had become too absorbing, and that my work had been neglected and become stagnant. Then I would savagely kick out of my way anything that had interrupted the creative flow. This was bound to cause great suffering to others, especially to those I wished only well. It made me remorseful and miserable, but it was a form of self-preservation that could not be helped. It is no wonder that so many great artists had the reputation of being scoundrels, since they often sacrificed decency in human relationships in order to further their art.

I have never been content unless I have had some *opus magnum* to occupy me. In spite of the fact that what always sold were the things that I dashed off in the intervals between large works, or did as sketches, it was the larger conceptions that kept me alive and believing in my work.

Now that my arthritis [1] keeps me from holding a brush, I can no longer hope to find myself in the pursuit of nature in art. My *opus magnum* must be my notes for an autobiography, and I race with time to set them down. I remember that just before I began to feel the last painful symptoms of arthritis I had written an ode to old age. I praised my freedom from sexual drive, my new and purer relationships with women, my keener vision of the objects at my bedside, my heightened knowledge of life's truth. It is true, in one sense, that some of the urgency to solve life's problems is lessened, but it is because neither I nor anyone else can answer the questions that concern me now.

My ode to old age has become a dirge. "Old age is a slow way of dying" someone has said—a slow and painful ordeal it is, made infinitely worse by the terrible loss of friends and my own physical inability to comfort those who are left. Neith Hapgood wrote me a few years ago, after Hutch had died. Her letter was beautiful and sad, and in its closing lines there is an accurate summary of what old age is really like:

> I am very lonely for Hutch—a life of forty-five years with him must be paid for now, and it comes high.

When my dear friend Margaret Lewisohn died, I felt what Neith had written, and for a few terrible hours I hung on the edge of a precipice, wondering whether it might not be best to let go. Margaret was the only woman, beside Vera, who aroused in me a higher and more idealized love. My respect and affection for her husband, Sam Lewisohn, killed any erotic impulses I might have felt for her, and she, herself, had great self-control and never permitted our relationship to enter the bloodstream. She was a beautiful, noble, and gracious woman, and only in one sense am I consoled at her loss. When

---

[1] Sterne obviously knew he was dying and wrote frankly about it. Many people who saw him during the last years report that he knew he had cancer. However, in his notes, he regularly refers to his illness as "arthritis."

I was young I would sometimes realize, when it was too late, how much people had meant to me. I have no such remorse about Margaret; there was hardly a day, in the long years I knew her, that I was not aware of her lovely spirit. The devoted loyalty to my work of both Sam and Margaret Lewisohn was only one of the many indications I had of the regard they returned to me.

These last years have not been without rewards of the tangible sort for my work. The Whitney Museum bought a painting, "Bali Bazaar," and a drawing, "Composition xix," in 1954; one of my paintings was chosen to hang in President Eisenhower's office at the White House; in February of 1957, "Benares on the Ganges" was awarded the $500 Andrew Carnegie Prize by the National Academy of Design.

However, a market that praised amateurs, where Grandma Moses and a multitude of less aged and less gifted prodigies were in command, was as much responsible for my discarding the brush as was my disability. The honored criterion that time is the final test of art is no longer valid. Now, not only excellence, like cream, rises to the top, but also the scum of fermentation. However, though I sometimes feel like a lost sheep in the art world, I am not pessimistic about the future of painting. I already see signs that abstract art is in its last convulsions. It cannot develop because it does not contain the seed of life within itself, and consequently it cannot blossom. It is sterile.

The art world requires no policemen to do its evolutionary job, nor are they needed in our political life. In their zeal to protect us from threats to our freedom, McCarthy and other self-appointed public custodians rob us of the very thing they pretend to preserve. Our rights are quickly being stuffed into their pockets, and the best way to combat them is not our present feeble protests, but a strong compaign of righteousness.

In the same way, it will take more than futile conferences to save the world from nuclear extinction. The splitting of the atom has split time, creating a new era not unlike our old marking of B.C. and A.D. The Christian era gave its followers an ideology to strive for, a promise for the future. Now, the hereafter must wait; nuclear warfare is too urgent to be put into the deep freeze. Survival on earth is of more pressing concern than any future heaven or hell.

I believe that the basic solution lies in the obvious precept that nationalism and nuclear weapons do not go together. We must learn to give up a certain degree of national sovereignty, or face the alternative—extinction. Nations should be deprived of their stockpiles of nuclear weapons and prohibited their manufacture. Weapons should be placed in a number of stations on all the five continents and should be under strict international control. The United Nations would then be more than the anemic infant it is today.

On the edge of this precipice it is hard for humanity to escape from a sense of insecurity. I am old and ill and it is tempting to shrug my shoulders and say *après moi, le déluge*. But I am concerned with our civilization. The fear engendered by the tyranny of one's fellow creatures is degrading, and may lead to revolt against the dictators; but our fear-haunted humanity seems to be completely submissive to total destruction by atomic bombs, because this represents a *force majeure* over which they feel they have no control. There is, I believe, still time to renounce our skepticism in the power of humanity and to save ourselves.

For me, there is little time left. Vera has had a breakdown and needs me, but every day I look into the mirror and raise my head, and watch the image there do the same. We stand and move toward each other, but each time there rises up an impenetrable wall of glass to separate us. One more step, one hurling of my own body pressure against the wall and it would crash to earth and take me with it. But I stop again, and again that face in the mirror takes on an abstracted expression, squints vaguely back at me.

The violent pain seems senseless, but after a night of it I

wake and sink deep into the past. A poem I learned when I was four years old races through my mind, although I'm sure I had long forgotten it.

Veronica Gockel, the Sternes' beloved and loyal house-keeper-companion, continues:
"He would never complain about the pain, but always had a cheerful joke for me. The only way we could tell when he was having a very bad time was to watch the bottle of Demerol to see how many pain-killing pills he was needing. He would work on his notes whenever he had the strength . . . having that big job to do kept him alive. . . ."

A few days before he died, Sterne scribbled the drawing of a feeble old man—himself—in a stenographer's notebook. He has written faintly, across the top, "pass resolutions— moral pressure— I'm all washed up." He died on July 23, 1957.
A tribute which Sterne himself might have liked best came in a letter to Vera Sterne dated August 8, 1959, from the Mayor of the Commune di Anticoli Corrado, province of Rome. It read:

Dear Madame,
I have the honor and the pleasure of announcing to you that the Communal Council of Anticoli Corrado has decided, that on the occasion of the celebration that 150 years ago, the beauty of Anticoli was revealed by the first group of Italian and foreign artists, of naming and dedicating three streets of Anticoli for three great deceased artists, who have lived a large part of their lives in our midst.

The chosen artists are: Maurizio Sterne (Your husband), Pietro Gaudenzi, Arturo Martini.

With this decision we have first of all thought of your lamented husband, great as a painter and great as a sculptor, at the same time for so many Anticolani also a living memory.

On a beautiful piece of marble we have had carved: "Via Maurice Sterne American Painter who lived in Anticoli from 1905 to 1934."

This stone will be placed on the wall of the street where it joins the Piazza of the Town, near to the house where you and your husband had lived.

On the 23 of August the Stone will be unveiled by the Director of the American Academy of Rome, in the presence of friends of your husband like the Toppi family, Rudolf Bennet, Peppino Sebasti, Guiseppe son of Pasquale, la Signora Checca Ciucci, Selva. . . .

INDEX